# RTI Toolkit:
## A Practical Guide for Schools

*by Jim Wright*

**DUDE PUBLISHING**
A Division of
**National Professional Resources, Inc.**
*Port Chester, New York*

**Publisher's Cataloging-in-Publication**
*(Provided by Quality Books, Inc.)*

Wright, Jim, 1959-
 RTI toolkit : a practical guide for schools / by Jim
Wright.
 p. cm.
 Includes bibliographical references.
 ISBN-13: 9-7819-3403205-3
 ISBN-10: 1-934032-05-0

 1. Inclusive education--Handbooks, manuals, etc.
2. Children with disabilities--Education--Handbooks,
manuals, etc.    I. Title.  II. Title: Response to
intervention toolkit.

 LC1200.W75 2007          371.9'046
                          QBI07-600086

Acquisitions Editor: Helene M. Hanson
Associate Editor: Lisa L. Hanson
Production Editor, Cover Design: Andrea Cerone,
National Professional Resources, Inc., Port Chester, NY

Dude Publishing
A Division of National Professional Resources, Inc.
25 South Regent Street
Port Chester, New York 10573
Toll free: (800) 453-7461
Phone: (914) 937-8879

Visit our web site: www.NPRinc.com

Printed in the United States of America

ISBN 978-1-934032-05-3

To Carol, who loved us—all the same.

# Contents

# Acknowledgements

RTI is about teamwork and collaboration. While much of the material in this book have been reproduced from the web site that I founded six years ago as a source for free RTI resources: Intervention Central (*http://www.interventioncentral.org*), I certainly required the help of my own team to create it.

First, I am indebted to my colleague Seth Aldrich for his willingness to engage in occasional meandering discussions with me about RTI . Whenever I was hung up on a point about RTI that I could not resolve on my own, I would introduce it into one of our conversations, and we would settle the question together. A school psychologist and personal friend, Seth also serves as a positive role model for me, eager to try out aspects of RTI in classrooms to see for himself what works and what does not.

My friend Stephanie Pelcher, a staff developer with Syracuse (NY) City Schools, was generous in allowing me to adapt materials from that school district's School-Based Intervention Team project. A teacher herself, Stephanie is always able to cut through the theoretical underbrush of RTI to determine exactly what supports a classroom teacher in the real world will need to help a struggling student.

I also want to acknowledge the pivotal assistance of Karen Norlander, Esq., who first recommended to my publisher that the company approach me to write this book. As both a lawyer practicing in educational law and a sought-after speaker, Karen has thought deeply about the potential benefits and challenges of incorporating RTI into the special education referral process.

I wish to express my appreciation to Bob Hanson and Helene Hanson of National Professional Resources, Inc., my publisher. Bob is the president of the publishing house and was so enthusiastic at the prospect of my writing a book on RTI that I became pretty excited about the project myself. As my editor, Helene was always the consummate professional, providing me with prompt, specific editorial feedback and maintaining a positive attitude even when I missed deadlines.

Thanks also to Lisa Hanson for her excellent technical editing, and Andrea Cerone for her outstanding design and production skills.

And finally, I thank my wife Mimi for her support during the writing of this book. Every day, she shares with me her inestimable gift of seeing the world through practical eyes.

# Introduction

This book, *RTI Toolkit: A Practical Guide for Schools*, was written to provide educators with the necessary guidance and tools to implement **Response to Intervention (RTI)** in a school setting. A guiding philosophy of this book is that "the quality of a school as a learning community can be measured by how effectively it addresses the needs of struggling students." (Wright, 2006, p.1). Schools are judged by their success in working with marginal learners who would otherwise fall through the cracks and become lost. RTI is a means to expand schools' capacity to reach and support diverse learners.

As will be discussed in the first chapter, the RTI model encompasses three Tiers of intervention: Tier I, universal strategies for all children; Tier II, interventions individualized to the needs of at-risk learners; and Tier III, intensive interventions for students with severe, chronic academic or behavioral needs. It is clear that RTI has the potential to grow into an immense, sprawling initiative, spanning the breadth of programs and services available within a school or district. A school that is just beginning the RTI process should choose its initial goals carefully to avoid becoming overwhelmed at the magnitude of the task.

For example, Tier I, universal strategies fall squarely within the domain of general education. And many forces, e.g., Boards of Education, staff and community expectations, state and federal regulations, exert a controlling influence on the content of general education, including its curricula and grading and testing criteria. Those implementing RTI must recognize, therefore, that, at least in the short term, their ability to reform the domain of general education is probably limited. In a similar manner, Tier III, intensive, intervention resources in many schools are largely restricted to those available through special education. Because special education services tend to be both expensive and highly regulated, those spearheading RTI in a school are likely to have only a limited impact in changing the manner in which these Tier III resources are allocated.

The book operates with the expectation that a group introducing the RTI process to a school is likely to have only limited resources with which to work and will be most successful if it concentrates the majority of its initial energy at the Tier II, individualized, intervention level. It was written expressly to help administrators, teachers, school psychologists, parents, and other school stakeholders accomplish this task. Although it does provide suggestions to schools for inventorying and organizing their Tier I universal and Tier III intensive student supports to integrate them into RTI. In the first year, the initial task of an RTI, implementation group should be to build the school's capacity at the Tier II level to:

- Identify students at risk for learning or behavioral issues,

- Tailor intervention plans to meet their needs,

- Monitor these students' progress over time to ensure that they are closing the gap with their peers, and

- Adopt decision rules to know when struggling students have not responded to intervention and should be referred on to Special Education.

Three assumptions form the foundation of this book:

1. *The primary focus of Tier II (individualized) interventions is the classroom.* Under the RTI model (Fuchs, Mock, Morgan, & Young, 2003; Kovaleski, 2003, December), schools may choose to establish stand-alone programs for students who require individualized interventions using the standard protocol approach, develop unique intervention plans for every student that the classroom teacher is expected to carry out using problem-solving approach, or adopt a combination of classroom and stand-alone intervention options. This book assumes that most of the interventions that the school designs will be centered in the classroom with a problem-solving approach; furthermore, these interventions will require the full participation of the classroom teacher. (However, the resources in this volume will also be very useful to schools that opt instead to establish stand-alone intervention programs.)

2. *The best mechanism to plan and support Tier II, individualize, interventions is a multi-disciplinary problem-solving team.* To implement RTI correctly, schools must be familiar with: a structured format for problem-solving; effective research-based interventions to address a range of academic and behavioral concerns; methods for student progress-monitoring and data analysis; and other specialized skills and knowledge. In any school, the most efficient way to get quick access to these competencies is to assemble a problem-solving team made up of teachers, support staff, and administrators. A bedrock assumption throughout this book is that RTI Teams will serve as the vehicle to assist teachers in putting together and monitoring individualized student intervention plans. Recruiting and training such a team should be a primary objective for any school starting RTI.

3. *Response to Intervention is the dominant initiative of the school.* RTI is an ambitious undertaking. Among other things, RTI requires that a school change its culture so that classroom teachers feel empowered to put individualized intervention plans in place for struggling students with support from

the building's RTI Team. It will be difficult to win over "reluctant" teachers to RTI however, if school staff believe that this initiative is just a fad that will vanish in one or two years. To promote RTI, schools should make an effort to educate staff about the initiative and make clear that RTI is the dominant organizing framework to be used in the school when planning group or individual student intervention services. To reinforce this message, schools should explicitly link RTI to other school-wide initiatives (e.g., Positive Behavioral Interventions and Supports and services provided through Reading First grant funds).

This book is organized as a series of steps that are essential to creating a successful RTI project:

- Chapter 1: Decision-makers in a school educate themselves about the elements of the Response to Intervention model, including its 3-tier system for organizing intervention resources and the use of a dual-discrepancy formula to diagnose Learning Disabilities.

- Chapter 2: The school develops a plan to launch the RTI project, by informing stakeholders about the model, setting up an RTI Steering Group, and otherwise preparing the building for this initiative.

- Chapter 3: The school establishes an RTI Intervention Team, with the skills necessary to implement and monitor individualized student intervention plans.

- Chapter 4: The school builds its capacity to select evidence-based interventions, package those interventions into classroom-friendly plans, and monitor the quality with which those plans are implemented.

- Chapter 5: To monitor the effectiveness of its individualized student intervention plans, the school uses academic and behavioral measures that are valid, reliable, and sensitive to short-term progress.

- Chapter 6: The school adopts decision rules to judge student academic progress and decide whether the intervention plan is effective.

- Chapter 7: The school strives continuously to update and improve its Response-to-Intervention process to take advantage of advances in RTI research.

In closing, the reader is reminded that RTI is a vast and rapidly evolving topic. No single book, including this one, can hope to answer all questions about how to implement RTI in schools. Any attempt to write a truly comprehensive RTI book would result in a multi-volume set the size of an encyclopedia. But it would be outdated the moment that it was published. This book does, however, provide the essential framework and set of practical tools required to begin the very important process of implementing RTI in a school or district.

## References

Fuchs, D., Mock, D., Morgan, P. L., & Young, C. L. (2003). Responsiveness-to-Intervention: Definitions, evidence, and implications for the learning disabilities construct. *Learning Disabilities Research & Practice, 18*(3), 157-171.

Kovaleski, J. F. (2003, December). *The three tier model of identifying learning disabilities: Critical program features and system issues.* Paper presented at the National Research Center on Learning Disabilities Responsiveness-to-Intervention Symposium,Kansas City, MO.

Wright, J. (2005, Summer). Five interventions that work. *NAESP Leadership Compass, 2(4)* pp.1,6.

# Chapter 1

## Response to Intervention:
### A Model to Improve Systems of Support for Struggling Learners

The story is old and has many variations. In one commonly told version, a hungry peddler enters a poor town. Told by the townspeople to be on his way, he instead builds a fire, heats a large pot of water, and tosses in a small stone. As curious villagers look on, the peddler smacks his lips at the flavorful broth that he has made from the stone. He thinks aloud that the soup would be even tastier if he had a wedge of cabbage. A villager hesitantly produces a cabbage that goes into the soup. The peddler pronounces the soup delicious, but muses that it would be even more wonderful if he had a small piece of beef, some potatoes, an onion. The villagers are now lining up to contribute ingredients. Then the entire village joins the peddler in a joyous feast of soup. Later, they pass down to their descendents the legend of the magical stone that the peddler used to make a soup (*Stone Soup*, 2007). This story, *Stone Soup*, is most often interpreted as a humorous parable of how a single catalyst (the peddler) can help members of a community open their hearts and share. Let's apply that lesson to public education.

Schools in America have substantial populations of students who struggle to succeed and require some degree of individualized assistance. No single statistic exists that describes the percentage of students at-risk for academic failure. But consider these indicators:

- One in three students in the fourth grade reads below the 'basic' level of proficiency (U.S. Department of Education, 2005);

- One in five students across the nation misses three of more days of school per month (National Center for Education Statistics, 2005);

- Annually, about 5 percent of students in grades 9-12 leave school without graduating and eleven percent of youth ages 16-24 were found to have dropped out of school during the most recent national census (National Center for Education Statistics, 2001);

- Approximately 10 percent of students in this country receive special education services. Fully *half* of the special education population nationally is identified as Learning Disabled (LD), with the percentage of school-age students classified as LD having more than doubled since 1980 (Vaughn & Fuchs, 2003).

There is no doubt that schools must rise to the challenge of supporting the large numbers of academically marginal students in their classrooms. But intervention resources are limited in our current educational system, and the modest academic assistance that is available is often provided too late to benefit failing students. For example, children who experience minor delays in acquiring reading skills relative to peers in the early primary grades, and do not receive prompt individualized academic assistance, are likely to develop large and stubborn gaps before the end of elementary school (Stanovich, 1986). Intervention resources, such as individualized instruction that might be effective if given at the point when struggling learners begin to fall behind, are often compartmentalized and kept off-limits to those students until they experience profound and chronic failure.

What schools need is a model for providing early intervention, one that efficiently and flexibly delivers educational assistance to at-risk learners to close skill or performance gaps with peers. **Response to Intervention (RTI)** is that model. In its simplest terms, RTI can be defined as "the change in [a student's] behavior or performance as a function of an intervention" (Gresham, 2001, p. 2). While some details for implementing RTI in schools are still being debated, there is broad consensus on its core elements. RTI requires that schools organize their intervention resources into levels of increasing intensity. Students who are identified as being at-risk for school failure receive individualized academic support, have ambitious goals set for improving their school performance, and are closely monitored to ensure that they achieve those goals (Kovaleski, 2003, December). As a school-wide initiative, RTI can serve a role like that of the peddler with the magical soup-stone in our fable: it provides a philosophy and blueprint that empowers all school stakeholders to share their problem-solving resources to attain positive academic outcomes for the greatest number of students.

## RTI: A Description

Schools that adopt RTI organize their intervention resources in an efficient manner that allows them to provide more intensive, individualized support as students display increased learning difficulties. RTI is also diagnostic, providing evidence that students with significant learning delays may have a learning disability if they fail to catch up with peers despite well-implemented interventions.

*Intervention Resources Organized into Tiers.* Intervention resources are arranged in three levels, or tiers (Kovaleski, 2003, December; Vaughn, 2003, December).

- Tier I: Interventions are universal, and available to all students. Teachers often deliver these interventions in the classroom (e.g., providing additional drill and practice in reading fluency for students with limited decoding skills). Tier I interventions are those strategies that instructors are likely to put into place at the first sign that a student is struggling. Tier I interventions attempt to answer the question: *Are routine classroom instructional modifications sufficient to help the student achieve academic success?*

- Tier II: Interventions are individualized, and tailored to the unique needs of struggling learners. They are reserved for students with significant skill gaps who have failed to respond successfully to Tier I strategies. Tier II interventions attempt to answer the question: *Can an individual-*

*ized intervention plan carried out in a general-education setting bring the student up to the academic level of his or her peers?*

There are two different vehicles that schools can use to deliver Tier II interventions (Fuchs, Mock, Morgan, & Young, 2003; Kovaleski, 2003, December).

—Problem-solving (Classroom-Based Intervention): Individualized research-based interventions are selected to match the profile of a particular student's strengths and limitations. The classroom teacher is often responsible for carrying out these interventions. An advantage of the problem-solving approach is that the intervention can be customized to the student's needs. However, developing intervention plans for individual students can be time consuming.

—Standard-Protocol (Stand-alone Intervention): Group intervention programs based on scientifically valid instructional practices ('standard protocol') are created to address frequent student referral concerns. These services are provided outside of the classroom. A middle school, for example, may set up a structured math-tutoring program staffed by adult volunteer tutors to provide assistance to students with limited math skills. Students referred for a Tier II math intervention would be placed in this tutoring program. Benefits of the standard-protocol approach is that it is efficient and consistent: large numbers of students can be put into these group interventions to receive a highly standard-ized intervention. However, standard group intervention protocols often cannot be individualized easily to accommodate a specific student's unique needs.

- Tier III: Interventions are the most *intensive* academic supports available in a school and are generally reserved for students with chronic and severe academic delays or behavioral problems. In many schools, Tier III interventions are available only through special education. Tier III supports try to answer the question: *What ongoing supports does this student require and in what settings should they be provided to facilitate the greatest success possible?*

*Flexible Response to Struggling Learners.* By grouping its intervention resources into successive tiers, schools can act quickly to meet the needs of at-risk students as soon as those students demonstrate that they require more assistance. The following is a description of how a struggling student might receive support under RTI:

1. The classroom teacher notes that a student has begun to show signs of academic difficulty. The teacher independently puts Tier I (universal) interventions into place and monitors the student's performance.

2. If the student fails to make adequate progress with Tier I (classroom-based) interventions, the teacher refers that student for Tier II (individualized) interventions. Upon receiving the referral, the school:

   —collects data to estimate the size of the academic skill gap between the student and typically performing peers,
   —determines the likely reason(s) for the student's depressed academic performance,
   —sets a realistic but ambitious goal for improvement (Fuchs, Fuchs, Hamlett, Walz, & Germann, 1993) that is projected to close the academic gap between the referred student and peers.

3. The student is assigned to a Tier II, scientifically valid intervention matched to that student's needs.

   —If the school has adopted a child-centered "problem-solving" approach (Kovaleski, 2003, December), a multi-disciplinary team meets with the referring teacher to assemble a plan customized to the needs of the student.
   —Alternatively, the student may be assigned to a group intervention that follows a "standard protocol" (Fuchs, Mock, Morgan, & Young, 2003) and is designed to address the student's skill or performance deficits.

4. While the Tier II intervention plan is in place, the student is monitored frequently using brief, sensitive measures such as curriculum-based measurement (e.g., Shinn, 1989). Progress-monitoring data is repeatedly compared to the student's outcome goal to determine whether the intervention is successful. If the student fails to make adequate progress over a reasonable period of time (for example, six instructional weeks) with a particular intervention, the school changes the intervention while continuing to monitor the student's progress.

5. Under the RTI model, if a student at the Tier II level does not respond to several well-implemented, research-based interventions conducted in the general education setting, that student is referred on for Tier III (intensive) interventions. In many schools, however, Tier III intervention resources are grouped under special education. So, depending upon state education and district guidelines, a student who continues to show chronic and significant academic deficits despite a history of intervention attempts may need to be found eligible for special education before that student can receive the full range of Tier III services.

*RTI as a Diagnostic 'Test'.* As schools harness their intervention resources to support RTI, a resulting benefit is that students who are falling behind their peers in academics can receive assistance quickly. In addition, the RTI model can be regarded as a test of sorts that can provide valuable diagnostic information about whether a student has a learning disability.

Fuchs (2003) developed a two-part "Dual Discrepancy" formula to describe diagnostic indicators of LD under RTI. As evidence of the first discrepancy, a student suspected of having a learning disability must display a significant gap between his or her own academic performance and the average performance of grade or age peers. After being provided with a series of research-based interventions, a student who still fails to close the academic gap with classmates shows the second discrepancy, a gap in rate of learning relative to peers. Not all schools will accept the dual discrepancy formula as sufficient to identify LD. It should be noted, however, that, the *absence* of either discrepancy—no gap relative to peers in the student's academic skills or rate of learning—is probably good evidence that at student does *not* have a learning disability.

As a means of LD diagnosis, the RTI process does have the advantage of being less prone to measurement error than traditional IQ-Achievement testing. Instead of relying on testing data collected during one or two sessions, schools that follow the RTI process can evaluate the possible presence of LD by first drawing upon multiple sources of data (e.g., teacher interview, direct observation, permanent work products, etc.) and by analyzing multiple progress-monitoring data-points collected across time (Francis, Fletcher & Morris, 2003, December).

## History of RTI

The method for intervening with at-risk learners that we now know as RTI was developed over the past several decades. A major impetus behind the rise of RTI has been widespread dissatisfaction with existing methods for identifying and treating children with Learning Disabilities.

In 1975, Congress passed Public Law 94-142, the Education of All Handicapped Children Act. This historic legislation required that school districts proactively seek out and identify children with school-related disabilities and provide them with appropriate educational programs. As states put the new law into practice, most adopted some version of an IQ-achievement discrepancy approach (Fuchs, Mock, Morgan, & Young, 2003, p. 158) to diagnose learning disabilities. Students who were formally tested and found to have IQ scores that were significantly higher than scores in selected areas of academic achievement were often designated as Learning Disabled. The test results were then frequently interpreted to create a profile of the LD student's unique aptitudes or abilities. Based on this profile of abilities, the LD student would often be prescribed specific academic interventions matched to the student's pattern of aptitudes, a methodology now widely known as the Aptitude-Treatment Interaction model (Gresham, 2001; Kavale & Forness, 1999).

*Limitations of IQ-Achievement discrepancy for LD eligibility*. Nearly from the moment of its adoption over 30 years ago, the IQ-achievement discrepancy model for diagnosing learning disabilities has faced persistent criticism (e.g., *Finding common ground: Consensus statements,* 2002). One recent critic has stated that "the process by which public schools identify students as Learning Disabled often appears to be confusing, unfair, and logically inconsistent" (Gresham, 2001, p. 2). For example, researchers have noted that:

- Using a discrepancy between IQ and achievement test scores to identify Learning Disabled students provides no useful information about what academic treatments, or interventions, might benefit a student (Barnett, Daly, Jones & Lentz, 2004; Gresham, 2001). For example, on formal reading tests students classified as LD using the test score discrepancy method perform in a similar manner as poor readers who do *not* qualify as LD (Fuchs, Mock, Morgan, & Young, 2003).

- No uniform statistical formula has been adopted nationally to determine "severe discrepancy" between IQ and achievement test scores (Bennett, & Clarizio, 1988). Instead, many states use different statistical formulas, resulting in inconsistencies between states in the numbers and characteristics of students identified as LD.

- IQ-Achievement discrepancies are based on single test scores collected at one point in time, compromising the reliability of these scores for high-stakes decisions such as LD identification (Francis, Fletcher & Morris, 2003, December).

- The test-score discrepancy model is not responsive to the learning needs of struggling students. In fact, students must experience academic failure for months or even years in order to demonstrate a statistically significant gap between higher IQ and lower achievement scores.

*Limitations of aptitude-treatment interaction as a means of selecting student interventions*. Many school practitioners found the notion of mapping out a student's cognitive aptitudes through psycho-educational testing and then matching those aptitudes to educational treatments, or interventions, to make intuitive sense. Unfortunately, research has not shown the aptitude-treatment interaction model to result in strong student outcomes (e.g. Gresham, 2001; Kavale & Forness, 1999). While LD students certainly possess unique patterns of aptitudes (*Finding common ground: Consensus statements*, 2002), at the present time it is not possible to reliably assign students to effective academic treatments based solely on knowledge of their profile of processing strengths and weaknesses.

*RTI: Inception and growth of a new paradigm.* The roots of RTI stretch back at least to the middle of the twentieth century, as influential figures in the field of behavior analysis identified the importance of using that discipline's methods of experiment and data analysis to solve meaningful problems in social settings (e.g., Baer, Wolf, & Risley, 1968). Over time, researchers developed the single-subject research techniques needed to accurately monitor individual students' response to school-based interventions (e.g., Barnett, Daly, Jones & Lentz, 2004; Horner, Carr, Halle, Odom, & Wolery, 2005). There was also an emerging understanding that students with learning problems do not exist in isolation, but rather that their instructional environment plays an enormously important role in these students' eventual success or failure (e.g., Lentz & Shapiro, 1986).

By the 1980s, schools started to acquire academic monitoring tools that allowed them to regularly track and chart student academic progress in basic skill areas and to use that information to judge in weeks rather than months whether an intervention plan is effective (e.g., Deno, 1986; Shinn, 1989). In 1991, Frank Gresham wrote an influential article introducing the term "resistance to intervention" to describe a student who failed to show the expected positive response to educational treatments (Gresham, 1991). Later, "resistance to intervention" was recast as the more neutral phrase "response to intervention" and a new problem-solving paradigm found its name.

In 2004, Congress reauthorized the Individuals With Disabilities Education Improvement Act (IDEIA 2004) and included landmark language in that law to encourage schools to break free of their reliance on the discredited IQ-Achievement Discrepancy method for identifying Learning Disabilities. The U.S. Department of Education then developed regulations based on IDEIA 2004 to guide state practices. These regulations (34 C.F.R. 300 & 301, 2006) direct that states cannot "require the use of a severe discrepancy between intellectual ability and achievement for determining whether a child has a specific learning disability". Furthermore, states "must permit the use of a process based on the child's response to scientific, research-based intervention" (34 C.F.R. 300 & 301, 2006; p. 46786). The federal regulations also require that schools "ensure that underachievement in a child suspected of having a specific learning disability is not due to lack of appropriate instruction" (34 C.F.R. 300 & 301, 2006; p. 46787) by:

- demonstrating that "the child was provided appropriate instruction in regular education settings, delivered by qualified personnel" and;

- collecting "data-based documentation of repeated assessments of achievement at reasonable intervals, reflecting formal assessment of student progress during instruction."

IDEIA 2004 therefore gives schools a new freedom to use the student's "response to scientific, research-based intervention" diagnostically as a prime indicator of whether the child has a Learning Disability. At the same time, this legislation prevents schools from classifying students too hastily as LD because it requires that they first demonstrate that the student has received adequate instruction in the general education classroom and that the student's academic progress in that setting has been closely monitored. In sum, IDEIA 2004 was the signal national event that opened the door to bring RTI into the schools on a large scale.

## RTI: A Work in Progress

Response to Intervention has much to recommend it as a method for identifying at-risk learners at an early stage, matching them to appropriate research-based interventions, and flexibly providing these students with additional support as needed. Schools that adopt RTI, however, should realize that the model is still under development (Barnett, Daly, Jones & Lentz, 2004; Gresham, 2001). Some current limitations to RTI include:

- *Scarcity of RTI research studies.* Few studies have been conducted on the effectiveness of RTI. Those studies that have been done often lack important information, such as the details regarding the strategies used for Tier II (individualized) interventions or the percentage of students who fail to respond to intervention and are then identified for special education services (Fuchs, Mock, Morgan, & Young, 2003).

- *Indeterminate decision rules.* There is not yet consensus among researchers on key RTI decision rules, including the length of time a student should be on an intervention plan before that plan can be evaluated (Gresham, 2001; Kovaleski, 2003, December), the intensity of intervention that a student might require (Barnett, Daly, Jones & Lentz, 2004; Gresham, 2001), and the number of intervention plans that should be attempted before a non-responding student is referred to special education.

- *Gaps in the intervention literature.* As defined by federal regulations, RTI hinges on "the child's response to scientific, research-based intervention" (34 C.F.R. 300 & 301, 2006). Yet it is surprising how much we still have to learn about "research-based" strategies for working with difficult-to-teach students. First, there is lack of agreement about what is required to certify an intervention as research-based (Kratochwill & Shernoff, 2003). Another concern is that the intervention knowledge bank is uneven. Some intervention areas, such as reading, have been extensively explored while others, such as spelling or mathematics, have received less attention. Also, interventions suitable for students in middle and high school have been studied less than those intended for students in the elementary grades (Vaughn & Fuchs, 2003). Even when scientifically valid interventions are selected and matched appropriately to students, these school-based interventions must be monitored to ensure that they are carried out with integrity (Gresham, 1989). However, measuring treatment integrity can be problematic in school settings (Gresham, 2001), due to limited time and potential teacher resistance.

- *Questions of scalability and cost-effectiveness.* As students move to higher tiers of support in the RTI model, they require significantly more adult attention. Team meetings are convened to create student intervention plans. School staff supervise and carry out these student plans, and monitor their effectiveness. Faced with RTI's staffing requirements, schools are justified in asking whether it is realistic to expect that such a labor-intensive model can be scaled up to address the needs of struggling learners across an entire school building or district. There are promising studies suggesting that RTI can indeed grow to accommodate large numbers of children without compromising its effectiveness. For example, Minneapolis successfully adopted an intervention model that anticipated many of the elements of RTI (Marston, Muyskens, Lau & Canter, 2003). The Heartland Area Educational Agency, which serves about one quarter of the school children in Iowa, has also put an RTI process in place across multiple schools and districts (Grimes & Kurns, 2003). But more research is needed on the benefits, potential trade-offs, and pitfalls of scaling up the RTI model to meet the needs of large schools and districts.

  A second question is whether RTI is worth the overall cost of resources that it requires (Gresham, 2001). Few, if any, comprehensive cost-benefit analyses have been conducted to date that compare the resources that schools are allocating to assist at-risk students under traditional models of special education to those that schools would allocate to help those children under RTI.

- *Lack of clarity regarding RTI & due process.* There is uncertainty as to whether a school that refers a child to an intervention team (Tier II: individualized interventions) as part of its RTI process may, in fact, have exercised its "child find" responsibilities under special education regulations (IDEIA 2004) and formally initiated a special education referral. This book adopts the viewpoint that student referrals to school-based intervention teams do *not* necessarily start the "special education" clock. Before considering a referral to special education, schools are required by federal regulation to document that they have first provided a struggling student with "appropriate instruction in regular education settings, delivered by qualified personnel"" and formally assessed "student progress during instruction" (34 C.F.R. 300 & 301, 2006; p. 46787). Tier II interventions that take place in the general education setting can be interpreted as a vehicle for collecting this necessary documentation *prior* to a special education referral. Still, the relation of RTI activities to special education due process has yet to be clarified by most state education departments or the courts.

## RTI: A Promise Unfolding

Limitations in the current version of RTI should by no means be regarded as fatal flaws. Rather, they reflect the fact that RTI is a new model, one that quite naturally is experiencing rapid change and growth as researchers and practitioners stretch it to meet the pressing needs of schools. But even now, in the early stages of its development, RTI offers a specific blueprint for schools that promises to greatly expand their capacity to support marginal, struggling students. That RTI blueprint includes guidelines for:

- Launching RTI throughout a school community;

- Establishing a strong intervention team;

- Creating research-based intervention plans that can actually work in classroom settings;

- Monitoring student progress using sensitive and time-efficient measures;

- Applying decision rules to determine in weeks not months whether a student has responded successfully to the interventions tried.

In the remainder of this book, we will explore each of these components in detail. And even as it explores today's best practices in academic and behavioral problem solving, the book also sketches emerging features of the next generation of the model now just over the horizon: *Response to Intervention 2.0*, Chapter 7.

# References

34 C.F.R. 300 & 301 (2006). Assistance to States for the Education of Children With Disabilities and Preschool Grants for Children With Disabilities.

Baer, D. M., Wolf, M. M., & Risley, T. R. (1968). Some current dimensions of applied behavior analysis. *Journal of Applied Behavior Analysis, 1,* 91–97.

Barnett, D. W., Daly, E. J., Jones, K. M., & Lentz, F.E. (2004). Response to intervention: Empirically based special service decisions from single-case designs of increasing and decreasing intensity. *Journal of Special Education, 38,* 66-79.

Bennett, D.E., & Clarizio, H.F. (1988). A comparison of methods for calculating a severe discrepancy. *Journal of School Psychology,* 26, 359-369.

Deno, S. L. (1986). Formative evaluation of individual student programs: A new role for school psychologists. *School Psychology Review, 15,* 358-374.

*Finding common ground: Consensus statements*. (2002). Nashville, TN: National Research Center on Learning Disabilities. Retrieved January 3, 2007, from http://www.nrcld.org/publi cations/digests/digest2.shtml

Francis, D. J., Fletcher, J. M., & Morris, R. (2003, December). *Response to Intervention (RTI): A conceptually and statistically superior alternative to discrepancy.* Paper presented at the National Research Center on Learning Disabilities Responsiveness-to-Intervention Symposium, Kansas City, MO.

Fuchs, L. (2003). *Assessing intervention responsiveness: Conceptual and technical issues*. Learning Disabilities Research & Practice, 18(3), 172-186.

Fuchs, L.S., Fuchs, D., Hamlett, C.L., Walz, L., & Germann, G. (1993). Formative evaluation of academic progress: How much growth can we expect? *School Psychology Review, 22,* 27-48.

Fuchs, D., Mock, D., Morgan, P. L., & Young, C. L. (2003). Responsiveness-to-Intervention: Definitions, evidence, and implications for the learning disabilities construct. *Learning Disabilities Research & Practice, 18*(3), 157-171.

Gresham, F. M. (1989). Assessment of treatment integrity in school consultation and prereferral intervention. *School Psychology Review, 18*, 37–50.

Gresham, F. M. (2001). *Responsiveness to intervention: An alternative approach to the identification of learning disabilities*. Paper presented at the Learning Disabilities Summit, Washington, DC.

Gresham, F. M. (1991). Conceptualizing behavior disorders in terms of resistance to intervention. *School Psychology Review*, 20, 23–36.

Grimes J. & Kurns, S. (2003, December). *An intervention-based system for addressing NCLB and IDEA expectations: A multiple tiered model to ensure every child learns*. Paper presented at the National Research Center on Learning Disabilities Responsiveness-to-Intervention Symposium, Kansas City, MO.

Horner, R. H., Carr, E. G., Halle, J., Odom, S., & Wolery, M. (2005). The use of single-subject research to identify evidence-based practice in special education. *Exceptional Children, 71,* 165-179.

Kavale, K., & Forness, S. (1999). Effectiveness of special education. In C. R. Reynolds & T. B. Gutkin (Eds.), *Handbook of school psychology* (3rd ed., pp. 984–1024). New York: Wiley.

Kovaleski, J. F. (2003, December). *The three tier model of identifying learning disabilities: Critical program features and system issues*. Paper presented at the National Research Center on Learning Disabilities Responsiveness-to-Intervention Symposium, Kansas City, MO.

Kratochwill, T. R. & Shernoff, E. S. (2003). Evidence-based practice: Promoting evidence-based interventions in school psychology. *School Psychology Quarterly, 18*, 389-408.

Lentz, F. E. & Shapiro, E. S. (1986). Functional assessment of the academic environment. *School Psychology* Review, 15, 346-57.

Marston, D., Muyskens, P., Lau, M., & Canter, A. (2003). Problem-Solving model for decision making with high-incidence disabilities: The Minneapolis experience. *Learning Disabilities Research & Practice, 18(3)*, 187–200.

National Center for Education Statistics. (2001). *Dropout rates in the United States: 2000*. Retrieved January 2, 2007, from http://nces.ed.gov/pubs2002/2002114.pdf

National Center for Education Statistics. (2005). *Student effort and academic progress*. Retrieved December 18, 2006, from http://nces.ed.gov/programs/coe/2006/section3/indicator24.asp#info

Simmons, D.K., Kame'enui, E.J. & Good, R .H. (2002). Building, implementing, and sustaining a beginning reading improvement model: Lessons learned school by school. In M. Shinn, H. Walker and G. Stoner (Eds.), *Interventions for academic and behavior problems II: Preventive and remedial approach* (pp. 537- 570). Bethesda, MD. National Association of School Psychologists.

Shinn, M. (1989). *Curriculum-based measurement: Assessing special children*. New York: Guilford.

Stanovich, K. E. (1986). Matthew effects in reading: Some consequences of individual differences in the acquisition of literacy. *Reading Research Quarterly, 21*, 360-406.

*Stone soup*. (2007). Wikipedia. Retrieved February 4, 2007, from http://en.wikipedia.org/wiki/Stone_soup

U.S. Department of Education. (2005). *1992–2005 reading assessments*. Retrieved January 23, 2007, from http://nces.ed.gov/programs/coe/2006/section2/table.asp?tableID=560

Vaughn, S. (2003, December). *How many tiers are needed for Response to Intervention to achieve acceptable prevention outcomes?* Paper presented at the National Research Center on Learning Disabilities Responsiveness-to-Intervention Symposium, Kansas City, MO.

Vaughn, S. & Fuchs, L. S. (2003). Redefining learning disabilities as inadequate response to intervention: The promise and potential problems. *Learning Disabilities Research & Practice, 18(3),* 137-146.

# Chapter 2

## Launching RTI in Your School:
### Gauging School Readiness, Educating Stakeholders, and Inventorying Resources

Schools that adopt the Response to Intervention model are taking on an ambitious project. To implement RTI effectively, schools must become familiar with a specialized set of tools and competencies, including a structured format for problem-solving, knowledge of a range of scientifically based interventions that address common reasons for school failure, and the ability to use various methods of assessment to monitor student progress in academic and behavioral areas.

To ensure eventual success, schools should first take steps to lay a firm foundation on which to build the RTI project. Those steps include:

- Assembling an RTI Steering Group;

- Gauging the school's level of RTI Readiness;

- Educating stakeholders in the school community about the RTI model;

- Inventorying resources throughout the school that can be used to support student intervention planning and progress-monitoring.

Subsequent chapters of this book will provide detailed instructions for constructing each essential element of RTI. This chapter, however, serves as a starting point, intended to guide schools as they take measure of their current capacity to implement RTI, expand their capacity for intervention planning, and plot the next steps that they will take as they set out on the ambitious journey of transforming the vision of RTI into a reality.

## Creating the RTI Steering Group

The collective knowledge and skills that teams offer make them an ideal vehicle for high-level decision-making. The school principal or other administrator should appoint an RTI Steering Group to oversee the introduction of RTI to the school. While schools have great flexibility in the personnel that they select to serve on the Steering Group, it is recommended that the team be multidisciplinary, with representation from administrators, teachers, and support staff (e.g., school psychologist). Many schools also choose to include a parent representative on the team. Of course, the Steering Group will have greater credibility and persuasive power if its members are respected and influential staff members. The Steering Group meets periodically (e.g., monthly) on an ongoing basis to evaluate the RTI project, shape its future direction, determine what resources the project requires, and allocate those resources. (Exhibit 2-A, *RTI Steering Group sample all-purpose agenda and minutes form provided.*)

## Rating a School's "RTI Readiness"

When schools decide to adopt a Response to Intervention model, they must identify both the barriers and the enabling factors that will influence the success of RTI in their buildings. One useful exercise that the Steering Group should undertake right away is to analyze the school's level of "RTI Readiness". Each team member should be given a copy of the *Response to Intervention School Readiness Survey* (Exhibit 2-B). This survey is an informal measure that rates a school community's RTI preparedness in the following areas: knowledge of the RTI model among school administrators and staff; existence of a skilled student problem solving (intervention) team; capacity to select and "package" intervention plans; ability to monitor student progress during intervention plans; and knowledge of methods and tools for graphing student baseline and progress-monitoring data for visual analysis. The Steering Group then pools its members' ratings on the survey to determine those areas in which the school is relatively prepared to bring in the RTI model and those areas in which improvements are needed. When completed, this exercise yields a road map for the school to follow as it implements RTI.

## Sharing the RTI Model With the School Community

Stakeholder groups in the school community must be informed about Response to Intervention before they can be expected to participate meaningfully in this initiative. Administrators, faculty and parents should all be provided with professional development about the RTI problem-solving framework and should be encouraged to share their views about the initiative. Schools can access a free PowerPoint (Wright, 2006) that can be shown to stakeholder groups to give them a concise overview of RTI. In addition to sharing a general message about RTI, the RTI Steering Group should also tailor its communication to match the unique needs of each stakeholder group.

- **Administration.** The backing of educational leaders at the district and building level is absolutely central to the success of RTI. A key requirement in rolling out RTI, then, is to educate administrators about the elements of RTI and to enlist their full support for the project. Whether convened as a group or in individual meetings, leaders ranging from the district superintendent down to building administrators should understand minimum requirements, including:

  —Allocation of scarce resources to purchase intervention and progress-monitoring resources; staff time to permit regular intervention team meetings (discussed further in Chapter 3 of this book); staff development to build capacity in the various elements of RTI;
  —A willingness to work with faculty and support staff to redefine job duties and work expectations to better meet the needs of the RTI model;

—Administrative endorsement of RTI in the face of possible resistance to change from school faculty or parents.

On the positive side, administrators should also realize that RTI can bring real benefits to a school or district. The goals of the RTI model are to provide more flexible, timely, and cost-effective intervention supports to struggling students, to reengineer the special education referral process to result in more appropriate (and perhaps fewer) referrals of children for special services, and to expand the range of accommodations that classroom teachers are routinely able to make available to diverse learners.

- **Teachers and Support Staff**. When introducing the concept of RTI to faculty and support staff, the RTI Steering Group has two key objectives: to provide general information about the RTI model; to have staff identify potential barriers to RTI within the school system, as well as possible enabling factors in the educational environment that might increase the probability of RTI's success.

  Schools often roll out RTI to staff by presenting an overview of the model at a faculty meeting (e.g., showing a PowerPoint presentation such as that of Wright, 2006). As part of that presentation, faculty are given a fact sheet about the RTI model and the role played by school-based intervention teams (Exhibit 2-C, *Frequently Asked Questions about Response to Intervention and RTI Teams: A Handout for Teachers*). After the RTI presentation, staff members are asked to respond anonymously to a questionnaire, sharing their opinion of whether the school is ready to implement the RTI process (see Exhibit 2-D *Response to Intervention (RTI): Staff Feedback Form*). The RTI Steering Group collects these questionnaires, summarizes staff comments, and tallies the percentage of respondents who vote YES on the question of whether they believe the school is ready to put RTI into practice successfully. While this anonymous vote is non-binding, the RTI Steering Committee should keep in mind that if the percentage of affirmative staff votes falls below *80 percent*, the school should consider putting substantial effort into winning over faculty to support the RTI process. Otherwise, negative staff attitudes toward RTI may become a significant blocker to its success.

- **Parents.** Through traditional channels such as district or school newsletters and Parent Teacher Association meetings, the school can inform parents of the RTI model and its potential positive benefits for at-risk students. In particular, parents are likely to seek assurance that the RTI model will not block them from their due process rights to access a special education evaluation or special services. However, parents will also probably be pleased to know that under the RTI initiative students can be referred quickly to a problem-solving team for Tier II interventions if they are beginning to experience academic delays or problem behaviors. The school may decide to show an RTI PowerPoint presentation at a parent inservice or distribute to parents a brief information sheet about RTI (see Exhibit 2-E, *Response to Intervention and Your School: A Handout for Parents*).

## Identifying Resources to Be Used for RTI

Schools that are able to identify every available resource in the building or school district that can support RTI and coordinate those resources effectively will gain a powerful advantage in the competition to successful implementation the Response to Intervention model. One method of systematically inventorying resources is for members of the RTI Steering Group to pool their knowledge of programs, personnel with specialized training, and other assets throughout the school that can be harnessed for RTI. A second and complimentary approach is to survey staff members directly about resources they are willing to make available to promote RTI.

*Completing a School-Wide Inventory.* An early and essential step for any school that adopts the Response to Intervention model is to inventory all available programs and services to plan and carry out interventions. Once this master list of inventory resources has been assembled, the RTI Steering Group can group those intervention resources under the appropriate Tier (I, II, or III).

- *Tier I, universal* supports are those academic and behavioral strategies and resources that are available to all students who need them. Possible examples of Tier I supports are teacher behavior notes sent home daily to the parent, signed homework agenda, and extra credit work that students can complete to improve their grades and build their skills.

- *Tier II, individualized* supports are not available to all students. Instead, they are individualized interventions reserved for students with more significant academic delays or behavioral problems. Examples of Tier II supports include instructional time in a small group with a math or reading instructional specialist, enrollment in a cross-age peer tutoring program, or participation in a counseling group that teaches social skills.

- *Tier III, intensive* supports are reserved for students with significant, chronic deficits that require the most intensive services available in a school building or district. Examples of Tier III supports include special education programming such as speech services, individual counseling, and direct instruction from a special education teacher.

Inventorying intervention resources throughout the school is a useful exercise for several reasons:

1. Allows the school to review its list of intervention resources organized by Tier to judge whether it has exhausted all supports at any Tier level before referring a student to the next Tier for higher-level interventions.

2. When putting together Tier II intervention plans, the RTI Team (discussed at length in Chapter 3) can conveniently consult the inventory to ensure full use of intervention resources available in the building.

3. A single, comprehensive list will reveal gaps that may exist in intervention resources. For example, a school might discover that it has few Tier I (universal) supports available for struggling readers ,even though many students are then referred to the RTI Team (Tier II) for reading-fluency issues.

4. A resource list exposes possible duplications of service. For example, a school may find that its school psychologist and school social worker each run informal counseling groups to build social skills. If the school decides that these two groups are redundant, one of the mental health professionals might instead organize a group to teach students effective study skills or to reduce bullying behaviors.

The Form *Guidelines for Creating an Inventory of Intervention Program Resources Throughout Your School* (Exhibit 2-F) can be used for collecting and organizing a listing of school-wide RTI resources by Tier.

***Distributing a Resource Inventory to Staff.*** Faculty and support staff can be a hidden reservoir of intervention and progress-monitoring resources that can advance RTI. The RTI Steering Group can ask interested staff to complete a simple inventory sheet on which they volunteer such resources as their direct services for intervention, progress-monitoring, or creating training materials. The Steering Group then collects these inventory sheets to create a comprehensive resource directory. A sample inventory sheet can be found as Exhibit 2-G, *Response to Intervention (RTI) Team: Staff Resource Inventory*.

# RTI: Next Steps

Once an RTI Steering Group is in place, the school has the necessary leadership and guidance to push the RTI project forward. By following the blueprint for launching RTI outlined in this chapter the Steering Group will complete the *RTI School Readiness Survey* to gain a sense of the school's relative strengths and weaknesses related to implementing RTI. The school will also reach out to administrators, teachers and support staff, and parents, educating them about the RTI model and getting their feedback about the initiative. Finally the Steering Committee will compile an inventory of programs, services, personnel, and other resources that can be accessed to support RTI. With this firm grounding, the Steering Committee will be ready to advance through the rest of this manual, which provides specific advice on creating a well-functioning intervention team, putting together research-based intervention plans, frequently monitoring student progress to document whether interventions are effective, and adopting decision rules to judge whether a student is responding appropriately to interventions.

## References

Wright, J. (2006). *Getting started with Response to Intervention: A guide for schools*. Retrieved on Retrieved January 2, 2007, from http://www.jimwrightonline.com/ppt/ rti_intro_wright.ppt

# Exhibit 2-A
## Response to Intervention Steering Group Meeting Minutes Form

Date: _____ Attendance: _____

**Meeting Topics**

School-Wide RTI Coordination & Direction: _____

_____

_____

Intervention Planning: _____

_____

_____

Student Assessment (Baseline/Progress-Monitoring): _____

_____

_____

Staff/Professional Development: _____

_____

_____

RTI & Special Education Referral Process: _____

_____

_____

General Staff Questions/Issues About RTI: _____

_____

_____

Other: _____

_____

# Exhibit 2-B
## Response to Intervention School Readiness Survey

**Introduction**. The *RTI School Readiness Survey* is an informal measure designed to help schools identify which elements of RTI they are already skilled in, and which elements they should continue to develop.

**Directions**. This survey is divided into the following sections:

1.  RTI: Understand the Model
2.  RTI: Use Teams to Problem-Solve
3.  RTI: Select the Right Intervention
4.  RTI: Monitor Student Progress
5.  *RTI: Graph Data for Visual Analysis*

Complete the items in each section that follows. After you have finished the entire survey, identify any sections in which your school needs to improve its performance.

Next, go to RTI_WIRE, the online directory of free Response to Intervention resources, at:

*http://www.jimwrightonline.com/php/rti/rti_wire.php*

RTI_WIRE is organized into categories matched to those on this survey, so that you can conveniently look up the information that your school needs to successfully put the RTI model into place.

| 1. RTI: Understand the Model | 0 | 1 | 2 | 3 |
| --- | --- | --- | --- | --- |
| | Lack skills or basic knowledge of this model | Just starting to learn this model (Beginning Phase) | Developing awareness of this model (Intermediate Phase) | Fully knows this model (Advanced Phase) |
| **Staff members of successful RTI schools understand the RTI model and believe that this approach will benefit teachers as well as struggling learners.** | | | | |
| At my school: | | | | |
| • the principal strongly supports Response to Intervention as a model for identifying educational disabilities. | | | | |
| • the staff has received an overview of the RTI model, understands its general features, and knows how RTI differs from the traditional 'test discrepancy' approach | | | | |
| • the majority of the staff (80 percent or more) appears ready to give the RTI model a try, believing that it may benefit teachers as well as students. | | | | |
| • all programs or resources that are intended to improve students' academics or behaviors are inventoried and organized into three levels, or Tiers. (Tier I contains programs available to all students, such as classwide tutoring. Tier II addresses the needs of students who show emerging deficits and includes individualized intervention plans designed by the school's RTI Team. Tier III is the most intensive level of assistance available in a school and includes special education services as well as such supports as Wrap-Around Teams for psychiatrically involved students.) | | | | |

| 2. RTI: Use Teams to Problem-Solve | 0 Lack skills or basic knowledge of this practice | 1 Just starting to learn this practice (Beginning Phase) | 2 Developing skill with this practice (Intermediate Phase) | 3 Fully competent in this practice (Advanced Phase) |
|---|---|---|---|---|
| **Successful RTI schools support teachers in the RTI process by encouraging them to refer struggling students to an RTI Team. This Team is multi-disciplinary and follows a structured problem-solving model.** | | | | |
| My school's RTI Team… | | | | |
| • is multi-disciplinary, and has members who carry a high degree of credibility with other staff in the building. | | | | |
| • follows a formal problem-solving model during meetings. | | | | |
| • creates an atmosphere in which the referring teacher feels welcomed and supported. | | | | |
| • collects background information / baseline data on the student to be used at the initial Team meeting. | | | | |
| • has inventoried school-wide resources that it can use in Team interventions. | | | | |
| • selects academic & behavioral interventions that are 'scientifically based' | | | | |
| • sets clear, objective, measurable goals for student progress. | | | | |
| • selects methods of assessment (e.g., Curriculum-Based Measurement, DIBELS) to track student progress at least weekly during the intervention. | | | | |
| • documents the quality of the referring teacher's efforts in implementing the intervention ('intervention integrity'). | | | | |
| • holds 'follow-up' meetings with the referring teacher to review student progress and judge whether the intervention was effective. | | | | |

| 3. RTI: Select the Right Intervention | **0**<br>Lack skills or basic knowledge of this practice | **1**<br>Just starting to learn this practice (Beginning Phase) | **2**<br>Developing skill with this practice (Intermediate Phase) | **3**<br>Fully competent in this practice (Advanced Phase) |
|---|---|---|---|---|
| **Successful RTI schools select interventions that match the student's underlying deficits or concerns, are scientifically based, and are feasible given the resources available.** | | | | |
| My school… | | | | |
| • has put together a library of effective, research-based intervention ideas for common student referral concerns—such as poor reading fluency and defiant behavior. | | | | |
| • considers the likely 'root causes' of the student's academic or behavioral difficulties (e.g., skill deficit, lack of motivation) and chooses intervention strategies that logically address those root causes. | | | | |
| • tailors intervention ideas as needed to be usable in real-world classrooms while being careful to preserve the 'treatment' qualities that make each intervention effective. | | | | |
| • formats intervention strategies as step-by-step teacher-friendly 'scripts' containing enough detail so that educators can easily understand how to put them into practice. | | | | |
| • follows up with teachers soon after a class-room intervention has been put into place to ensure that the instructor has been able to start the intervention, and is implementing it correctly. | | | | |

| 4. RTI: Monitor Student Progress | 0 Lack skills or basic knowledge of this practice | 1 Just starting to learn this practice (Beginning Phase) | 2 Developing skill with this practice (Intermediate Phase) | 3 Fully competent in this practice (Advanced Phase) |
|---|---|---|---|---|
| **Successful RTI schools have the capacity to collect baseline data, as well as to conduct frequent progress monitoring of students in academic and behavioral areas.** | | | | |
| My school can… | | | | |
| • conduct structured classroom observations of students to determine rates of on-task behavior, academic engagement, work completion, and rates of positive or negative interactions with adults. | | | | |
| • collect and assess student work products to assess the completeness and accuracy of the work—and to estimate the student time required to produce the work. | | | | |
| • administer and score curriculum-based measurement (CBM) probes in basic skill areas: phonemic awareness, reading fluency, math computation, and writing. | | | | |
| • use local or research norms (e.g., CBM), or criterion-based benchmarks (e.g., DIBELS) to judge the magnitude of a student's delays in basic academic skills. | | | | |
| • create Daily Behavior Report Cards (DBRCs) or other customized rating forms to allow the instructor to evaluate key student academic and general behaviors on a daily basis. | | | | |

| 5. RTI: Graph Data for Visual Analysis | 0 Lack skills or basic knowledge of this practice | 1 Just starting to learn this practice (Beginning Phase) | 2 Developing skill with this practice (Intermediate Phase) | 3 Fully competent in this practice (Advanced Phase) |
|---|---|---|---|---|
| **Successful RTI schools routinely transform progress-monitoring data into visual displays such as time-series graphs to share with teachers, Team members, parents, and others. These displays demonstrate whether the student is benefiting from the intervention.** | | | | |
| My school can… | | | | |
| • convert progress-monitoring data into visual displays such as time-series graphs to aid in instructional and behavioral decision-making. | | | | |

# Exhibit 2-C
## Frequently Asked Questions about Response to Intervention and RTI Teams: A Handout for Teachers*

Schools across the nation have steadily raised their academic expectations in recent years. While most students are able to meet these higher learning standards, some children struggle with the demands of school and begin to fall behind their peers in academics or show behavior problems. There are many possible reasons why students experience school difficulties. To better accommodate the learning needs of all students, our school has adopted a school-wide approach called *Response to Intervention* or RTI.

**What is RTI?** RTI is a flexible problem-solving model in which schools provide timely assistance to students and match that help to each learner's level of need. Schools who use RTI organize their school intervention services into three levels, or *Tiers*.

**What do these three levels of RTI support look like?** Students with emerging difficulties in school are first given *Tier I,* universal support. If that help is not sufficient, they are next provided with *Tier II,* individualized assistance. Students with significant school delays who do not 'respond' to Tier I and Tier II interventions may be eligible for *Tier III,* intensive supports.

*Tier I Supports.* Universal, or Tier I, supports are those academic and behavioral strategies that all teachers routinely use at the first sign that a student is having problems in their classrooms. As examples of Tier I supports, instructors may change their method of instruction, provide a child with additional individual help, or check the child's homework each day. Teachers who use Tier I supports with students should keep a log of their intervention efforts and the student's progress.

*Tier II Supports.* If the student continues to fall significantly behind peers despite classroom supports, the teacher can refer the child to the school's Response to Intervention (RTI) Team for Tier II, individualized support. The RTI Team contacts the student's parent(s) and meets with the teacher to collect detailed information about the child's academic levels, study and learning habits, and general classroom behaviors. With that information, the team and teacher identify possible reasons why a student is experiencing academic or behavioral difficulties and put together a practical, research-based, classroom-friendly 'intervention plan' to address those student problems. This individualized plan is tailored to the student's specific learning needs. The classroom teacher may carry out the intervention plan alone. Or other school staff, such as reading or math specialists, may help the teacher put the plan into place.

While the intervention plan is in action, the RTI Team regularly monitors the student using academic or behavior measures—such as curriculum-based measurement or daily behavior report cards— to see if the child is making satisfactory progress. Information about the student's progress is shared with the parent(s) and classroom teacher. If the data collected show that the student is not achieving his or her expected goals for improvement, the RTI Team and classroom teacher meet again to change the intervention plan.

*Tier III Supports.* If the RTI Team finds—after trying several individualized intervention plans—that a student still has not make significant progress, the school may refer the student for Tier III supports. In many schools, Tier III supports include services available under Section 504 or Special Education. Students may need to go through a formal evaluation process, including specialized testing, to determine if they qualify for Tier III services.

**How does an RTI Team differ from a Clinical Evaluation Team?** Clinical Evaluation Teams are responsible for identifying children who may have educational disabilities and be eligible for Special Education or §504 Services. Clinical Evaluation Teams are typically composed largely of clinical evaluation staff such as school psychologists and speech/language pathologists. In contrast to Clinical Evaluation Teams, RTI Teams focus solely on creating strategies to help children to be more successful in general-education classrooms. Classroom teachers are central and highly valued members of RTI Teams. Among its core components, the RTI Team model promotes a collegial atmosphere in which teachers work together to solve student problems, employs research-based intervention ideas to promote student success, and uses dependable but time-friendly assessment methods to measure the progress of struggling learners.

**Who serves on an RTI Team—and what do they do?** The RTI Team consists of a group of educators who work together as effective problem-solvers. Any school staff member can serve on an RTI Team. To help RTI Team meetings run more smoothly, team members take on structured roles. The *facilitator* runs the meeting, keeps participants on task, and checks in with the referring teacher to make sure that he or she agrees with the interventions being proposed. The *recorder* takes notes on the meeting proceedings in sufficient detail to create a detailed, written intervention plan. The *time-keeper* tracks elapsed time during the meeting to ensure that team members use valuable meeting time efficiently. The *case manager* assists the referring teacher in collecting information about the student prior to the meeting and may also support the teacher in starting the intervention plan. Additionally, RTI Teams have a *coordinator* who takes care of logistical issues such as scheduling meetings, maintaining a meeting calendar, and, when possible, arranging substitute teacher coverage for those attending an RTI Team meeting.

**What happens when a student is referred to the RTI Team?** Any teacher in the school can refer a student to the RTI Team. The RTI Team meeting process is based on an efficient, research-based problem-solving model. To initiate an RTI Team meeting, the classroom teacher first completes a referral form, providing relevant background information about the student. An initial RTI Team meeting is then scheduled. At that meeting, the team and teacher explore reasons for the student's learning or behavioral difficulties. They also identify student strengths. Then the group and referring teacher brainstorm about interventions likely to meet the needs of the referred student. The team notes those intervention ideas that the teacher finds most acceptable and collaborates with the instructor to turn them into a formal intervention plan. Additionally, the RTI Team and teacher come up with methods to track the student's improvement during the intervention. Before the meeting adjourns, a follow-up meeting date is set to review the student's progress.

**How do I get more information about the RTI process in our school?** If you would like to know more about your school's RTI Team or overall RTI process, talk with your principal or RTI Team coordinator.

* Sections of this handout were adapted from Wright, J. (n.d.) *Frequently asked questions about the Syracuse School-Based Intervention Team Project*... Retrieved December 22, 2006, from http://www.jimwrightonline.com/pdfdocs/sbit/sbit_Forms_Sept05/sbitFAQs.pdf

# Exhibit 2-D
## Response to Intervention (RTI): Staff Feedback Form

Directions: We want to know your thoughts about bringing a Response to Intervention (RTI) model to our school. Please respond to the questions below. (You can answer this form anonymously if you choose.)

Name [Optional]:_____ Date:_____

What are some *benefits* you think could result from having our school adopt the RTI model?

_____

_____

_____

What are some *concerns* you might have about having our school adopt the RTI model?

_____

_____

_____

What are *questions* you still have about having our school adopt the RTI model?

_____

_____

_____

Overall, do you support bringing the RTI model to our school at this time?
_____ Yes  _____ No

Who would you nominate to serve on a school team that will meet with teachers to help them to plan academic and behavioral interventions for students at risk? (Please feel free to nominate yourself if interested.)

1. _____  2. _____

3. _____  4. _____

# Exhibit 2-E
## Response to Intervention and Your School: A Handout for Parents

Schools across the nation have steadily raised their academic expectations in recent years. While most students are able to meet these higher learning standards, some children struggle with the demands of school and begin to fall behind their peers in academics or show behavior problems. There are many possible reasons why students experience school difficulties.

To better accommodate the learning needs of all students, your school has adopted a school-wide approach called *Response to Intervention* or RTI. RTI is a flexible problem-solving model in which schools provide timely assistance to students and match that help to each learner's level of need. Schools that use RTI organize their school intervention services into three levels, or *Tiers*. Students with emerging difficulties in school are first given *Tier I,* universal support. If that help is not sufficient, they are next provided with *Tier II,* individualized assistance. Students with significant school delays who do not 'respond' to Tier I and Tier II interventions may be eligible for *Tier III,* intensive supports.

- *Tier I Supports*. Universal, or Tier I, supports are those academic and behavioral strategies that all teachers routinely use at the first sign that a student is having problems in their classrooms. As examples of Tier I supports, instructors may change their method of instruction, provide a child with additional individual help, or check the child's homework each day.

- *Tier II Supports.* If the student continues to fall significantly behind peers despite classroom supports, the teacher will refer the child to your school's Response to Intervention (RTI) Team for Tier II, individualized support. The RTI Team contacts the student's parent(s) and meets with the teacher to collect detailed information about the child's academic levels, study and learning habits, and general classroom behaviors. With that information, the team and teacher identify possible reasons why a student is experiencing academic or behavioral difficulties and put together a practical, research-based, classroom-friendly 'intervention plan' to address those student problems. This individualized plan is tailored to the student's specific learning needs. The classroom teacher may carry out the intervention plan alone. Or other school staff, such as reading or math specialists, may help the teacher to put the plan into place.

  While the intervention plan is in action, the RTI Team regularly monitors the student with academic or behavior measures—such as curriculum-based measurement or daily behavior report cards—to see if the child is making satisfactory progress. Information about the student's progress is shared with the parent(s) and classroom teacher. If the data collected show that the student is not achieving his or her expected goals for improvement, the RTI Team and classroom teacher meet again to change the intervention plan.

• *Tier III Supports*. If the RTI Team finds after trying several individualized intervention plans that a student still has not make significant progress, the school may refer the student for Tier III (intensive) supports. In many schools, Tier III supports include services available under Section 504 or Special Education. Students may need to go through a formal evaluation process, including specialized testing, to determine if they qualify for Tier III services.

You are welcome to contact your school's principal, if you have concerns about your child's academic performance or would like to know more about the RTI process.

# Exhibit 2-F
## Guidelines for Creating an Inventory of RTI Program Resources Throughout Your School

An early and essential step for any school that adopts the Response to Intervention model is to inventory all programs and services that are available to plan and carry out interventions. Once this 'master list' of inventory resources has been assembled, the RTI Steering Group can group those intervention resources as Tier I, II, or III.

A recommended process for creating the inventory of RTI resources for your school follows:

1. *Get Tier I Teacher Input.* Many Tier I resources are modest but important accommodations that can easily be overlooked because they are a natural part of classroom instruction. To capture the full range of Tier I support available in your school, give teachers the worksheet that follows: *Common Student Academic and Behavior Problems: What Works in Your Classroom?*, based upon a list of frequently encountered classroom problems, have teachers write down their preferred Tier I strategies for dealing with these common student problems, and then collect these sheets.

2. *Brainstorm as a Team.* Assemble your RTI Steering Group and give each team member several blank copies of the *Inventorying Your School's RTI Resources: A Brainstorming Activity* that follows. Direct team members to write down as many resources as they can think of at each Tier Level.

3. *Analyze Brainstorming Lists and Categorize Responses.* Collate the intervention-resource ideas collected in steps 1 and 2. Discard any ideas that do not appear to be true intervention resources. Organize the remaining ideas by Tier level, using the *Tier I, II, & III Resource Listing* sheets that follow.

## Common Student Academic and Behavior Problems: What Works in Your Classroom? (Exhibit 2-F continued)

Teacher Name: _____ Grade or Program: _____

Please review the list of common student academic and behavior problems below. Next to each entry, jot down preferred strategies that you commonly use to help these students in the course of your teaching.

• Reading Decoding: _____

_____

_____

• Reading Comprehension: _____

_____

_____

• Math Computation/Word Problems: _____

_____

_____

• Remaining On-Task: _____

_____

_____

• In-Class Work Completion: _____

_____

_____

• Homework Completion: _____

_____

_____

• Compliance With Adult Requests: _____

_____

_____

# Inventorying Your School's RTI Resources:
## A Brainstorming Activity (Exhibit 2-F continued)

Directions: List any resources in your building that you believe can help your school to provide intervention support to students. Examples include existing programs (e.g., peer tutoring program in reading), specialized staff training (e.g., school psychologist who can train teachers to set up a classroom token economy), and available personnel (e.g., a paraprofessional who has 30 minutes available every other day to assist with interventions). [Optional: For each resource that you list, check the intervention Tier(s) under which you believe the resource should be categorized.]

- _____ Tier __I __II __III
- _____ Tier __I __II __III
- _____ Tier __I __II __III
- _____ Tier __I __II __III
- _____ Tier __I __II __III
- _____ Tier __I __II __III
- _____ Tier __I __II __III
- _____ Tier __I __II __III
- _____ Tier __I __II __III
- _____ Tier __I __II __III
- _____ Tier __I __II __III
- _____ Tier __I __II __III
- _____ Tier __I __II __III
- _____ Tier __I __II __III
- _____ Tier __I __II __III
- _____ Tier __I __II __III

## Tier I, Universal Resource Listing (Exhibit 2-F continued)

*Tier I, universal,* supports are those academic and behavioral strategies and resources that are available to all students who need them. Possible examples of Tier I supports are teacher behavior notes sent home daily to the parent, signed homework agenda, and 'extra credit' work that students can complete to improve their grade and build their skills.

List all Tier I supports that are available in your school:

- _____

- _____

- _____

- _____

- _____

- _____

- _____

- _____

- _____

- _____

- _____

- _____

- _____

- _____

- _____

# Tier II, Individualized Resource Listing (Exhibit 2-F continued)

*Tier II, individualized,* supports are those that are not available to all students. Instead, they are reserved for those students who have more significant academic delays or behavioral problems. Examples of Tier II supports are additional time with a math or reading instructional specialist, enrollment in a cross-age peer tutoring program, and group counseling.

List all Tier II supports that are available in your school:

- _____

- _____

- _____

- _____

- _____

- _____

- _____

- _____

- _____

- _____

- _____

- _____

- _____

- _____

- _____

## Tier III, Intensive Resource Listing (Exhibit 2-F continued)

*Tier III, intensive,* supports are reserved for students with extreme, chronic deficits that require the most intensive services available in a school building or district. Examples of Tier III supports include special education programming such as speech services, individual counseling, and direct instruction from a special education teacher.

List all Tier III supports that are available in your school:

- _____

- _____

- _____

- _____

- _____

- _____

- _____

- _____

- _____

- _____

- _____

- _____

- _____

- _____

- _____

# Exhibit 2-G
## Response to Intervention (RTI) Team: Staff Resource Inventory

Our school's RTI Team is seeking help from staff members who can volunteer expertise, time, and/or materials to support the intervention plans of struggling learners. Please complete the brief questionnaire below, listing any resources that you might be able to contribute. Thank you!

Please return your completed form to: _____

| | | |
|---|---|---|
| Your Name: _____ | Position: _____ | Date: _____ |

**'Helper' Roles**. Please check any helper roles for which you would volunteer (if your schedule allows) to assist students with RTI intervention plans:

❑ Tutor a student: Subject area(s)?: _____

❑ Mentor a student: Preferred age(s) or grade(s)?_____

❑ 'Check in' with students briefly each day to ensure that they have their homework assignments written down and the necessary work materials

❑ Monitor student academic progress: Using what methods?_____

❑ Monitor student behavior progress: Using what methods?_____

❑ Create materials to help with interventions (e.g., sticker charts, student worksheets): What types of materials?: _____

❑ Other 'helper' role ideas? _____

**Training**. List any topics relating to student academic or behavioral interventions, progress-monitoring, etc., in which you have expertise and would be willing to train staff:

• _____

• _____

**Professional Development or Instructional Materials**. List educator training manuals or student instructional materials (books, computer software, etc.) that you are willing to make available if needed to plan or carry out interventions:

• _____

• _____

• _____

# Chapter 3

## Harnessing Your School's Collective Intelligence:
### Creating a Multi-Disciplinary RTI Team

The engine that powers any school-wide Response to Intervention program is the RTI Problem-Solving Team referred to in the remainder of this book as the RTI Team). This group of school professionals meets with referring teachers to assist them in identifying their central concerns about struggling students and to design intervention plans to help those students achieve success.

The greatest strength of any RTI Team is the diversity of experience, skills, and knowledge that its combined membership can draw upon to identify the best intervention plan for a student. This collective intelligence far exceeds the abilities of even the most skilled and gifted individual teacher. Organizational expert Ken Blanchard captures the collaborative spirit of RTI Teams in his quote, "None of us is as smart as all of us." RTI Teams enhance the power of diverse membership by following a structured problem solving model that includes: identifying and analyzing the nature of the student's presenting problem(s); selecting intervention ideas matched to the student's profile of need; collecting ongoing progress-monitoring data on the student to judge whether the intervention plan is effective (Kovaleski, 2003).

The activities of RTI Teams fall within Tier II of the Response to Intervention model (Kovaleski, 2003). A teacher may encounter a student in his or her classroom who is difficult to teach and who is not successful in school despite that teacher's best instructional efforts. This student's performance can be viewed as evidence that the Tier I (universal) academic or behavioral supports that the teacher has made available to all children in the classroom are simply not intensive or targeted enough to support this specific student. The struggling student therefore crosses into the territory of Tier II interventions, because he or she requires more intensive interventions that are specifically tailored to match his or her unique needs. As a Tier II support, the RTI Team typically is trained to collect information about the student, review appropriate research-based interventions, work collaboratively with the referring teacher to decide what specific intervention ideas would be a good fit for that particular classroom, and, when necessary, make additional resources available to implement the intervention plan.

This chapter explains how to structure RTI Teams so that they can work most effectively with referring teachers to create intervention plans. It also describes the steps that RTI Teams follow in their problem-solving meetings. The chapter closes with ideas for overcoming challenges that RTI Teams commonly face. The RTI Team model presented in this book is adapted from the School-Based Intervention Team (SBIT) Project, a pioneering initiative piloted in the early 1990s by the Syracuse (NY) City School District (School-Based Intervention Team Project, 2005). Research demonstrates that School-Based Intervention Teams improved academic and behavioral outcomes for large numbers of at-risk students in the urban school districts where they originated (McDougal, Clonan & Martens, 2000).Since its inceptions, the SBIT Intervention Team model has been adopted by a number of school districts across the country (e.g., Albemarle County Public Schools, 2006). This author was part of the founding group that designed, implemented, and refined the SBIT model—an initiative that continues to this day.

## Essential Elements of the Team Problem-Solving Model

RTI Teams must function within a larger school culture, therefore it is natural for schools to wish to tinker with their team's structure or problem-solving process; for instance to accommodate limited building resources, or make the team process more user-friendly for instructional staff. There is nothing wrong with tailoring minor aspects of RTI Teams to match school needs. However, the RTI Team model depends upon a handful of essential core elements, that are central to its success and should not be changed (S. Pelcher, [Coordinator, SBIT Project, Syracuse, NY], personal communication, August 23, 2006). These core elements include:

- *Diverse representation.* The RTI Team is composed of a mix of educational staff, including teachers. Teams whose membership is truly multidisciplinary possess the breadth of experience and professional skills to find superior solutions for behaviorally challenging or difficult-to-teach children. Also, having classroom instructors on the RTI Team increases its credibility with referring teachers.

- *Collegiality.* Educators who refer students to the RTI Team are treated as respected colleagues. Teachers may initially be intimidated when bringing a student to the problem-solving team, believing that they will be judged as a failure because the student is not successful. The RTI Team can reassure referring teachers that they are esteemed colleagues by using a respectful tone, encouraging the visiting teacher to participate as a full member of the group, and pausing at various points in the meeting to ensure that the teacher is in full agreement with the team's decisions before moving on.

- *Structured Problem-Solving.* The RTI Team follows a structured format when analyzing possible reasons for a student's academic or behavioral difficulties and planning interventions. Adopting a structured problem-solving approach when exploring, defining, and prioritizing the referring teacher's concerns helps the team make efficient use of time and increases the probability that it will select the right intervention(s) to meet the student's needs.

- *School Focus.* The RTI Team focuses its energies on helping the student in the school setting. Many students come from difficult circumstances, and may have factors in their medical background, family situation, home environment, or neighborhood that present potential barriers to school success. However, the RTI Team realizes that it is not in a position to reengineer the student's life outside of school. Instead, the team works to identify strategies that will benefit the student within the school environment.

- *Research-Based Interventions*. The RTI Team recommends academic and behavioral strategies that have been researched and found to be effective in school settings. Schools have the responsibility to use scientifically validated intervention methods to prevent wasting time and effort, and to give students the best chance to be successful.

- *Parent Involvement*. Parents are kept informed of RTI Team meetings and are welcomed as full participants. Parents bring unique and valuable information about their child to RTI Team discussions. They should routinely be invited to problem-solving meetings. If parents cannot attend an RTI Team meeting, they should be sent a courtesy copy of the student's intervention plan.

## Roles of RTI Team Members

For each meeting, RTI Team members are assigned to one of four rotating roles: facilitator, timekeeper, recorder, and case manager (School-Based Intervention Team Project, 2005). Each role is essential to the team process; therefore, the team should ensure that at least four members attend each meeting (not counting the referring teacher). RTI Team members are trained so that they are able to assume any of the four roles. In addition, the RTI Team coordinator (an important non-rotating role), helps to ensure that the team's day-to-day operations are maintained.

- *Facilitator.* The role of facilitator can be challenging and requires that this person have a solid working knowledge of the RTI Team process, as well as good meeting-facilitation skills. The facilitator opens the meeting with a brief overview of what the team and referring teacher expect to accomplish in the session. The facilitator also describes the general problem-solving process to be used at the RTI Team meeting. A key objective of the facilitator is to establish and maintain a supportive atmosphere. While all team members are encouraged to take an active part in the problem-solving discussion, the facilitator pays special attention to "process" issues such as:

—encouraging participation from others,

—helping redirect the discussion if the group begins to get off task

—clarifying and summarizing information being communicated during the meeting.

The facilitator attempts to elicit an appropriate level of team agreement throughout the process, and helps resolve any conflicts that may emerge in the group.

- *Recorder*. The recorder is responsible for completing the meeting minutes forms (see Exhibit 3-A, *RTI Problem-Solving Team: Initial Meeting Minutes Form*). Because the recorder must capture the important information shared at the meeting, he or she may need to interrupt the meeting occasionally to ask for clarification about various points under discussion. It is helpful if the recorder and facilitator sit near each other in the meeting so that they can work together to ensure that all of the relevant information needed is obtained and recorded. As the recorder writes the meeting notes, he or she should take care to include enough detail so that a person not able to attend the meeting can still read the notes and, from them, understand the key details of the intervention plan developed by the team.

- *Timekeeper*. Because a large number of tasks must be accomplished in a short span of time at the RTI Team meeting, keeping track of time is very important. The timekeeper's role is to monitor the team's use of time and politely remind team members when time is running out during a particular stage of the meeting.

- *Case Manager*. The case manager's job is to support the referring teacher throughout the problem-solving process. The case manager may perform roles such as:

—helping the referring teacher complete the referral form,
—consulting with the teacher about the types of student background or assessment information that might be useful during the initial RTI Team meeting,
—assisting the teacher in collecting student data before the initial meeting.

After the initial RTI Team meeting, the case manager also makes a point to check in with the referring teacher to ensure that he/she is able to implement the intervention plan developed at that meeting. The case manager may also be the person on the team to assess the degree to which interventions and assessment procedures were implemented as designed.

• *Coordinator.* In addition to the four rotating roles, the RTI Team coordinator plays an important non-rotating role, helping to ensure that the day-to-day operations of the team are maintained. The coordinator reviews teacher referrals, ensuring that each referral is complete and that a case manager is assigned to each case. The coordinator notifies RTI Team members of days, times and locations of meetings and coordinates the assignment of substitutes for teachers attending team meetings.

## An Overview of the RTI Team Meeting Process

The RTI Team follows a structured problem-solving process that makes the most efficient use of time to achieve the goal of developing effective student intervention plans. The RTI Team problem-solving process is implemented when a teacher completes the *RTI Team Teacher Referral Form* (Exhibit 3-B). When the RTI Team receives this completed form, it schedules an initial meeting with the referring teacher. Prior to the initial meeting, the case manager meets with the referring teacher to review the referral form, answer any questions that the teacher may have about the RTI Team process, and decide what background and baseline information should be collected before the meeting. Chapter 5 provides a detailed explanation of methods of student assessment commonly used in schools. Additional information on Curriculum-Based Measurement is also found in Appendix B.

At the start of the initial RTI Team meeting, the facilitator explains to the referring teacher the purpose and structure of the problem-solving meeting. RTI Teams can use the sample *RTI Team Introductory Script* (Exhibit 3-C) as a guide for making opening comments. The RTI Team meeting then conducts a general review of the referring teacher's concerns. The team and referring teacher quickly narrow down those concerns to a manageable number, set goals for student improvement, create intervention plans matched to concerns, and identify methods for monitoring the student's response to the intervention strategies. The referring teacher leaves the initial meeting with a detailed intervention plan. A follow-up meeting is scheduled (typically within six to eight weeks of the initial meeting), at which time the team will reconvene with the teacher to determine whether the intervention plan was successful or needs to be modified or replaced.

## Steps in the Initial RTI Team Meeting

Experienced RTI Teams can be expected to complete initial student referral meetings in about 30 minutes. Below is a brief explanation of the eight steps of the RTI Team meeting process (adapted from the model developed by the School-Based Intervention Team Project, 2005). For more in-depth coverage of these meeting steps, refer to the *RTI Problem-Solving Team: Initial Meeting Companion Guide (Exhibit 3-D)* and *RTI Problem-Solving Team: Initial Meeting Minutes Form* (Exhibit 3-A).

- *Step 1: Assess Teacher Concerns*. At the opening of the RTI Team meeting, the referring teacher presents his or her primary concerns about the student's behavioral or academic difficulties. Team members ask questions as needed to clarify their understanding of the teacher's concerns.

- *Step 2: Inventory Student Strengths/Talents*. The teacher and team list the student's strengths, talents, and interests. This information is often used later in the meeting to design interventions that are motivating to the student.

- *Step 3: Review Baseline or Background Data.* Information that had been collected on the student prior to the meeting is presented to assist the team in understanding the nature of the referral concern. Examples of baseline or background information that teams often find useful are highlights from the student's cumulative folder, Curriculum-Based Measurement data in Oral Reading Fluency, attendance and office disciplinary records, and classroom observation data.

- *Step 4: Select Target Teacher Concerns*. Because the RTI Team has limited time available, it can realistically expect to create intervention plans for no more than one or two teacher concerns during a typical problem-solving meeting. If, at the start of the meeting, the referring teacher has brought up more than two concerns, the team takes a moment at this stage to help the teacher in trim the list to the top one or two concerns that will be the focus of the remainder of the meeting. These key concerns should be stated in measurable, observable terms.

- *Step 5: Set Academic and/or Behavioral Outcome Goals and Methods for Progress-Monitoring*. The RTI Team is able to judge that an intervention is successful if, at the conclusion of the intervention, the student has achieved a pre-determined improvement goal. At this point in the initial meeting, the team and referring teacher set a specific goal that the student is expected to reach in several weeks when the follow-up RTI Team meeting is held. The team also selects at least two methods for monitoring the student's response to intervention for each of the one or two referral concerns. The team decides who will be responsible for collecting and charting the progress-monitoring data and bringing it to the follow-up RTI Team meeting.

- *Step 6: Design an Intervention Plan.* The team generates a list of research-based intervention ideas that match the student's referral concern(s). The referring teacher selects those ideas that seem most feasible to use in the classroom. The team and teacher fill in all of the relevant details of each intervention strategy and identify any staff members who will assist the teacher in putting the intervention in place.

- **Step 7: Plan for How Information will be shared with the Student's Parent(s)**. If the parent cannot attend the RTI Team meeting, a staff member (usually the classroom teacher) is delegated to contact the parent after the problem-solving meeting to communicate the main details of the intervention plan. This can be most effectively accomplished by sharing a copy of the meeting minutes.

- **Step 8: Review Intervention & Monitoring Plans**. The team thoroughly reviews details of the intervention and progress-monitoring plans at the close of the meeting to ensure that the teacher and other team members understand the elements of these plans and that each person with a role in carrying out the plans knows his or her responsibilities.

## Troubleshooting Common RTI Team Challenges

No one likes to think about worst-case scenarios. However, successful RTI Teams adopt a realistic attitude, recognizing that they stay strong and effective by anticipating challenges and adequately preparing for them *before* they occur. In particular, teams should have strategies in place to start off on a strong footing, guarantee sufficient time to meet, recruit new members, handle a large number of student referrals, and work with reluctant teachers.

- **First Steps: Establishing an Effective Team**. The success of any new RTI Team will depend upon thorough preparation. Establishing a clear team process and meeting procedures increases the likelihood of a positive outcome. Other important steps include: getting the word out to faculty, other staff, and parents about the team and its services; inventorying resources in the building that can be used by the intervention team; holding several practice team meetings to build the new team's meeting and problem-solving skills before accepting the first actual staff referral. The handout, *RTI Team: A Checklist for Getting Started* (Exhibit 3-E), provides a step-by-step guide for starting an RTI Team.

- *Finding Time to Meet*. The RTI process requires time for team problem-solving, but time is a scarce and precious commodity in educational settings. Ideally, schools are able to supply substitutes to cover classrooms or otherwise free RTI Team members and the referring teacher to attend intervention meetings. Schools with limited funds must find their own creative ways to pull teams together. Possible ideas include:

  —*Holding meetings outside of the instructional day.* Some schools have pockets of time before or after school when staff could take part in RTI Team meetings.
  —*Scheduling meetings during common non-instructional periods.* Identify times when a substantial number of team members have a shared planning period and plan to meet at these times.
  —*Recruiting a large pool of team members.* If sufficient staff are signed up to serve on the team, individual members can be scheduled to participate in RTI Team meetings only every other week or so. With a longer interlude between RTI meetings, teachers on the team will miss less classroom instruction time and have fewer teaching plans to write up for substitutes who cover their classroom.
  —*Scheduling team meetings at different times each week.* If RTI Team meetings are held at the same time each week, some members may find that they are repeatedly missing important activities in their classrooms. Schools might consider alternating weekly meetings between the morning and the afternoon to vary the times that teachers will be out of their classrooms.

- *Recruiting Team Members.* Gradual turnover of membership on RTI Teams is healthy. It is to be expected that, after several years of service, veterans might want to cycle off the team to make room for new members who bring a fresh perspective. While vacancies on the team will occasionally occur, the RTI Team can prepare in advance by recruiting teachers or other staff whose skills will complement those of current team members. Midway through each school year, the RTI Team should survey its membership to determine who might be departing the team in the coming year. Recruitment of new members then begins and can be done informally or formally. For example, the principal may approach a teacher known for her strong instructional skills and ask whether she is interested in filling an upcoming vacancy on the RTI Team. Or the school may put invitations in staff mailboxes or make an announcement at a faculty meeting, encouraging those who are interested to submit their names to the principal for consideration. Once new members have been recruited, they can attend a brief orientation session that covers the RTI process and their responsibilities as team members. If possible, new recruits should be permitted to observe at several problem-solving meetings before being asked to take on more demanding roles such as meeting facilitator.

- **Handling a Large Volume of Student Referrals**. RTI Teams can become victims of their own success. As word gets around that the team provides teachers with useful and effective ideas for interventions, the number of student referrals may increase beyond the team's capacity to handle them all! To prevent or better manage large numbers of student referrals, consider the following:

  —*Encourage referrals early in the school year*. The least busy period for most RTI Teams is during the first half of the school year, a time when teachers are just getting to know their students and may not yet have decided which students need specialized interventions. However, when a student is struggling, teachers can sometimes delay too long before referring and then encounter a delay of several weeks or more before they are able to meet with the now fully booked RTI Team. The team may want to announce at a faculty meeting near the start of the school year that it is actively accepting referrals. Encourage teachers to refer early if they see clear evidence of students who are not making it in their classrooms. By filling up its calendar early in the school year, the RTI Team will make optimal use of its time and will be able to promptly meet the needs of a greater number of teachers.

—*Create one intervention plan to apply to several similar referrals from the same teacher.* If a teacher refers several students from the same classroom for similar concerns (e.g., off-task, lack of homework, non-compliance), the RTI team may ask the teacher to pick one student from that referred group to discuss at an RTI Team meeting. The teacher can then be encouraged to apply the intervention plan created at that meeting to other students in the classroom.

—*Create building-level programs to target common referral concerns.* A significant number of referrals are for similar student concerns, the RTI team may decide that rather than meeting to discuss each individual case, it would be more efficient to create a building-wide program to address these students' shared needs. If an elementary school discovers, for example, that a sizable number of RTI Team referrals are for students with poor reading fluency, the school might set up a cross-age peer-tutoring program that uses a research-based, fluency-building technique such as paired reading. Or, a middle school that receives frequent referrals for students who do not complete homework might create a study course to teach struggling students good study and homework habits. The RTI Team can determine who is placed in these programs and also monitor students' progress. Of course, students who fail to show improvement in a building-wide program would be referred back to the RTI Team for more intensive, individualized interventions.

—*Provide targeted staff development.* By analyzing the referrals that it receives, the RTI Team may identify shared teacher needs that can be met most quickly and efficiently through staff development. For example, if it is evident that a large number of referrals from different instructors center on issues of student behavior and discipline, the team may consult with the building administrator to provide all teachers with training in classroom management strategies.

- **Encouraging Reluctant Teachers to Collaborate with the RTI Team**. It is virtually inevitable at some point that the RTI Team will need to work with resistant or reluctant teachers. These instructors might entirely avoid referring students to the RTI team, appear resistant to ideas offered at team meetings, or even say negative things about the team to their colleagues in private. There are many reasons that a teacher might be reluctant to view the team positively and use it as a problem-solving resource. For example, the teacher may wrongly believe that the team cannot offer any new ideas to help with the problem, or may be unhappy because the principal forced that teacher to refer a student to the team. While there are many strategies for working effectively with reluctant teachers, the team must first understand the source of the teacher's reluctance and then craft a response calculated to reduce or eliminate the teacher's resistance.(See Exhibit 3-F, *Motivating the Reluctant Teacher: Six Strategies for RTI Teams,* for ideas to energize reluctant teachers.)

• ***Maintaining the Quality of the RTI Team Process****.* Over time, RTI Teams can drift away from the core elements of the problem-solving process, making them less effective. One way that teams can maintain the quality of the services that they provide is to periodically set aside time as a group to rate practices. (See Exhibit 3-G, *RTI Team Effectiveness Self-Rating Scale*).  Another method that teams can use to monitor how supportive and helpful they are perceived as being in the school community is to survey the satisfaction of teachers who have referred students to the RTI Team. (See Exhibit 3-H, *RTI Team Teacher Feedback Questionnaire)*. Within four to eight weeks of attending an initial RTI Team meeting, referring teachers receive a copy of this survey in their school mailbox, (they can complete the survey anonymously). The team collects these teacher feedback questionnaires and reviews the information each year to judge the level of consumer satisfaction with the problem-solving support it provides.

# References

Albemarle County Public Schools. (2006). *School-Based Intervention Teams: Process/concept.* Retrieved on November 18, 2006, from http://schoolcenter.k12albemarle.org/education/dept/deptinfo.php?sectiondetailid=17968&sc_id=1168909757

Kovaleski, J. F. (2003). *The three tier model for identifying learning disabilities: Critical program features and system issues.* Paper presented at the National Research Center on Learning Disabilities Responsiveness-to-Intervention Symposium, Kansas City, MO. Retrieved October 23, 2006, from http://www.nrcld.org/symposium2003/kovaleski/kovaleski.pdf

McDougal, J. L., Clonan, S. M. & Martens, B. K. (2000). Using organizational change procedures to promote the acceptability of prereferral intervention services: The school-based intervention team project. *School Psychology Quarterly, 15,* 149-171.

School-Based Intervention Team Project. (2005). *School-based intervention teams forms & related resources: Complete set.* Retrieved on September 8, 2006, from http://www.interventioncentral.org/htmdocs/interventions/sbit.php

# Exhibit 3-A
## RTI Team: Initial Meeting Minutes Form
### (See Exhibit 3-D for Guidelines)

| Step 1: Assess Teacher Concerns | Allotted Time: 5 Minutes |
|---|---|

Review concerns listed on the RTI Team Teacher Referral Form, see Exhibit 3-B, with the referring teacher and team. List primary concerns:

_____

_____

_____

| Step 2: Inventory Student Strengths & Talents | Allotted Time: 5 Minutes |
|---|---|

List student strengths, talents, and/or any preferred activities or incentives that motivate the student:

- _____

- _____

- _____

| Step 3: Review Background/Baseline Data | Allotted Time: 5 Minutes |
|---|---|

Review any background or baseline information collected on the student (e.g., attendance and office disciplinary referral records, student grades, Curriculum-Based Measurement data, Daily Behavior Report Card ratings, direct-observation data, etc.)

_____

_____

_____

_____

_____

_____

Adapted from the School-Based Intervention Team Project Complete Forms & Related Resources, available at: http://www.interventioncentral.org/htmdocs/interventions/sbit.php. Used with permission.

| Step 4: Select Target Teacher Concerns | Allotted Time: 5-10 Minutes |
|---|---|

Define the top 1-2 concerns in **observable terms** (top 1-2 difficulties that most interfere with the student's functioning in the classroom):

Hint: Behavior problems should include relevant information about *frequency*, *duration*, and/or *intensity* of behavior (e.g., using data from Teacher Behavior Report Cards, direct observations). Academic problems should have data regarding student *fluency* and *accuracy* in the area of concern (e.g., curriculum-based assessment), as well as information about *work completion*.

1. _____
_____
_____
_____
_____
_____
_____
_____
_____
_____

*Reasons/Functions for Behavior*

**Behavioral**
- ❏ Lacks necessary skills
- ❏ Has limited motivation
- ❏ Seeks att'n from adults
- ❏ Seeks att'n from peers
- ❏ Reacts to teasing/ bullying
- ❏ Tries to escape from work demands or setting
- ❏ Seeks access to privileges, rewards
- ❏ Seeks sensory stimulation (e.g., playing with objects)
- ❏ _____

**Academic**
- ❏ Lacks necessary skills
- ❏ Has limited motivation
- ❏ Struggling academically in current instructional placement
- ❏ Needs drill & practice
- ❏ _____

2. _____
_____
_____
_____
_____
_____
_____
_____
_____

*Reasons/Functions for Behavior*

**Behavioral**
- ❏ Lacks necessary skills
- ❏ Has limited motivation
- ❏ Seeks att'n from adults
- ❏ Seeks att'n from peers
- ❏ Reacts to teasing/ bullying
- ❏ Tries to escape from work demands or setting
- ❏ Seeks access to privileges, rewards
- ❏ Seeks sensory stimulation (e.g., playing with objects)
- ❏ _____

**Academic**
- ❏ Lacks necessary skills
- ❏ Has limited motivation
- ❏ Struggling academically in current instructional placement
- ❏ Needs drill & practice
- ❏ _____

| Step 5: Set Academic and/or Behavioral Outcome Goals and Methods for Progress-Monitoring | Allotted Time: 5 Minutes |
|---|---|

Fill out the details for each intervention goal (to a maximum of two) in the table below. At the bottom of the table, you will combine the elements of the goal into a single student 'goal-statement'. NOTE: For help in completing this section, refer to the *RTI Team Companion Guide,* Exhibit 3-D.

| Intervention Goal 1 | Intervention Goal 2 |
|---|---|
| 1. Describe in measurable, observable terms the behavior that is to be changed (taken from Step 4): _____ | 1. Describe in measurable, observable terms the behavior that is to be changed (taken from Step 4): _____ |
| 2. What is the target date to achieve this goal? _____/_____/_____ | 2. What is the target date to achieve this goal? _____/_____/_____ |
| 3. Is the goal for the behavior listed in Step 2 to be: ___ increased? *or* ___ decreased? | 3. Is the goal for the behavior listed in Step 2 to be: ___ increased? *or* ___ decreased? |
| 4. What are the conditions under which the behavior *typically appears* (problem behaviors) or *should be displayed* (desired behaviors)? _____ | 4. What are the conditions under which the behavior *typically appears* (problem behaviors) or *should be displayed* (desired behaviors)? _____ |
| 5. What is the goal (level of proficiency) that the student is expected to achieve by the date listed above? _____ | 5. What is the goal (level of proficiency) that the student is expected to achieve by the date listed above? _____ |
| 6. What measure(s) will be used to monitor student progress? a._____ b._____ | 6. What measure(s) will be used to monitor student progress? a._____ b._____ |
| 7. How frequently will this student goal be monitored? (e.g., weekly?, daily?) _____ | 7. How frequently will this student goal be monitored? (e.g., weekly?, daily?) _____ |
| 8. Who is responsible for monitoring this student goal? _____ | 8. Who is responsible for monitoring this student goal? _____ |
| 9. Write a goal statement based on your responses: By the target date of _____, <br> [# 2: Target date] <br> when_____, <br> [# 4: Conditions in which the behavior is likely to appear] <br> the student will increase / decrease the behavior_____ <br> [# 1: Definition of behavior] <br> to achieve the goal of_____. <br> [# 5: Proficiency goal] | 9. Write a goal statement based on your responses: By the target date of _____, <br> [# 2: Target date] <br> when_____, <br> [# 4: Conditions in which the behavior is likely to appear] <br> the student will increase / decrease the behavior_____ <br> [# 1: Definition of behavior] <br> to achieve the goal of_____. <br> [# 5: Proficiency goal] |

| Step 6: Design an Intervention Plan | Allotted Time: 15-20 Minutes |
|---|---|

**Intervention Script Builder**     Date the intervention will begin: _____

| Intervention Check | Intervention Preparation Steps: Describe any preparation (creation or purchase of materials, staff training, etc.) required for this intervention. | Person(s) Responsible |
|---|---|---|
| This step took place Y___ N___ | 1. _____ | |
| This step took place Y___ N___ | 2. _____ | |
| This step took place Y___ N___ | 3. _____ | |

| Intervention Check | Intervention Steps: Describe the steps of the intervention. Include enough detail so that the procedures are clear to all who must implement them. |
|---|---|
| This step took place Y___ N___ | 1. _____ |
| This step took place Y___ N___ | 2. _____ |
| This step took place Y___ N___ | 3. _____ |
| This step took place Y___ N___ | 4. _____ |
| This step took place Y___ N___ | 5. _____ |
| This step took place Y___ N___ | 6. _____ |

Research Citation(s) / References: If possible, list the published source(s) that make this a 'scientifically based' intervention.

_____

_____

Intervention Quality Check: How will data be collected to verify that this intervention is put into practice as it was designed? (Select at least one option.)

❑ Classroom Observation: Number of observations planned?_____

   Person responsible for observations?: _____

❑ Teacher Intervention Rating Log: How frequently will the teacher rate intervention follow-through?

   Daily _____    Weekly _____

❑ Teacher Verbal Report: Who will check in with the teacher for a verbal report of how the intervention is progressing? _____

   Approximately when during the intervention period will this verbal 'check in' occur?

   _____

❑ Rating Intervention Follow-Through: Select either the classroom teacher/teaching team or an outside observer to rate the quality of the intervention and check the appropriate set of directions below.

   _____ *Teacher/Teaching Team Directions*: Make copies of this intervention script. Once per week, review the steps in the intervention script and note (Y/N) whether each step was *typically* followed. Then write any additional notes about the intervention in the blank below

   _____ *Independent Observer Directions*: Make copies of this intervention script. At several points during the intervention, make an appointment to observe the intervention in action. While observing the intervention, go through the steps in the intervention script and note (Y/N) whether each step was typically followed. Then write any additional notes about the intervention in the space below

Intervention Observation Notes:_____

_____

_____

## Step 7: Plan to Share Meeting Minutes with Parents        Allotted Time: 5 Minutes

Who will share a copy of the minutes of this meeting with the student's parent(s), and when?

_____

## Step 8: Review the Intervention and Monitoring Plans        Allotted Time: 5 Minutes

At the close of the meeting:

❑ The recorder reviews the main points of the intervention and monitoring plans with the team.

❑ The team selects a date and time for the follow-up RTI Team meeting on this student. (NOTE: Generally, follow-up meetings are scheduled 6-8 instructional weeks from the start date of the intervention (Step 6).

Next meeting date and time: _____

❑ The case manager reviews the agreed-upon time within the next school week to meet with the referring teacher(s):

Date and time for case manager to meet with the referring teacher(s):

_____

❑ The team completes the RTI Team Debriefing Form.

# RTI Team Meeting Debriefing Form

Directions: As a Team, rate your group's performance at today's initial RTI meeting on the items below. If your group rates any of the items as "No" or "Partly", take a moment to discuss what factors led to this rating.

|  | YES | PARTLY | NO |
|---|---|---|---|
| 1. Does the Team feel that overall it closely followed the steps of the initial meeting format? | 1 | 2 | 3 |
| 2. Is the meeting minutes form filled out completely? | 1 | 2 | 3 |
| 3. Were all the team members given an opportunity to participate? | 1 | 2 | 3 |
| 4. Was the referring teacher supportive about the intervention plan? | 1 | 2 | 3 |
| 5. Did the team use the meeting time efficiently? | 1 | 2 | 3 |
| 6. Was Baseline Data on the student: | | | |
| • reviewed at the meeting? | 1 | 2 | 3 |
| • used to make decisions? | 1 | 2 | 3 |
| 7. Were the target behavioral and/or academic concern(s) clearly defined in observable terms? | 1 | 2 | 3 |
| 8. Were the intervention plans clearly and specifically defined? | 1 | 2 | 3 |
| 9. Did the team determine how the intervention integrity would be monitored? | 1 | 2 | 3 |

(Optional) What are some additional ideas that the group has for helping this particular teacher to successfully carry out the intervention plan?

_____

_____

_____

# Exhibit 3-B
## RTI Team Teacher Referral Form

Please answer the questions below so that we will be better prepared at the initial RTI meeting to talk with you about the needs of this student.

### *General Information*---------------------------------------------

Person Making Referral: _____ Date: _____

Student Name: _____ Date of Birth: _____

Dominant Language: _____ Grade: _____

Address: _____ Phone: _____

Date Parent Was Contacted About RTI Referral: _____ By Whom?: _____

Medical or health concerns for this student: _____

_____

How is the student's attendance this year? _____

Current school or agency support services or program(s) in place for this student (e.g., counseling, tutoring, etc.):

_____

What are several strengths, talents, or specific interests for this student?

     1. _____

     2. _____

     3. _____

### *Instructional Information*---------------------------------

What makes this student *difficult to teach*? List any academic, social, emotional, or medical factors that seem to negatively affect the student's progress. (If the problem is primarily *behavioral*, how often does the problem occur, how intense is it, and for how long does the problem last? If the problem is primarily *academic*, what specific deficits does the student have in particular academic skills or competencies?)

_____

_____

How do this student's academic skills compare to those of 'average' children in your classroom? (e.g., How does the student compare to peers in reading, math, writing, organizational skills?.):

_____

_____

What is this child's estimated current reading level?_____

List any other general information about the student's academic levels or abilities (e.g., test results) that may shed light on your referral concern:

_____

***Problem-Identification Information----------------------***
Interventions Attempted: Please describe specific attempts that you or others have made this year to meet this student's academic, social, and/or emotional needs:

| *Intervention* | *Dates Began-Ended* (Approximate) | *Person(s)* Responsible | *Outcome* |
|---|---|---|---|
|  |  |  |  |
|  |  |  |  |
|  |  |  |  |

If the referral concern is in academics, how much time during the period/day does the student receive instruction in the area(s) of difficulty?

_____

When have you observed the problem occurring the most?_____
Are there settings or situations in which the problem is *less* severe or *minimized*? If so, when?_____
Please list members of your instructional team/building staff whom you would like:
❑ To receive an invitation to the initial     ❑ To receive a copy of the RTI Intervention
   RTI meeting:        Plan(s) after the initial meeting:

_____     _____

What would be the best day(s)/time(s) for a member of the RTI team to observe the student having the difficulties that you describe above? (Please attach a copy of the student's daily schedule, if available):

_____

Adapted from the School-Based Intervention Team Project Complete Forms & Related Resources, available at: http://www.interventioncentral.org/htmdocs/interventions/sbit.php. Used with permission.

# Exhibit 3-C
## RTI Team Introductory Script:
## Share With Referring Teacher at the Start of the Initial Meeting

"Welcome to this initial RTI Team meeting. We are meeting with you today to discuss concerns that you have about a student, _____ .

The purpose of this meeting is for us all to work together to come up with practical ideas to help this student to be more successful in school. I am the facilitator for today's meeting. The person taking notes during the meeting will be_____.
The case manager for this student is _____ . The time-keeper for the meeting is _____ .

You can expect this meeting to last about _____ minutes. By the time you leave, we should have a complete student intervention plan put together to help address your concerns.

Our team and you have a lot to do today and only limited time in which to do it. To help us to work efficiently and not waste your time, we will follow a structured problem-solving model that goes through several stages. Together, our team and you will:
- Assess your major concerns about the student,
- Help you to pick the one or two most important student concerns for us to work on today,
- Set specific student goals for improvement,
- Design an intervention plan with strategies to help that student improve, and
- Decide how to share information about this plan with the student's parent(s).

As the student's teacher, you are the most important participant in this meeting. Please let us know at any time if you disagree with, or have questions about, our suggestions. Our meeting will not be a success unless *you* feel that the intervention ideas that we offer will address the student's difficulties and are feasible for you to do.

Our meeting notes will document the student's referral concerns and the intervention plan that we come up with. These notes may be shared with others who are not here today, including child's parent(s) and the building administrator. However, we ask that everyone here keep the *conversations* that take place at this meeting confidential.

Do you have any questions?"

Adapted from the School-Based RTI Team Project Complete Forms & Related Resources, available at: http://www.interventioncentral.org/htmdocs/interventions/sbit.php. Used with permission.

# Exhibit 3-D
## RTI Team: Initial Meeting 'Companion Guide' (See Exhibit 3-A)

| Step 1: Assess Teacher Concerns | Allotted Time: 5 Minutes |
|---|---|

GOALS:
- The case manager or facilitator reviews information from the referral form.
- The referring teacher is encouraged to discuss his or her major referral concerns.

SAMPLE QUESTIONS:
- *Given the information that you wrote down on the referral form, what are the specific difficulties that you would like to have us address today?*
- *How is this student problem interfering with the student's school performance?*
- *What concern(s) led you to refer the student to this team?*

The RTI Team is ready to move on to the next meeting step when…
- Team members have a good knowledge of teacher concerns.

TIP:
To save time, the case manager or meeting facilitator can:
- Open with a short script about how the meeting will be conducted.
- Review information from the *RTI Team Teacher Referral Form.*
- Ask the teacher if there are any additional concerns or questions not documented on the *Referral Form.*

| Step 2: Inventory Student Strengths & Talents | Allotted Time: 5 Minutes |
|---|---|

GOALS:
- Discuss and record the student's strengths and talents, as well as those incentives that motivate the student. This information can be valuable during intervention planning to identify strategies that will motivate the student to participate.

SAMPLE QUESTIONS:
- *Please tell us a few of the student's strengths, talents, or positive qualities that might be useful in designing interventions for him or her.*
- *What rewards or incentives have you noted in school that this child seems to look forward to?*
- *What are classroom activities that the student does well or seems to enjoy?*
- *What are hobbies or topics that interest this student?*

The RTI Team is ready to move on to the next meeting step when…
- The team has identified personal strengths, talents, and/or rewards that are likely to motivate the student if integrated into an intervention plan.

TIP:
- The referring teacher may want to meet with the child *prior* to the RTI Team meeting to collect information about those incentives or activities that the student finds motivating.

| Step 3: Review Background/Baseline Data | Allotted Time: 5 Minutes |

GOALS:
- Review background or baseline data to better understand the student's abilities and potential deficits.
- Determine the student's current level(s) of performance in areas of academic or behavioral concern.

SAMPLE QUESTIONS:
- *What information has been collected to document the student's current level of functioning in the academic or behavioral area of concern?*
- *What is student's frequency of absences and tardies this year?*
- *What number and type of disciplinary office referrals has the student received this year?*
- *What information from the student's cumulative folder (e.g., test results, teacher comments, past report card grades) might give insight into the student's academic or behavioral difficulties?*

The RTI Team is ready to move on to the next meeting step when…
- The team has reviewed and discussed all pertinent background and baseline data.

TIP:
The student's classroom teacher knows that student best. Set the expectation that the referring teacher be responsible for pulling together essential archival information about the student for the initial meeting (for example, attendance and office disciplinary data, key highlights from the student's cumulative folder).

| Step 4: Select Target Teacher Concerns | Allotted Time: 5-10 Minutes |

GOALS:
- Define the top 1-2 teacher concerns in easily observable, measurable terms.
- For behavioral concerns, understand the dimensions of the problem (e.g., the frequency, duration, and/or intensity of the challenging behavior).
- For academic concerns, identify any underlying skill deficits, note whether the student is appropriately matched to the level of difficulty of classroom instruction, and estimate the current rate of student work completion.
- For each teacher concern, decide what underlying reasons, or functions, best explain the student's difficulties.

SAMPLE QUESTIONS:
- *From the list of concerns that you have shared with our team, what are the top ONE or TWO problems that you would like us to concentrate on today?*
- *(Academic) What can you tell us about the student's current skill levels, rate of homework and classwork completion, attention to task, general level of motivation?*
- *(Behavioral) How long does each behavioral outburst last? About how frequently do episodes occur?*

- *(Behavioral) What kinds of events happen in the room just before the student has an outburst or displays problem behavior? How do adults react to the student's problem behavior? How do classmates react to the problem behavior? What is the outcome or consequence for the student after he or she engages in the problem behavior?*
- *What do you think is a reason that the student shows the behavior(s) of concern? How does this behavior help the student to get his or her needs met?*

The RTI Team is ready to move on to the next meeting step when…
- The team has selected one or two primary teacher concerns.
- Everyone on the team can visualize the target concerns because they are stated in specific, observable, measurable terms.
- The referring teacher and team agree on possible underlying reasons ('functions') for the student's academic or behavioral concerns.

TIP:
- The team can save time and run a more efficient meeting if team members list all teacher concerns at the start of the meeting but postpone engaging in an extended discussion about any particular concern until the teacher selects that problem as a TOP concern.

| Step 5: Set Academic and/or Behavioral Outcome Goals and Methods for Progress-Monitoring | Allotted Time: 5 Minutes |
|---|---|

GOALS:
- For each of the academic or behavioral referral concerns, set ambitious but realistic goals for improvement that are likely to be attained within 6-8 instructional weeks. Select methods to monitor student progress during the intervention.

SAMPLE QUESTIONS:
- *Given the student's current functioning, what gains do you expect that the student will make in 6-8 weeks if the intervention that we design for him or her is successful?*
- *What is a realistic rate of progress for this student in oral reading fluency?*
- *Have we picked monitoring methods that are most efficient for monitoring the student's goal? Does the research support using these monitoring methods for tracking progress toward this particular goal?*
- *How frequently should data be collected using this progress-monitoring method?*
- *Is the monitoring method selected sufficiently sensitive to short-term student growth?*
- *Are there simple, already-existing sources of data to monitor progress toward this goal (e.g., using student homework grades to monitor completion and accuracy of homework assignments, collecting completed student work products as a means of tracking completion and accuracy of in-class assignments)?*

In the Goal-Setting section, the recorder fills out a table with the key information about the goal that will be monitored and the assessment methods to be used in tracking student progress. Here are the specific questions asked in this section, with advice on how to respond:

1. *Describe in measurable, observable terms the behavior that is to be changed (taken from Step 4).*
   Refer to the definition that you used in Step 4 to define the target behavior. Also, check out the section, *Common Methods for Monitoring Student Progress Toward Behavioral and Academic Goals* that appears at the end of this *Companion Guide*. You may find the column 'Suggested Behavior Goals' in this section to be helpful!

2. *What is the target date to achieve this goal?*
   Generally, RTI Teams allow 6-8 instructional weeks for interventions to take effect. Your team can choose a shorter or longer time period however.

3. *Is the goal for the behavior listed in step 2 to be:___ increased?  or___ decreased?*
   If your target behavior is a **problem** behavior (e.g., hitting), your team will want to decrease it. If the target behavior is **desired** (e.g., reading fluency), your team will want to increase it.

4. *What are the conditions under which the behavior typically appears (problem behaviors) or should be displayed (desired behaviors)?*
   Here are examples of 'condition' statements that give information about where, when, and under what circumstances the student's target behavior will be monitored: "When given a book at the fourth grade level', 'when given a directive by the teacher', 'when moving through the hallway', 'during math instruction'.

5. *What is the goal (level of proficiency) that the student  is expected to achieve by the date listed above?*
   Levels of proficiency should be described in measurable, quantifiable terms. Examples of proficiency levels include 'on-task 80% or more', 'turning in homework at least 4 days per week', '85 correctly read words per minute'.

6. *What measure(s) will be used to monitor student progress?*
   Refer to the section, *Common Methods for Monitoring Student Progress Toward Behavioral and Academic Goals* for widely used student monitoring methods (see last two pages of this Exhibit).

7. *How frequently will this student goal be monitored? (e.g., weekly?, daily?)*
   It is recommended that interventions be monitored at least weekly if possible, to provide sufficient information for the RTI Team to decide within 6-8 weeks whether the intervention plan is effective.

8. *Who is responsible for monitoring this student goal?*
   Often RTI Team members or other school staff assist the referring teacher to monitor student progress. Be sure to list the names of ALL personnel who take part in the monitoring effort.

The RTI Team is ready to move on to the next meeting step when…
- The team has selected ambitious but realistic goals for improvement in the target academic or behavioral area.
- The referring teacher agrees that the outcome goals are appropriate for this student case.
- Each student goal is matched with at least two appropriate methods of progress-monitoring.

TIPS:
- Review the teacher's prioritized concerns to ensure that they are stated in specific, observable, measurable terms. It is much easier to set goals when concerns are clearly defined rather than vaguely worded.
- At the end of this Companion Guide is a section, *Common Methods for Monitoring Student Progress Toward Behavioral and Academic Goals.* This section lists suitable instruments or methods for assessing student academics and general behaviors. Refer to this document when writing student goal statements.
- Review additional information about assessment methods in Chapter 5 of this manual.
- Creative RTI Teams can often save time and effort by making full use of simple, already-existing sources of data to monitor progress toward student goals (e.g., using student homework grades to monitor completion and accuracy of homework assignments, collecting completed student work products as a means of tracking completion and accuracy of in-class assignments).

| Step 6: Design an Intervention Plan | 15-20 Minutes |
|---|---|

GOALS:
- Select at least one intervention that addresses each of the selected referral concerns.
- Spell out the details of the intervention as a series of specific STEPS so that the teacher or other person(s) designated to implement it can do so correctly and efficiently.
- Note any important additional information about the intervention, including:
    — When and where the intervention will take place;
    — Whether specialized materials or training are required to implement the intervention;
    — Names of individuals responsible for carrying out the intervention.
- Review the intervention plan with the teacher to ensure that she or he finds the plan acceptable and feasible;
- Select a method to check up on how well the intervention is carried out ('intervention follow-through').

SAMPLE QUESTIONS:
- *Given the underlying reasons for this student's academic or behavioral problems, what research-based intervention ideas are most likely to address the student's needs?*

- What aspect of this particular intervention idea is likely to improve the student's academic or behavioral functioning in the area(s) specified?
- Are there specialized materials or training needed to implement this intervention successfully?
- How can our team assist you, the referring teacher, with the intervention?
- How can we work the student's strengths, talents, or interests into the intervention to make it more effective or motivating?
- What is a simple method that our team can use to track how successfully the intervention was put into practice (e.g., creation of a checklist of key steps to be implemented)?

The RTI Team is ready to move on to the next meeting step when…
- The referring teacher and team members agree that the intervention:
    - Directly addresses the identified concern(s);
    - Is judged by the referring teacher to be acceptable, sensible, and achievable;
    - Is realistic, given the resources available;
    - Appears likely to achieve the desired goal for student improvement within the timeline selected.
- The team has selected a method for evaluating whether the intervention has been carried out as designed ('treatment integrity').

TIP:

Consider inviting staff members with expertise in a particular type of referral problem to attend your RTI Team meeting as 'intervention consultants' whenever you have students that present specialized concerns. For example, your team might invite a speech/language pathologist to a meeting for a student who appears to have difficulty acquiring language concepts.

| Step 7: Plan to Share Meeting Minutes With Parents | Allotted Time: 5 Minutes |
| --- | --- |

GOALS:
- If the parent(s) cannot attend the RTI Team meeting, the team selects an individual to contact the parent(s) after the meeting to review the main points of the student's intervention plan.

SAMPLE QUESTIONS:
- Who will contact parents after this meeting to share the main points of our intervention plan?
- What specific details about the intervention plan would the parent(s) be most interested in hearing about?

The RTI Team is ready to move on to the next meeting step when…
- At least one team member (often the referring teacher) has taken responsibility to contact the parent to share information about the student's intervention plan.

**TIP:**
It is important for a representative from the RTI Team (usually the referring teacher) to contact parents prior to the initial RTI Team meeting to explain the purpose of the meeting and to extend an invitation to attend. This proactive outreach to parents establishes a tone of trust and open communication between school and home.

| Step 8: Review the Intervention & Monitoring Plans | Allotted Time: 5 Minutes |
|---|---|

**GOALS:**
- Review the main points of the intervention and monitoring plans with the referring teacher and other team members.
- (Case Manager) Schedule a time within a week of the initial meeting to meet with the referring teacher to:
  — review the intervention plan,
  — offer any needed assistance in carrying out the intervention,
  — ensure that the intervention plan is being put into practice as planned.
- Schedule a follow-up RTI Team meeting (usually within 6-8 weeks of the initial problem-solving meeting).
- As a team, take a moment to complete the *RTI Team Meeting Debriefing Form* (once the referring teacher has left the RTI Team meeting) at the end of the Minutes Form, Exhibit 3-A.

**SAMPLE QUESTIONS:**
- *Do the referring teacher and other members of our team all know what their responsibilities are in carrying out the intervention and monitoring plans for this student?*
- *(Meeting debriefing) Was our team able to support the referring teacher in identifying the most important referral concern(s)?*
- *(Meeting debriefing) Did our team help the teacher to put together a good intervention plan that is feasible and can be carried out with currently available resources?*

Adapted from the School-Based RTI Team Project Complete Forms & Related Resources, available at: http://www.interventioncentral.org/htmdocs/interventions/sbit.php. Used with permission.

# Common Methods for Monitoring Student Progress Toward Behavioral and Academic Goals

Directions: The selected measures listed below can be used to monitor student academic and behavioral goals. Select those measures that your RTI Team will use to monitor a particular student. Write the monitoring procedures you have chosen into Step 5 ('Goal-Setting') on the *RTI Team Meeting Minutes Form*.

## ACADEMIC PROBLEMS

### DIBELS: Dynamic Indicators of Basic Early Literacy Skills

| | Description of Measure | Suggested Behavior Goals |
|---|---|---|
| ☐ | Initial Sound Fluency (ISF) | Increase ISFs Correctly Per Minute to ___ |
| ☐ | Letter Naming Fluency (LNF) | Increase LNFs Correctly Per Minute to ___ |
| ☐ | Phonemic Segmentation Fluency (PSF) | Increase CSFs Correctly Per Minute to ___ |
| ☐ | Nonsense Word Fluency (NWF) | Increase NWFs Correctly Per Minute to ___ |
| ☐ | Oral Reading Fluency (ORF): Specify Reading/Monitoring Level | Increase Words Correctly Per Minute to ___ |

### CBM: Curriculum-Based Measurement

| | Description of Measure | Suggested Behavior Goals |
|---|---|---|
| ☐ | Oral Reading Fluency | Increase __ Correct Read Words Per Minute to ___ |
| ☐ | Maze Passages (Reading Comprehension) | Increase __ Correct Maze Responses in 3 Minutes to ___ |
| ☐ | Math Computation: Specify Computation Problem Type(s) | Increase __ Correct Digits Per 2 Minutes to ___ |
| ☐ | Writing: Total Words | Increase __ Total Words in 3 Minutes to ___ |
| ☐ | Writing: Correctly Spelled Words | Increase __ Words Spelled Correctly in 3 Minutes to ___ |
| ☐ | Writing: Correct Writing Sequences | Increase __ Correct Writing Sequences in 3 Minutes to ___ |

### Permanent Work Products (Classroom Assignments)

| | Description of Measure | Suggested Behavior Goals |
|---|---|---|
| ☐ | Amount of Work Completed | Increase the Average Percentage of Work Completed to __% |
| ☐ | Accuracy of Work Completed | Increase the Average Percentage of Work Done Correctly to __% |
| ☐ | Quality of Work Completed | • Increase the Average Grade in [Subject Area] to ____ <br> • Increase Teacher Ratings on a [Subject Area] Rubric to ____ |

### Homework Assignments

| | Description of Measure | Suggested Behavior Goals |
|---|---|---|
| ☐ | Work turned in | Increase the Average Number of Times per Week When Homework is Turned in to ____ |
| ☐ | Amount of Work Completed | Increase the Average Amount of Homework Completed Correctly to ____ |
| ☐ | Accuracy of Work Completed | Increase the Average Percentage of Homework Completely Correctly to ___ |
| ☐ | Quality of Work Completed | Increase the Average Student Grade on Homework to ___ Increase Teacher Ratings of the Quality of Student Work Using an Evaluation Rubric to ____ |

# BEHAVIORAL PROBLEMS

## Behavior Observations of Students in Schools (BOSS) Shapiro, 1996

| | Description of Measure | Suggested Behavior Goals |
|---|---|---|
| ❑ | Active Engaged Time (AET) | Increase the Average Percentage of Student AET to ___% |
| ❑ | Passive Engaged Time (PET) | [Increase/Decrease] the Average Percentage of Student PET to ___% |
| ❑ | Off-Task Motor (OFT-M) | Decrease the Average Percentage of Student OFT-M to ___% |
| ❑ | Off-Task Verbal (OFT-V) | Decrease the Average Percentage of Student OFT-V to ___% |
| ❑ | Off-Task Passive (OFT-P) | Decrease the Average Percentage of Student OFT-P to ___% |
| ❑ | Teacher-Directed Instruction (TDI) | Decrease the Average Percentage of TDI to ___% |

## Classroom Behaviors Observation Form (C-BOF) Adapted from Wright, 1995 (See Exhibit 5-I in Chapter 5 of this manual to learn more about the C-BOF)

| | Description of Measure | Suggested Behavior Goals |
|---|---|---|
| ❑ | Schoolwork (SW) | Increase the Average Percentage of Student SW to ___% |
| ❑ | Out of Seat (OS) | Decrease the Average Percentage of Student OS to ___% |
| ❑ | Playing With Objects/Motor Activity (PLO/MO) | Decrease the Average Percentage of Student PLO/MO to ___% |
| ❑ | Calling Out (CO) | Decrease the Average Percentage of Student CO to ___% |
| ❑ | Peer Interaction (PI) | [Increase/Decrease] the Average Percentage of Student PI to ___% |
| ❑ | Teacher Interaction: Positive (TI+) | Increase the Average Percentage of TI+ to ___% to ___% |
| ❑ | Teacher Interaction: Negative (TI-) | Decrease the Average Percentage of TI- |

## Daily Behavior Report Card (DBRCs)

| | Description of Measure | Suggested Behavior Goal |
|---|---|---|
| ❑ | [Each DBRC rating item is customized to match the student's presenting concern(s)] | • Increase the Average Teacher Ratings of 'Satisfactory' or Better on the DBRC Item [Insert Item] to ___ <br> • Increase the Frequency of Teacher Ratings of 'Satisfactory' or Better on the DBRC Item [Insert Item] to ___ Times Per Week. |

## Attendance/Tardiness

| | Description of Measure | Suggested Behavior Goal |
|---|---|---|
| ❑ | Student Attendance | • Reduce the Percentage of Days Absent During the Next [Insert Weeks] Weeks to ___% <br> • Reduce the Number of Days Absent During the Next [Insert Weeks] Weeks to No More Than ___ |
| ❑ | Student Tardiness | • Reduce the Percentage of Days Tardy During the Next [Insert Weeks] Weeks to ___% <br> • Reduce the Number of Days Tardy During the Next [Insert Weeks] Weeks to No More Than ___ |

## References

Shapiro, E.S. (1996). Academic skills problems: Direct assessment and intervention. (2nd ed.). New York: `Guildford Press.

Wright, J. (1995). ADHD: A school-based evaluation manual. Retrieved July 23, 2006, from http://www.jimwrightonline.com/pdfdocs/adhdManual.PDF.

# Exhibit 3-E
## The RTI Team:
## A Checklist for Getting Started...

Early in the school year your new RTI Team can take steps that will greatly increase its chances of success. By carefully setting up your team process and meeting procedures, informing teachers about the services that your team offers, and inventorying your school's intervention-related resources, your team will be far better prepared to take on challenging teacher referrals. The checklist below offers a framework for quickly establishing your team as an effective teacher support.

**1. Establish a clear team process and meeting procedures.** Within the first two weeks of the school year, your team should:

❑ Select a regular meeting time that is most convenient for team members and referring teachers. Be sure to allow enough time in these sessions to meet on a student and, afterwards, to debrief as a group about the team's performance.

❑ Find a suitable meeting place. At minimum, the site selected for your team meetings should offer privacy (to safeguard the confidentiality of information being shared about the referred student) and sufficient space to comfortably seat the referring teacher and other members of the team.

❑ Establish a system for responding promptly to teacher referrals. Teachers should have convenient access to the referral forms. Your team should also coordinate with the team in your building that handles Special Education referrals to work out a method for deciding which initial teacher referrals may be more appropriate for the intervention team and which should instead be routed to the Special Education team.

❑ Work out procedures for communicating efficiently among all team members. Typically, the team communication plan includes procedures for all team members to review teacher referrals and related information prior to the initial meeting on the student, and a uniform system for team members to use in communicating with the rest of the team (e.g., via staff mailboxes, email, telephone tree, general discussion time reserved at the end of weekly meetings).

**2. Publicize your team and its services to your faculty, other staff, and parents.** Some tried-and-true methods for getting the word out to the school community about your intervention team include these ideas:

❑ Schedule time at a faculty meeting early in the school year to present an overview of your team to staff. During the presentation, members from your team can introduce themselves and describe the structured problem-solving process that your team uses to help teachers with struggling learners to come up with effective intervention ideas. The presenters might also hand out intervention-team referral forms and invite teachers to refer students.

❑ Periodically present brief 'updates' about your intervention team at faculty meetings throughout the school year. One use of these updates would be to have teachers who have used your team and found its services to be helpful to share their success stories with their teaching colleagues.

❑ Write up a short description of your team and place it in all teacher mail-boxes. The description could include the names of staff who serve on the team, description of services or supports that you team offers, and proce-dures for referring a student to the RTI team.

❑ Present a workshop on your intervention team to your school's Parent Teacher Organization (PTO). Parents would appreciate knowing how the RTI Team differs from other school teams, and how this team can help struggling learners be more successful. Or your school may want to spread the word by mailing each parent a brochure describing the intervention team and its role in promoting school success.

❑ Schedule occasional professional-development 'clinics' during the school year (e.g., after school or during a Superintendents' Conference Day), at which RTI Team members offer trainings to teachers on effective strategies to use for common referral concerns. These clinics can be a great way to expand the skill base of all teachers in the building while publicizing your intervention team as a consultation resource for teachers.

3. **Create an inventory of resources in your building that can be used by your intervention team.** RTI Teams can use all the help they can get when assisting teachers with student interventions. Here are some ideas to increase the interven-tion resources available to your team:

❑ Make a list of locations around the school that can be used as space for interventions (e.g., places with adult supervision where cross-age peer tutoring can take place).

❑ Solicit names of volunteers in your building who are willing to help with implementing and/or monitoring school-based interventions.

❑ Create a directory of staff willing to serve on your intervention team whose training or professional experience gives them expertise in key intervention topics (e.g., reading instruction, behavior management). Invite these staff to attend those team meetings in which the student's referral concern matches these staff members' area of expertise.

**4. Try out the team roles and meeting procedures at least two or three times in actual meetings before accepting your first staff referral.** It is a good idea for your team to practice its meeting skills before accepting referrals from all staff members. One 'safe' way for your new team to practice its problem-solving skills is to have team members refer a couple of students *from their own classrooms* to the intervention team. The referring team member, of course, will assume the role of the referring teacher in these practice meetings. In all other respects, however, these practice meetings follow the intervention problem-solving model and include these steps:

❑ The referring intervention-team member completes a written teacher referral.

❑ A case liaison is assigned to collect both classroom information and academic and behavioral-baseline data on the student prior to the initial team meeting.

❑ A formal intervention team meeting is scheduled, with at least 90 minutes reserved for discussion of the case.

❑ Team roles (i.e., facilitator, recorder, case liaison, time-keeper) are assigned prior to the meeting.

❑ Formal intervention and monitoring plans are developed at the initial meeting.

❑ A follow-up meeting is scheduled to review the student's progress during the intervention.

❑ Ample time is reserved at the conclusion of each 'practice' meeting for the team to debrief, with each member sharing his or her perceptions about what the team did well during the meeting and what areas of team-process may need improvement.

# Exhibit 3-F
## Motivating the 'Reluctant' Teacher: Six Strategies for RTI Teams

Schools are complex social organizations. Researchers have discovered a number of techniques that can be used in social settings, including schools, to increase people's motivation to express support for a process or carry out an action. Presented here are six key strategies (*reciprocation, consistency, social proof, liking, authority, scarcity*) for building social influence (Cialdini, 1984). RTI Teams might consider using one or more of them when attempting to energize 'reluctant teachers' to make full use of the team's services. Of course, as with all techniques designed to impact social influence, these approaches should be used in an ethical and responsible manner.

**Reciprocation.** When people are given a gift or have a service performed for them, they feel obligated to 'pay back' that gift or service. Often, the person who initiates the favor is in a position both to select what is given and to suggest an appropriate 'pay-back' favor. The impulse to reciprocate can also be triggered through the 3-step 'rejection-then-retreat' strategy: (1) One party makes a request that is within reason but also goes beyond what the second party can agree to. So the request is rejected. (2) The first party then retreats to a *milder* request (concession). (3) The second party now feels obligated to match the requester's initial concession with a reciprocal concession. So he or she is likely to accept this less ambitious request.

Here are some ideas for how RTI Teams can use ***reciprocation*** to energize teachers:
- Regularly stuff teacher mailboxes with intervention tips, along with a cover note inviting their referrals to the RTI Team.
- Sponsor teacher workshops on common academic or behavioral concerns (with attractive handouts, refreshments, etc.). During the workshop, invite teachers to refer to your team.
- Offer to meet with a teacher for an RTI Team meeting at a time most convenient to him or her, even if this accommodation is somewhat *inconvenient* for team members.
- Offer to collect baseline information on a problem student and to schedule a brief conference with the teacher to discuss findings (e.g., percentage of time on task). At the conference, invite the teacher to refer the student to the RTI Team.
- Canvass team members to compile a list of 'special services' they might offer to a struggling teacher. (E.g., a physical education teacher might offer to give high-energy kids an extra gym period twice per week, etc.). Approach that teacher with the list of RTI Team services and invite him or her to select one or two. After delivery of the service(s), invite the teacher to refer a student to the team.

**Consistency.** People strive, often unconsciously, to maintain consistency between their opinions or attitudes and their actions.

The 'foot-in-the-door' technique uses our need for internal consistency as an incremental motivational tool to get people to agree to a request that they would otherwise probably refuse. (1) First, the person is asked to perform a small act that signals support for a cause (e.g., signing a petition to keep our highways free from litter). (2) As a direct result of agreeing to that small act, the person realigns his or her internal attitudes to match the action (e.g., 'I am a person that will take action to support the cause of a litter-free environment.'). (3) The person will then be more likely in the future to say 'yes' to *larger* requests that support the same cause (e.g., agreeing to join a weekend cleanup group that volunteers time to clear trash from alongside scenic roadways).

The power of consistency between words and acts can be made even greater when the person's initial, small act supporting a cause is publicized for others (e.g., publishing the names of those signing an anti-litter petition in a local newspaper).

Here are some ideas for how RTI Teams can use **consistency** to energize teachers:
- Invite a 'reluctant teacher' to provide 'moral support' to a colleague by accompanying him or her to an intervention-team meeting. Once the teacher has participated in the RTI Team problem-solving process as a guest, follow up with an invitation to that teacher to submit his or her own student referral to the team.
- Approach 'reluctant teachers' who have specialized training or skills (e.g., in early literacy) to serve as 'consultant members' of the RTI Team. Invite them to meetings whenever their expertise is needed. Spread the word through the school that these teachers are serving as team members. Eventually, invite them to refer one of their own students to the RTI Team.
- Ask a teacher if he or she would keep a supply of RTI Team referral forms or other materials in the classroom for the convenience of colleagues. If the teacher agrees, approach him or her several weeks later about referring a student to the team.
- Organize a team -sponsored monthly school contest, in which teachers and other school staff are invited to submit academic or behavioral 'intervention tips'. Publicize the winners' names and distribute their strategies to all teachers on intervention-team letterhead. Later, invite winners to join the RTI Team or to refer students to the team.

**Social Proof.** People are influenced to take an action when they see that others are also doing it. Social proof influences us even more when we believe that those whom we observe doing the activity resemble us (e.g., in occupation, social class, etc.).

Here are some ideas for how RTI Teams can use *social proof* to energize teachers:

- Have teachers of varying backgrounds and seniority give occasional testimonials at faculty meetings about the success of the RTI Team's problem-solving process.
- If your school has a grade level (e.g., middle school) that sends few referrals to the RTI Team, invite a teacher from that grade level to join the team.
- Ask a teacher from an underrepresented grade level who had a successful RTI Team case for permission to publicize the main points of the intervention plan that other faculty from her or his teaching team or grade might want to try with their own students.
- Identify key qualities of selected 'reluctant teacher' groups (e.g., veteran teachers, middle school faculty). Bring in a small delegation of RTI Team members and referring teachers from a *different* school to talk about their successes at a faculty meeting. Be sure that some of those speakers are teachers with characteristics similar to those of reluctant teachers from your own school.
- Collect general statistics about teachers' use of your RTI Team and share those statistics with staff. For example, an RTI Team might announce, "We received 35 separate referrals last year from 20 teachers. That means that nearly half of our classroom instructors used our RTI Team. This year we want to see the number of teachers referring to our team to go even higher!"

**Liking.** People are motivated to carry out the requests of those whom they like. Friends are obviously the most persuasive, because we have already chosen to like them! If friends are not available, we typically find people whom we are familiar with (neutral acquaintances) to be more likeable than complete strangers. A person unknown to us can increase his or her likeability by having a connection to one of our friends, complementing us, or appearing similar to us (e.g., engaging in the same hobbies or interests or sharing similar attitudes or opinions).

Here are some ideas for how RTI Teams can use *liking* to energize teachers:

- Ask referring teachers who had a good experience with your RTI Team if they would be willing to encourage a colleague with whom they are friends to refer a student to the team.
- List groups or individuals who currently are not using your RTI Team very much. Assign the member of your team who has the most positive relationship with each group or individual on the list to seek them out to invite them personally to refer a student to the team.
- Whenever possible, strongly encourage teachers referring a student to the RTI Team to bring a colleague of their choice to the meeting for 'collegial support'. As friends of the referring teacher, these invited guests will themselves probably be open to a later invitation to refer a student to the team.

- At RTI Team meetings, compliment referring teachers on positive aspects of their instruction or behavior management. Keep praise brief, sincere, and specific.
- Sign up well-liked faculty to serve on the RTI Team. (You can quickly generate a list of respected faculty by having your staff nominate team members through an anonymous survey.)

**Authority.** People respect and follow authority. There are a number of types of authority that can be motivational. Examples of authority include organizational (e.g., school principal), experiential (e.g., veteran teachers), and professional (e.g., teacher with an advanced degree or specialized training).

Here are some ideas for how RTI Teams can use *authority* to energize teachers:
- Have your principal set a goal for each non-tenured new teacher to refer at least *one* student to the RTI Team that year.
- Have higher-level building or district administrators make supportive comments about the RTI team at faculty meetings or workshops.
- Ask teachers with experiential or professional authority to give public testimonials about the value of the RTI Team.
- Send individual 'Thank You' cards to teachers who refer to the RTI Team. Have your principal sign each card personally.
- If a respected speaker or presenter from outside your school comes in to present to faculty, consider approaching that person in advance to describe the RTI Team process and to request that the speaker make public, supportive statements about the project.

**Scarcity.** When items, resources, or opportunities are in short supply, people value them more. We become even *more* motivated when we have to compete *with others* for scarce resources!

Here are some ideas for how RTI Teams can use *scarcity* to energize teachers:
- Plan a moratorium (end-date) for accepting referrals to your school's RTI Team. Publicize this date as it approaches.
- Set a cap on the number of referrals that your team will accept during a school year. Post this number publicly. As new referrals are accepted, change the posted number to reflect the quantity of 'open' referral slots still available. Announce this figure regularly at faculty meetings or in the school newsletter.
- Teachers feel the pressure of low-performing students more acutely at predictable milestones in the school year (e.g., end of marking periods, around the time of state 'checkpoint' examinations). As these dates approach, send a supportive note to faculty from your team reminding them that the team is still accepting referrals but that slots are limited.

- Create an attractive packet of desirable intervention strategies or tips. Print off only enough copies of the packet so that teachers referring to your team can each receive a copy. As the supply of handouts dwindles, remind teachers that they can still get their copy by referring a student to the RTI Team.
- Enlist a building staff member with specialized behavior-management or instructional knowledge as a 'consultant member' of the RTI Team. Announce to staff that this team consultant has agreed to participate in only a limited number of cases (e.g., five slots)—and that your team will honor teacher requests for these select meeting slots on a first-come, first-serve basis.

## Reference

Cialdini, R.B. (1984). Influence: *How and why people agree to things.* New York: William Morrow & Company, Inc.

# Exhibit 3-G
## Response to Intervention Team Effectiveness Self-Rating Scale

1-*Strongly Disagree*  2-*Disagree*  3-*Agree*  4-*Strongly Agree*

*How Effective is Our Current RTI Team in…?*

**Coordinating Meetings ("How well do we coordinate & schedule?")**
- Reviewing teacher referrals & checking in with teacher as needed ........... **1 2 3 4**
- Scheduling meetings ................................................................................. **1 2 3 4**
- Notifying referring teachers and RTI Team members
  about upcoming meetings ........................................................................ **1 2 3 4**
- Finding substitutes (if necessary) for team members, referring teachers ..... **1 2 3 4**
- Taking good meeting notes ........................................................................ **1 2 3 4**

**Meeting Issues ("How well do we stick to a problem-solving framework and make referring teachers feel welcome & supported?")**
- Having team members follow a 'problem-solving' format
  and avoid digressions .............................................................................. **1 2 3 4**
- Creating an atmosphere in which the referring teacher(s)
  feel welcome & supported ....................................................................... **1 2 3 4**

**Interventions ("How well do we select, document, and monitor interventions?")**
- Identifying school-wide resources available for use in team interventions ..... **1 2 3 4**
- Selecting interventions that are research-based ...................................... **1 2 3 4**
- Recording interventions thoroughly in clearly outlined steps ..................... **1 2 3 4**
- Documenting intervention 'follow-through' by teachers ............................. **1 2 3 4**

**Communication and the RTI Team ("How well do we communicate our purpose and role to our audiences?")**
- Publicizing the purpose and role of the RTI Team to faculty
  and other staff ........................................................................................ **1 2 3 4**
- Publicizing the purpose and role of the RTI Team to parents ..................... **1 2 3 4**
- Sharing information about meeting results, interventions with parents ........ **1 2 3 4**

*1-Strongly Disagree  2-Disagree  3-Agree  4-Strongly Agree*

**RTI Team 'Process' Issues ("How well do we share our feelings and attitudes about the RTI Team?")**
- Encouraging team members to share opinions about the RTI Team's direction, overall success ...................................................... 1 2 3 4
- Encouraging team members to identify positive, negative events occurring at meetings .............................................................. 1 2 3 4
- Reserving sufficient time for team 'debriefings' to communicate about 'process' issues ................................................................. 1 2 3 4

**Additional Topics...**
- Recruiting future RTI Team members ............................................. 1 2 3 4
- Finding ways to save time in the RTI process ............................... 1 2 3 4
- Coordinating RTI Team and Special Education referrals ................ 1 2 3 4
- Observing appropriate confidentiality with team, teacher, and student information ................................................................. 1 2 3 4

- Other:_____ 1 2 3 4

- Other:_____ 1 2 3 4

Date Completed: _____

# Exhibit 3-H
## RTI Team: Referring Teacher Feedback Questionnaire

Date: _____ Name [Optional]: _____

We are contacting you because you referred a child to your building's RTI Team this year. As a teacher, your feedback is <u>very</u> important in helping us to assess the effectiveness of our RTI Team. Please take a few minutes to complete the items below. The questionnaire is anonymous. Your responses and comments will be compiled and shared with your building's RTI Team, but you will not be identified. Thank you in advance for helping us to evaluate the RTI program!

1a. How would you rate the severity of the student's target problem(s) <u>prior</u> to your referring the child to RTI?

   Not at all severe   **1   2   3   4   5   6**   Very severe

1b. How would you rate the severity of the student's target problem(s) <u>now</u> after referring the child to RTI?

   Not at all severe   **1   2   3   4   5   6**   Very severe

Regarding the interventions used, please circle the number which best describes your agreement/disagreement with each statement, using the following scale:

1=strongly disagree   2=disagree   3=slightly disagree   4=slightly agree   5=agree   6=strongly agree

2.  I liked the procedures used in this intervention.                    **1 2 3 4 5 6**
3.  This intervention was a good way to handle the problem.              **1 2 3 4 5 6**
4.  Overall, this intervention was beneficial for the child.            **1 2 3 4 5 6**
5.  I had the resources (time/materials) needed to implement            **1 2 3 4 5 6**
    this intervention.

6.  To what extent were you and/or others able to implement the RTI intervention as designed?

   Not at all **1   2   3   4   5   6**   Every day/Exactly as planned

7.  Through your involvement with the RTI Team, do you feel that you have gained intervention ideas or knowledge that you will be able to use with other students?

   Definitely NO **1   2   3   4   5   6**   Definitely YES

8.  In general, how helpful was the RTI Team in helping you to achieve a positive outcome for the student?

   Not at all helpful **1   2   3   4   5   6**   Very helpful

Adapted from the School-Based Intervention Team Project Complete Forms & Related Resources, available at: http://www.interventioncentral.org/htmdocs/interventions/sbit.php. Used with permission.

# Chapter 4

## Interventions:

### How to Select, Package, and Use Them

Interventions are specific strategies adopted to help students make progress toward academic or behavioral goals. Because students' response to individually tailored interventions drives the entire RTI problem-solving process, the interventions themselves are certainly of central importance indeed, they may be thought of as the foundation upon which the entire structure of RTI rests.

As mentioned earlier in this book, the RTI model commonly groups interventions into 3 levels, or tier. Tier I interventions are universally available to all students in a classroom or school. Tier II interventions are tailored to the unique needs of students who display academic or behavioral deficits and who have not responded to the supports available to all students. Tier III interventions are the most intensive supports available in a school setting.

This chapter will focus solely on Tier II interventions. While each of the three tiers of intervention holds a significant place within the RTI process, the RTI Team typically invests most or all of its time and effort in creating student plans at the Tier II level, designing interventions, to maintain struggling students in general education classrooms. Furthermore, the discussion of interventions that follows will have an academic rather than a behavioral focus, as the RTI model is tied primarily to the identification of learning disabilities. (Keep in mind, however, that the intervention concepts explored in this chapter can be applied equally well to behavioral interventions.)

The RTI Team tilts the odds of achieving a successful academic intervention in its favor by:

- Identifying the driver(s) or underlying reason(s) for the student's poor school performance by completing a schoolwork motivation assessment and analyzing the student's acquisition, fluency, and generalization of target academic skills;

- Coming up with one or more research-based strategies matched to the student's academic needs;

- Organizing the chosen strategies into a plan formatted as a teacher-friendly intervention script;

- Assessing the intensity of the intervention plan to ensure that it is feasible, given the school's resource;.

- Selecting at least one method to measure the quality of the teacher's intervention follow-through.

The remainder of this chapter will look individually at each of these elements of intervention planning, implementation, and assessment.

## Matching Interventions to Student Needs

Tier II interventions consist of individualized "treatments" designed to improve a student's functioning in targeted academic domains. There are at least two reasons why it is important to choose an intervention that will best match the student's needs. First, finding the intervention that research suggests will most likely address the child's area(s) of deficit or delay ensures that the intervention has a high probability of being effective. Second, the RTI Team wants to avoid the potential danger of choosing the *wrong* approach to help the student. An ineffective intervention will produce no positive impact on the child's learning problems and might even worsen those problems. A student with poor decoding skills, for example, probably needs to practice reading aloud while receiving corrective feedback along with generous amounts of encouragement. That same student may become frustrated if he or she is merely offered incentives for improved reading in the place of necessary instructional feedback and encouragement.

The process of selecting the appropriate intervention depends on careful detective work to uncover the underlying reason or reasons for the student's lack of academic success. This detective work can be condensed to a two-step process: First, check whether the student is motivated to apply his or her best effort on challenging academic assignments (motivation assessment); next, if the student's difficulties appear to be tied primarily to learning rather than motivation issues, identify the student's stage of learning (Instructional Hierarchy).

## Checking for Student Motivation

Academic motivation rests upon two interacting dimensions: the student must have a reasonable *expectation of success* on the learning task; and the student must place a *significant value on achieving success* on that learning task (Sprick, Borgmeier, & Nolet, 2002). If *either* of these factors (the student's expectation of success on the task or the student's valuing of that success) is lacking, then the student will not be academically motivated.

RTI Teams are sometimes uncertain as to whether a student's deficient academic performance stems, at least in part, from that student's lack of motivation and effort. The following is a simple method by which to check whether limited student motivation is blocking academic success (Witt & Beck, 1999; Witt, VanDerHeyden & Gilbertson 2004):

1. Give the student a timed worksheet to complete with items of the type that the student takes a long time to finish or that appear to challenge the student. Collect and score the worksheet.

2. Give the student a second worksheet to complete that is similar to the first. This time, offer the student a valued reinforcer (e.g., free time, a praise note to parents, a sticker). Collect and score the worksheet.

3. If the student performs substantially better (20 percent) when offered a reinforcer, this suggests that poor motivation is a significant factor in the student's lack of academic success and that the intervention plan should include specific strategies to boost the student's academic motivation.

For detailed instructions in how to conduct an assessment of academic motivation and interpret the results, see Exhibit 4-A, *Schoolwork Motivation Assessment*.

## Applying the Instructional Hierarchy

When mastering new academic skills or strategies, the student learner typically advances through a predictable series of learning stages.  At the start, a student is usually halting and uncertain as he or she tries to use the target skill. With teacher feedback and lots of practice, the student becomes more fluent, accurate, and confident in using the skill. It can be very useful to think of these phases of learning as a hierarchy. The learning hierarchy (Haring, Lovitt, Eaton, & Hansen, 1978) has four stages: *acquisition*, *fluency*, *generalization*, and *adaptation*.

1. **Acquisition:** The student has begun to learn how to complete the target skill correctly but is not yet accurate or fluent in the skill. The goal in this phase is to improve accuracy.

2. **Fluency:** The student is able to complete the target skill accurately but works slowly. The goal of this phase is to increase the student's speed of responding (fluency).

3. **Generalization:** The student is accurate and fluent in using the target skill but does not typically use it in different situations or settings. The student may confuse the target skill with similar skills. The goal of this phase is to get the student to use the skill in the widest possible range of settings and situations, or to accurately discriminate between the target skill and similar skills.

4. **Adaptation:** The student is accurate and fluent with the skill, and uses it in many situations or settings. However,

the student is not yet able to modify or adapt the skill to fit novel task-demands or situations. The goal is for the student to be able to identify elements of previously learned skills that he or she can adapt to the new demands or situation.

When the RTI Team has accurately identified a student's learning stage, the instructor can select instructional ideas that are more likely to be successful because these strategies match the student's learning needs. Exhibit 4-B, *Instructional Hierarchy*, contains a table with specific "look-fors" (behavioral indicators) to identify a student's learning stage and provide intervention ideas at each stage.

## Defining Academic Problems in Specific Terms

When the RTI Team receives teacher referrals that describe students as having global learning concerns, the team should attempt to define the student's academic problems in as detailed a manner as possible. After all, it is difficult to select effective interventions for such vaguely defined student problems as "poor reading comprehension" or "limited writing skills." The solution is to analyze a global academic skill and divide it into more narrow and specific subskills. The RTI Team can then select the focused subskills that appear to be areas of weakness and best explain the child's lack of academic success. For sample worksheets that break global reading and writing skills into a series of academic subskills, review Exhibit 4-C, *Reading Comprehension Checklist*, and Exhibit 4-D, *Writing Skills Checklist*.

## Packaging Interventions as Teacher-Friendly Scripts

In the Response to Intervention process, an intervention plan functions much like a map. Just as explorers can navigate with greater confidence when they possess an accurate map of the local terrain, teachers and other school staff are able to carry out interventions consistently and reliably when they have clear instructions for implementing the intervention strategies. But how thorough should an intervention plan be? Ideally, the plan should contain sufficient detail to allow educators who may be unfamiliar with the student to carry out the plan with an acceptable level of quality (e.g., Martens & Hiralall, 1997). The well-written intervention plan should also:

- Be formatted as a step-by-step script or numbered series of instructions for implementing all aspects of the intervention;
- List the person(s) responsible for carrying out each intervention step;

- Include information on preparing the intervention and putting the intervention into practice;

- Cite one or more research-based sources documenting the effectiveness of the selected intervention.

The *Intervention Script Builder* (Exhibit 4-E) provides a simple framework to package an academic or behavioral intervention plan.

## Determining the Intensity of an Intervention

No matter how simple or complex, all school-based interventions require time and energy to plan, carry out, and monitor. Within current Response to Intervention models, there are two quite different options for structuring Tier II interventions Fuchs, Mock, Morgan., & Young, 2003).

- ***Intervention plans customized to the student.*** In this approach, the RTI Team meets with the referring teacher to create an intervention plan unique to the needs of the student, usually one that can be carried out mostly or entirely within the student's classroom. The teacher would typically be responsible for carrying out the intervention, perhaps with training and other support from the RTI Team. By using the classroom as the intervention site, the RTI Team can discover whether the student will benefit from a range of research-based strategies that a teacher could feasibly put into place while juggling the many other demands of his or her class. A drawback of this approach, however, is that a busy teacher has only limited time to deliver individualized interventions. Even effective strategies designed to be feasible in a classroom setting may not be sufficiently intensive to help a student with significant academic delays or behavioral problems close the gap with peers.

- *Intervention plans as "standard protocols."* Some schools create external programs that provide students who need additional academic support with standardized interventions ("standard protocols") that are often more intensive than a classroom teacher could ordinarily be expected to provide. The rationale for using standard protocols in Tier II intervention plans is that these intensive "pull-out" programs have greater potential to improve problem behaviors or deficient academic skills more rapidly than does a classroom-based intervention. The trade-off, however, is that pull-out interventions often require substantial resources to set up (e.g., time to design the program or train staff, purchase of specialized materials) and to implement. Indeed, due to the effort that they require, pull-out interventions can resemble Tier III interventions, the most intensive available in a school setting. Also, because a pull-out intervention takes place outside the classroom, it does not give the RTI Team a direct answer to the question "What accommodations are necessary to help this student to be successful in a general education setting?"

As an example of an external intervention program based on a standard protocol, one school district had a large number of young students who could not read fluently. The district created a peer-tutoring program in several of its elementary buildings in which a group of older peers (fourth and fifth-grade students) were trained to work with younger students three to four times per week (Wright & Cleary, 2006). RTI Teams at each school selected at-risk readers to enroll in the peer-tutoring program. Peer tutors used "listening passage preview," a simple but effective intervention demonstrated to build reading fluency. The peer tutors were able to provide a scientifically valid intervention to their tutees, while also giving these younger readers more time (up to 90 minutes per week) and individualized attention than the classroom teacher was able to provide.

There is no clear-cut advantage to intervention plans that are customized to the student or based on a standard protocol. Schools must decide for themselves which type of intervention model best suits their needs and resources. It is important, however, that schools recognize the level of effort that an intervention requires before committing to it to ensure that the intervention plan can be sustained over time if it is successful. The *Intervention Intensity Rating Form* (Exhibit 4-F) contains 10 rating items that allow RTI Teams to assess the intensity of a particular intervention and to decide whether that plan more closely resembles a Tier II, moderate support, or Tier III intervention, intensive support.

## Measuring Intervention Follow-Through

When a classroom intervention has been painstakingly designed and is ready to be implemented, it still faces serious obstacles to success. For example, the teacher may lack the necessary materials, skills, or training to start the intervention or may perform the steps of the intervention incorrectly. If a specific intervention is implemented incorrectly or not at all, the student does not have a true opportunity to "respond to intervention."

The RTI Team, therefore, should always attempt in some manner to measure the quality with which classroom interventions are put into practice as a routine part of its data collection activities (Gresham, 1989; Gresham, Gansle, & Noell, 1993). When the team collects evidence showing that a research-based intervention has been carried out as designed, it has greater confidence that the student's progress-monitoring data truly shows whether or not the student benefited from that intervention.

A term that is used to describe how well an intervention is carried out is "intervention follow-through" (researchers also sometimes refer to this concept as "treatment integrity"). Educators demonstrate good intervention follow-through when they faithfully follow all the steps of the student's intervention script (without skipping any), and also use the intervention as frequently and for as long a duration as it was originally designed. To measure teachers' intervention follow-through, schools can use an independent observer, have teachers self-monitor with an intervention checklist, or direct teachers to rate their own performance with an intervention evaluation log.

***Independent Observer.*** One method for rating the quality of intervention follow-through is to have an independent observer (e.g., a fellow teacher, school psychologist, or school administrator) drop by the classroom occasionally when the intervention is occurring. The observer has a checklist defining the essential steps of the intervention. Each time that the observer notes that the instructor has completed an intervention step, the observer records this information with a checkmark on the corresponding section of the intervention checklist. Independent observations are the most objective method of measuring intervention follow-through. However, they are also the most time-intensive. Additionally, some teachers may feel uncomfortable with direct observations, at least initially, because they perceive that their own work performance is being evaluated. The *Intervention Script Builder* (Exhibit 4-E) has an "Intervention Check" column that an observer can use to rate the steps of the intervention.

***Self-Monitoring With Intervention Checklist.*** Having teachers rate their own adherence to an intervention is an alternative method for tracking intervention follow-through. Periodically, the teacher reviews a script listing all the steps of the intervention and rates whether he or she has successfully carried out each separate step. Having teachers closely monitor their own intervention follow-through offers a major advantage: with the checklist as a prompt, they are less likely to skip important steps (Hayes, 1981). However, teacher ratings can also be subjective in nature and must therefore be viewed with less confidence than other sources of data on intervention follow-through.

Teachers who self-monitor should evaluate the quality of their intervention efforts more frequently (e.g., everyday) when they are just beginning the intervention phase to ensure that they are implementing the strategy properly. Teachers can then reduce the frequency of monitoring (e.g., weekly) as they become more confident and practiced in the intervention procedures. Again, it is noted that The *Intervention Script Builder* (Exhibit 4-E) includes an "Intervention Check" column that the classroom teacher can use periodically to rate the steps of the intervention.

***Self-Monitoring With An Intervention Evaluation Log.*** A method for teachers to briefly self-monitor intervention follow-through is through use of a generic rating sheet. Each day, teachers rate the degree to which they were able to carry out the intervention as designed, with the option of including notes to explain any problems that they encountered with the intervention that day. Advantages to using a simple rating log are that this method is quick and convenient and that teachers are likely to attend more closely to the quality of their interventions when they must measure that quality on a daily basis (Hayes, 1981). Because the log is based solely on teacher judgment, however, and requires only a single global rating of the intervention each day, there is possibility that the results will be overly subjective. Schools should regard a teacher log as the least preferred method for monitoring intervention follow-through. However, its use is still far better than not monitoring the quality of classroom interventions at all. The *Teacher Intervention Evaluation Log* (Exhibit 4-G) provides a generic form on which instructors can rate the implementation of their interventions as frequently as daily.

## Assembling an "Intervention Bank"

An RTI Team must be prepared to discuss a wide range of student concerns but it can be difficult during busy problem-solving meetings for the team to select and format appropriate research-based interventions. One helpful idea that RTI Teams can use to build their intervention capacity is to create an "intervention bank." The team identifies common teacher referral concerns in their school. The team then locates descriptions of research-based interventions to address these concerns by consulting trusted sources (e.g., intervention articles taken from reputable peer-reviewed journals; print or web publications from respected organizations such as the Council for Exceptional Children or the National Association of School Psychologists; etc.). If necessary, the team rewrites the interventions described in these research articles as accessible, step-by-step teacher scripts. Over time, the RTI Team collects the intervention scripts that they have developed and organizes them. During meetings, the team can quickly turn to the relevant section of the intervention bank to review a series of scientifically valid interventions that might be appropriate to a particular student's needs. **Appendix A** contains a wealth of research-based interventions which address student problems with reading and writing. RTI Teams can use this collection of strategies as a starter set for building their own intervention bank.

# References

Fuchs, D., Mock, D., Morgan, P., & Young, C. (2003). Responsiveness-to-intervention: Definitions, evidence, and implications for the learning disabilities construct. *Learning Disabilities: Research and Practice, 18(3)*, 157-171.

Gresham, F. M. (1989). Assessment of treatment integrity in school consultation & prereferral intervention. *School Psychology Review, 18,* 27-50.

Gresham, F. M., Gansle, K. A., & Noell, G. H. (1993). Treatment integrity in applied behavior analysis with children. *Journal of Applied Behavior Analysis, 26(2),* 257-263.

Haring, N.G., Lovitt, T.C., Eaton, M.D., & Hansen, C.L. (1978). *The fourth R: Research in the classroom.* Columbus, OH: Charles E. Merrill Publishing Co.

Hayes, S. C. (1981). Theoretical explanations for reactivity in self-monitoring. *Behavior Modification, 5,* 3-14.

Martens, B. K., & Hiralall, A. S., (1997). A versatile, low-impact procedure for increasing appropriate behavior in a nursery school. *Behavior Modification, 21,* 308-323.

Sprick, R. S., Borgmeier, C., & Nolet, V. (2002). Prevention and management of behavior problems in secondary schools. In M. A. Shinn, H. M. Walker & G. Stoner (Eds.), *Interventions for academic and behavior problems II: Preventive and remedial approaches* (pp.373-401). Bethesda, MD: National Association of School Psychologists.

Witt, J., & Beck, R. (1999). *One minute academic functional assessment and interventions: "Can't" do it…or "won't" do it?* Longmont, CO: Sopris West.

Witt, J. C., VanDerHeyden, A. M., Gilbertson, D. (2004). Troubleshooting behavioral interventions: A systematic process for finding and eliminating problems. *School Psychology Review,* 33, 363-381.

Wright, J., & Cleary, K. S. (2006). Kids in the tutor seat: Building schools' capacity to help struggling readers through a cross-age peer-tutoring program. *Psychology in the Schools, 43(1)*, 99-107.

# Exhibit 4-A
## Schoolwork Motivation Assessment
(adapted from Witt & Beck, 1999; Witt, VanDerHeyden & Gilbertson, 2004)

Student:_____ Teacher/Classroom:_____

Date of Assessment: __/__/__ Person Completing Assessment:_____

| Step 1: Assemble an incentive menu. Create a 4-5 item menu of modest incentives or rewards that students in the class are most likely to find motivating. Examples of popular incentives include:<br>• Small prizes such as pencils or stickers,<br>• Five minutes of extra free time,<br>• Opportunity to play a computer game,<br>• Praise note or positive phone call to parent. | Incentive / Reward Menu<br><br>Idea 1:_____<br><br>Idea 2:_____<br><br>Idea 3:_____<br><br>Idea 4:_____<br><br>Idea 5:_____ |
|---|---|

**Step 2: Create two versions of a CBM probe or timed worksheet.** Make up two versions of a structured, timed worksheet with items of the type that the student appears to find challenging. Use one of the options below:

Option 1: Create Curriculum-Based Measurement probes. The probes should be at the same level of difficulty, but each probe should have different items or content to avoid a practice effect. NOTE: CBM probes in oral reading fluency, math computation, writing, and spelling can all be used.

Option 2: Make up two versions of custom student worksheets. The worksheets should be at the same level of difficulty, but each worksheet should have different items or content to avoid a practice effect. NOTE: If possible, the worksheets should contain standardized short-answer items (e.g., matching vocabulary words to their definitions) to allow you to calculate the student's rate of work completion.

**Step 3: Administer the first CBM probe or timed worksheet to the student WITHOUT incentives.** In a quiet, non-distracting location, administer the first worksheet or CBM probe under timed, standardized conditions. Collect the probe or worksheet and score.

| Step 4: Compute an improvement goal. After you have scored the first CBM probe or worksheet, compute a '20 percent improvement goal'. Multiply the student's score on the worksheet by 1.2. This product represents the student's minimum goal for improvement. | Student Score on First CBM Probe or Worksheet _____<br>Multiplied by: 1.2<br>Yields an improvement goal of: _____ |
|---|---|

**Step 5: Have the student select an incentive for improved performance.** Tell the student that if he or she can attain a score on the second worksheet that meets or exceeds your goal for improvement (Step 4), the student can earn an incentive. Show the student the reward menu. Ask the student to select the incentive that he or she will earn if the goal is met or exceeded.

| | |
|---|---|
| **Step 6: Administer the second timed worksheet to the student WITH incentives.** Give the student the second CBM probe. Collect and score. If the student meets or exceeds the pre-set improvement goal, award the student the incentive. | Student Score on Second CBM Probe or Worksheet _____ <br><br> Compared to: <br><br> Improvement goal of: _____ |

**Step 7: Interpret the results of the academic motivation assessment to select appropriate interventions.** Use the decision-rules below to determine recommended type(s) of intervention:

❑ ACADEMIC INTERVENTIONS ONLY. If the student fails to meet or exceed the improvement goal, an academic intervention should be selected to teach the appropriate skills or to provide the student with drill and practice opportunities to build fluency in the targeted academic area(s).

❑ COMBINED ACADEMIC AND PERFORMANCE INTERVENTIONS. If the student meets or exceeds the improvement goal but continues to function significantly below the level of classmates, an intervention should be tailored that includes strategies to both improve academic performance and to increase the student's work motivation. The academic portion of the intervention should teach the appropriate skills or provide the student with drill and practice opportunities to build fluency in the targeted academic area(s). Ideas for performance interventions include: providing the student with incentives or 'pay-offs' for participation and/or structuring academic lessons around topics or functional outcomes valued by the student.

❑ PERFORMANCE INTERVENTIONS ONLY. If the student meets or exceeds the improvement goal with an incentive and shows academic skills that fall within the range of 'typical' classmates, the intervention should target only student work performance or motivation. Ideas for performance interventions include: providing the student with incentives or 'pay-offs' for participation and/or structuring academic lessons around topics or functional outcomes valued by the student.

**References:**

Witt, J., & Beck, R. (1999). *One minute academic functional assessment and interventions: "Can't" do it…or "won't" do it?* Longmont, CO: Sopris West.

Witt, J. C., VanDerHeyden, A. M., Gilbertson, D. (2004). Troubleshooting behavioral interventions: A systematic process for finding and eliminating problems. School Psychology Review, 33, 363-381.

# Exhibit 4-B

## Instructional Hierarchy: Matching Interventions to Student Learning Stage (Haring, et al., 1978)

| Learning Stage | Student 'Look-Fors'… | What strategies are effective… |
|---|---|---|
| **Acquisition:** Exit Goal: The student can perform the skill accurately with little adult support. | • Is just beginning to learn skill<br>• Is not yet able to perform or earning task reliably or with high level of accuracy | • Teacher actively demonstrates target skill<br>• Teacher uses 'think-aloud' strategy—especially for thinking skills that are otherwise covert<br>• Student has models of correct performance to consult as needed (e.g., correctly completed math problems on board)<br>• Student gets feedback about correct performance<br>• Student receives praise, encouragement for *effort* |
| **Fluency:** Exit Goals: The student: (a) has learned skill well enough to retain; (b) has learned skill well enough to combine with other skills; (c) is as fluent as peers. | • Gives accurate responses to learning task<br>• Performs learning task slowly, haltingly | • Teacher structures learning activities to give student opportunity for active (observable) responding<br>• Student has frequent opportunities to *drill* (direct repetition of target skill) and *practice* (blending target skill with other skills to solve problems)<br>• Student gets feedback on *fluency* and *accuracy* of performance<br>• Student receives praise, encouragement for *increased fluency* |
| **Generalization:** Exit Goals: The student: (a) uses the skill across settings, situations; (b) does not confuse target skill with similar skills. | • Is accurate and fluent in responding<br>• May fail to apply skill to new situations, settings<br>• May confuse target skill with similar skills (e.g., confusing '+' and 'x' number operation signs) | • Teacher structures academic tasks to require that the student use the target skill regularly in assignments.<br>• Student receives encouragement, praise, reinforcers for using skill in new settings, situations<br>• If student confuses target skill with similar skill(s), the student is given practice items that force him/her to correctly discriminate between similar skills<br>• Teacher works with parents to identify tasks that the student can do outside of school to practice target skill<br>• Student gets periodic opportunities to review, practice target skill to ensure maintenance |
| **Adaptation:** Exit Goal: The Adaptation phase is continuous and has no exit criteria. | • Is fluent and accurate in skill<br>• Applies skill in novel situations, settings without prompting<br>• Does not yet modify skill as needed to fit new situations (e.g., child says "Thank you" in all situations, does not use modified, equivalent phrases such as "I appreciate your help.") | • Teacher helps student to articulate the '*big ideas*' or core element(s) of target skill that the student can modify to face novel tasks, situations (e.g., fractions, ratios, and percentages link to the 'big idea' of *the part in relation to the whole*; 'Thank you' is part of a larger class of *polite speech*).<br>• Train for adaptation: Student gets opportunities to practice the target skill with modest modifications in new situations, settings with encouragement, corrective feedback, praise, other reinforcers.<br>• Encourage student to set own goals for adapting skill to new and challenging situations. |

# Exhibit 4-C
## Reading Comprehension Checklist
### (National Reading Panel, 2000; Pressley & McDonald, 1997)

Student: _____ Date: _____ Person Completing: _____

**Directions:** Use this checklist to inventory students' reading comprehension skills.  Any comprehension sub-skill that is marked 'N[o]' should be targeted for intervention.

| Before reading the text, the student: |
|---|

__Y__ N__More data needed   • *Articulates his or her general purpose or reason for reading the text*

__Y__ N__More data needed   • *Sets specific goals, expectations, or outcomes to be attained by reading the selection*

__Y__ N__More data needed   • *Previews the text (e.g., looking over chapter and section headings, examining illustrations, tables, and figures) to build a preliminary mental map of the content*

__Y__ N__More data needed   • *Identifies sections of the text that are more relevant or less relevant to his/her  goals*

__Y__ N__More data needed   • *Adopts a 'reading plan' to most efficiently accomplish pre-set goals*

| While reading the text, the student: |
|---|

__Y__ N__More data needed   • *Accesses his/her 'prior knowledge' of the topic to more fully understand the meaning of the text*

__Y__ N__More data needed   • *Continually monitors his/her understanding of the reading*

__Y__ N__More data needed   • *Uses strategies, as needed, to define the meanings of unknown words, to memorize content, and to overcome other difficulties encountered during reading*

__Y__ N__More data needed   • *Engages in closer, more careful reading in those sections of the text that relate specifically to his/her reading goals*

__Y__ N__More data needed   • *Dialogs with the writer by recording information (e.g., in notes written in the page margin or in a reader's diary) about points of uncertainty, confusion, agreement, or disagreement, further elaborations of an idea presented in the text, etc*

__Y__ N__More data needed   • *Jumps back and forth in the text as needed to check facts, clear up confusion, or answer questions*

| When finished reading the text, the student: |
|---|

__Y__ N__More data needed   • *Makes use of 'text lookback', rereading sections of the text if needed to clarify understanding, clear up confusion, or more fully comprehend content*

__Y__ N__More data needed   • *Reviews notes from his or her reading to summarize the 'gist' (key ideas) of the text*

__Y__ N__More data needed   • *Continues to think about the text and the relation of its ideas or content to previous readings or the student's own knowledge and experiences*

**References:**

National Reading Panel. (2000). Teaching children to read: An evidence-based assessment of the scientific research literature on reading and its implications for reading instruction. (NIH Publication No. 00-4754). Washington, DC: National Institute of Child Health and Human Development.

Pressley, M., & Wharton-McDonald, R. (1997). Skilled comprehension and its development through instruction. School Psychology Review, 26(3), 448-467.

# Exhibit 4-D
## Writing Skills Checklist

Student:_____ Date:_____ Person Completing:_____

**Directions:** Use this checklist to inventory student's foundation writing skills. Any writing skill that is marked 'N[o]' should be targeted for intervention.

| Problem? | Writing Competency | Sample Intervention Ideas |
|---|---|---|
| **Physical Production of Writing** | | |
| ___Y ___N | *Writing Speed.* Writes words on the page at a rate equal or nearly equal to that of classmates | • Teach keyboarding skills<br>• Allow student to dictate ideas into a tape-recorder and have a volunteer (e.g., classmate, parent, school personnel) transcribe them |
| ___Y ___N | *Handwriting.* Handwriting is legible to most readers | • Provide training in handwriting<br>• Teach keyboarding skills |
| **Mechanics & Conventions of Writing** | | |
| ___Y ___N | *Grammar & Syntax.* Knowledge of grammar (rules governing use of language) and syntax (grammatical arrangement of words in sentences) is appropriate for age and/or grade placement | • Teach rules of grammar, syntax<br>• Have student compile individualized checklists of his/her own common grammar/syntax mistakes; direct students to use the checklist to review work for errors before turning in |
| ___Y ___N | *Spelling.* Spelling skills are appropriate for age and/or grade placement | • Have student collect list of own common misspellings; assign words from list to study; quiz student on list items<br>• Have student type assignments and use spell-check |
| **Writing Content** | | |
| ___Y ___N | *Vocabulary.* Vocabulary in written work is age/grade appropriate | • Compile list of key vocabulary and related definitions for subject area; assign words from list to study; quiz student on definitions of list items<br>• Introduce new vocabulary items regularly to class; set up cooperative learning activities for student to review vocabulary |
| ___Y ___N | *Word Choice.* Distinguishes word-choices that are appropriate for informal (colloquial, slang) written discourse vs. formal discourse | • Present examples to the class of formal vs. informal word choices<br>• Have student check work for appropriate word choice as part of writing revision process |
| ___Y ___N | *Audience.* Identifies targeted audience for writing assignments and alters written content to match needs of projected audience | • Direct student to write a 'targeted audience profile' as a formal (early) step in the writing process; have student evaluate the final writing product to needs of targeted audience during the revision process |
| ___Y ___N | *Plagiarism.* Identifies when to credit authors for use of excerpts quoted verbatim or unique ideas taken from other written works | • Define plagiarism for student. Use plentiful examples to show acceptable vs. unacceptable incorporation of others' words or ideas into written compositions |

## Writing Preparation

| | | |
|---|---|---|
| __Y___N | *Topic Selection.* Independently selects appropriate topics for writing assignments | • Have student generate list of general topics that that interest him/her; sit with the student to brainstorm ideas for writing topics that relate to the student's own areas of interest |
| __Y___N | *Writing Plan.* Creates writing plan by breaking larger writing assignments into sub-tasks (e.g., select topic, collect source documents, take notes from source documents, write outline, etc.) | • Create generic pre-formatted work plans for writing assignments that break specific types of larger assignments (e.g., research paper) into constituent parts. Have student use these plan outlines as a starting point to making up his/her own detailed writing plans |
| __Y___N | *Note-Taking.* Researches topics by writing notes that capture key ideas from source material | • Teach note-taking skills; have student review note-cards with the teacher as quality check |

## Writing Production & Revision

| | | |
|---|---|---|
| __Y___N | *Adequate 'Seat Time'.* Allocates realistic amount of time to the act of writing to ensure a quality final product | • Use teacher's experience and information from proficient student writers to develop estimates of minimum writing 'seat time' needed to produce quality products for 'typical' writing assignments (e.g., 5-paragraph opinion essay; 10-page term paper). Share with student.<br>• Have student keep a writing diary to record amount of time spent in act of writing for each assignment. Require that this information be submitted along with the student's assignment (Additional idea: Consider asking parents to monitor and record their child's writing time.) |
| __Y___N | *Oral vs. Written Work.* Student's dictated and written passages are equivalent in complexity and quality | • Allow student to dictate ideas into a tape-recorder and have a volunteer (e.g., classmate, parent, school personnel) transcribe them<br>• Permit the student to use speech-to-text software (e.g., Dragon Naturally Speaking) to dictate first drafts of writing assignments |
| __Y___N | *Revision Process.* Revises initial written draft before turning in for a grade or evaluation | • Create a rubric containing the elements of writing that student should review during the revision process; teach this rubric to the class; link a portion of the grade on writing assignments to student's use of the revision rubric |
| __Y___N | *Timely Submission.* Turns in written assignments (class work, homework) on time | • Provide student incentives for turning work in on time<br>• Work with parents to develop home-based plans for work completion and submission<br>• Institute school-home communication to let parents know immediately when important assignments are late or missing |

# Exhibit 4-E
## Intervention Script Builder

Student Name: _____ Grade: _____

Teacher/Team: _____ Intervention Start Date: ___ / ___ / ___

Description of the Target Academic or Behavior Concern:_____

| Intervention Check | Intervention Preparation Steps: Describe any preparation (creation or purchase of materials, staff training, etc.) required for this intervention. | Person(s) Responsible |
|---|---|---|
| This step took place Y___ N___ | 1. _____ | |
| This step took place Y___ N___ | 2. _____ | |
| This step took place Y___ N___ | 3. _____ | |
| **Intervention Check** | **Intervention Steps:** Describe the steps of the intervention. Include enough detail so that the procedures are clear to all who must implement them. | **Person(s) Responsible** |
| This step took place Y___ N___ | 1. _____ | |
| This step took place Y___ N___ | 2. _____ | |
| This step took place Y___ N___ | 3. _____ | |
| This step took place Y___ N___ | 4. _____ | |
| This step took place Y___ N___ | 5. _____ | |
| This step took place Y___ N___ | 6. _____ | |

Research Citation(s) / References: List the published source(s) that make this a 'scientifically based' intervention.

_____

Intervention Quality Check: How will data be collected to verify that this intervention is put into practice as it was designed? (Select at least one option.)

❑ Classroom Observation: Number of observations planned? _____

   Person responsible for observations?:_____

❑ Teacher Intervention Rating Log: How frequently will the teacher rate intervention follow-through?

     Daily _____ Weekly_____

❑ Teacher Verbal Report: Who will check in with the teacher for a verbal report of how

   the intervention is progressing?_____

   Approximately when during the intervention period will this verbal 'check in' occur?

                                                   _____

❑ Rating Intervention Follow-Through: Select either the classroom teacher/team or an outside observer to rate the quality of the intervention and check the appropriate set of directions below.

   _____Teacher Directions: Make copies of this intervention script. Once per week, review the steps in the intervention script and note (Y/N) whether each step was _typically_ followed. Then write any additional notes about the intervention in the blank below

   _____ Independent Observer Directions: Make copies of this intervention script. At several points during the intervention, make an appointment to observe the intervention in action. While observing the intervention, go through the steps in the intervention script and note (Y/N) whether each step was typically followed. Then write any additional notes about the intervention in the space below

Intervention Observation Notes: _____

_____

_____

# Exhibit 4-F

## Intervention Intensity Rating Form

**Directions:** The *Intervention Intensity Rating Form* provides an informal estimate of the resources and effort required to carry out a particular intervention. Tier I interventions are universally available to all students in a classroom or school. Tier II interventions are tailored to the unique needs of students who display academic or behavioral deficits and who have not responded to the supports available to all students. Tier III interventions are the most intensive supports available in a school setting.

For each of the intervention elements below, check the box in the Tier I, II, or III column that *best* matches the specific intervention you are rating. (If you are unsure of a rating, make your best guess.) Count up the checks in each column.

Guidelines for Interpreting Results. If 7 or more of your ratings on this 10-item form fall under any *single* Tier, it is likely that the intervention has a level of intensity matching that Tier as well. An intervention with 8 checks under the Tier II column, for example, should be considered a Tier II intervention. If you have a *mixed* pattern of ratings—with no single column containing 7 or more checks—count up the number of checks in each column. The intervention should be considered equivalent in intensity to the *highest* column that contains 3 or more checks. (Tier I is the lowest column. Tier III is the highest.) An intervention with more than 3 checks under the Tier III column, for example, would be considered a Tier III intervention.

Intervention Description: _____

| Intervention Element | Tier I | Tier II | Tier III |
|---|---|---|---|
| **Preparation of the Intervention** | | | |
| 1. Certification or other formal credentials required to qualify person(s) to implement the intervention | ☐ No certification or specialized credentials required | ☐ Certification or specialized credentials required (e.g., Reading Specialist, School Psychologist) but commonly available in school setting | ☐ Certification or specialized credentials required: in highly specialized area or in form of advanced degree (e.g., Ph.D.) |

| Intervention Element | Tier I | Tier II | Tier III |
|---|---|---|---|
| 2. On a per-pupil basis, the cost to purchase or effort needed to create intervention materials | ☐ Intervention materials not needed or do not entail significant expense or effort | ☐ Intervention materials required but can be obtained at a modest cost or with reasonable effort or effort | ☐ Intervention materials per pupil are costly or require substantial effort to create |
| 3. Initial training required to use the intervention | ☐ Little or no training needed | ☐ Modest amount of training (1 or 2 sessions) needed | ☐ Significant training (more than 2 sessions) required |

### Implementation of the Intervention

| Intervention Element | Tier I | Tier II | Tier III |
|---|---|---|---|
| 4. Amount of preparation required for each session of the intervention | ☐ Little or no preparation is needed | ☐ Some preparation is needed (up to 15 minutes per session) | ☐ Substantial preparation is needed (more than 15 minutes per session) |
| 5. Average time needed each session to implement the intervention | ☐ Little or no extra time is needed | ☐ Some time is needed (up to 30 minutes per session) | ☐ Substantial time is needed (more than 30 minutes per session) |
| 6. Degree to which the intervention is tailored to the unique needs of the target student | ☐ Intervention is likely to be effective with a wide range of students (e.g., use of praise statements) | ☐ Intervention is tailored to the target student but could also be applied to other students who show similar, somewhat common presenting problems (e.g., poor reading fluency; inattention) | ☐ Intervention is highly individualized to the needs of the target student, unlikely to be applicable to many other students in the class or school (e.g., middle school student requiring early-elementary level reading instruction) |
| 7. Degree to which the intervention can be carried out by the educator as part of his or her "typical" instructional routine | ☐ Intervention can be fully integrated into the teacher's instructional routine | ☐ Intervention requires that the educator expend moderate amount of additional effort or time beyond the usual instructional routine | ☐ Intervention requires that the educator expend significant additional effort or time beyond the usual instructional routine |

| Intervention Element | Tier I | Tier II | Tier III |
|---|---|---|---|
| 8. Size of the developmental gap between the stated intervention outcome goal(s) of the target student and the 'typical' academic or behavioral levels of the classroom or grade level | ☐ Intervention goal approaches or matches the academic or behavioral levels of most students at that grade level | ☐ Intervention goal falls somewhat below the academic or behavioral levels of most students at that grade level | ☐ Intervention goal falls significantly below the academic or behavioral levels of most students at that grade level |
| 9. Potential of the intervention to distract other students or disrupt their learning | ☐ Intervention can be implemented with little or no distraction of other students or disruption to their learning | ☐ Intervention is likely to result in mild distraction of other students or mild disruption to their learning | ☐ Intervention is likely to result in significant distraction of other students or disruption to their learning |
| *Monitoring of the Intervention* | | | |
| 10. Effort required to monitor the success of the intervention (e.g., a teacher who rates a student on a Daily Behavior Report Card would be considered 'low effort', a psychologist who carries out twice-weekly direct observations of student behavior would be 'high effort') | ☐ Method(s) of intervention monitoring requires little additional effort | ☐ Method(s) of intervention monitoring requires moderate additional effort | ☐ Method(s) of intervention monitoring requires significant additional effort |
| | TIER I TOTAL = _____ | TIER II TOTAL = _____ | TIER III TOTAL = _____ |

# Exhibit 4-G
## Teacher Intervention Evaluation Log

Student:_____ Date: _____

Staff Member(s) Implementing Intervention: _____

Classroom/Location: _____ Intervention Description:_____

_____

*Complete form below, with a rating of '1' as **Not At All**, & '9' as **Fully**.*

. . . . . . . . . . . . . . . . . . . . . . . . . . . . . . . . . . . . . . . . . . . . . . . . . . . . . . . .

Date:_____

To what degree were you able to carry out the intervention as designed?

| 1 | 2 | 3 | 4 | 5 | 6 | 7 | 8 | 9 |

Not at all : Somewhat : Fully

If your rating fell below a '7', descirbe the reason(s) the intervention could not be carried out as planned:

_____

_____

_____

- - - - - - - - - - - - - - - - - - - - - - - - - - - - - - - - - - - - - - - - - - - - -

Date:_____

To what degree were you able to carry out the intervention as designed?

| 1 | 2 | 3 | 4 | 5 | 6 | 7 | 8 | 9 |

Not at all : Somewhat : Fully

If your rating fell below a '7', descirbe the reason(s) the intervention could not be carried out as planned:

_____

_____

_____

- - - - - - - - - - - - - - - - - - - - - - - - - - - - - - - - - - - - - - - - - - - - -

Date:_____

To what degree were you able to carry out the intervention as designed?

| 1 | 2 | 3 | 4 | 5 | 6 | 7 | 8 | 9 |

Not at all : Somewhat : Fully

If your rating fell below a '7', descirbe the reason(s) the intervention could not be carried out as planned:

_____

_____

_____

- - - - - - - - - - - - - - - - - - - - - - - - - - - - - - - - - - - - - - - - - - - - -

Date:_____

To what degree were you able to carry out the intervention as designed?

| 1 | 2 | 3 | 4 | 5 | 6 | 7 | 8 | 9 |

Not at all : Somewhat : Fully

If your rating fell below a '7', descirbe the reason(s) the intervention could not be carried out as planned:

_____

_____

_____

# Chapter 5

## Methods to Monitor Academic & Behavioral Interventions

The RTI problem-solving model requires reliable information about the student, and lots of it. The RTI Team that tries to accurately pinpoint the reasons why a student is struggling in school and to design an effective intervention plan without good data is like the pilot who tries to fly across an unknown continent without navigation instruments. The RTI Team that lacks good data about the student's academic skills, work habits, and general behaviors can only guess blindly about the nature of the student's problems and what interventions would benefit that student. The outcomes of such a random process would probably be poor. With the right assessment tools, though, the Team can collect data, analyze it to match the student to those research-based interventions most likely to be successful, and then verify that the student is indeed benefiting from the intervention.

The assessment process for a student referred to the RTI Team is ongoing and makes use of data from many sources. The classroom teacher who refers the child can provide much valuable information about the student's academic skills, work habits, and general classroom behaviors. Schools maintain rich records on students, storing data on attendance, disciplinary office referrals, grades, performance on group achievement tests, and more. This archival information can provide clues and insights into factors that may be hindering a student's school success. When the RTI

Team implements an intervention plan that is tailored to the unique needs of the student, it collects data frequently to monitor the student's progress. The RTI Team analyzes this stream of progress-monitoring information to determine in a short time whether the selected intervention strategies are having the expected positive impact on the student's performance.

In this chapter, we review key concepts of school assessment that can save RTI Teams time and effort, while assisting them in making better judgments about the meaning of the assessment data they have collected. The chapter also presents examples of essential assessment tools that RTI Teams can use to gauge the nature and severity of a student's presenting concerns and to track the student's progress once interventions have been put into place.

## Common Types of Assessment Data

When collecting information on students, RTI Teams have many methods of data collection from which to choose. Some sources of information offer one-time glimpses of the student's functioning, while other sources of data can be collected repeatedly over time to provide an evolving narrative of the student's progress. Below is a listing of the most common sources of student assessment data used by RTI Teams (see Exhibit 5-A, *Common Types of Student Assessment & Progress-Monitoring Data*).

- *Grade Report Cards*. Grades provide evidence of student performance in previous years. Teacher comments describe academic performance and general behaviors. (see Exhibit 5-B, *Student Archival Information Sheet*).

- *Test/Screening Data*. Test records from the student's cumulative folder illustrate academic strengths and weaknesses. Results from group tests and universal screenings given during the current school year provide a useful comparison to peer performance.

- *Student Interview or Self-Completed Learning Survey*. The student is given the opportunity to inform adults about perceived academic or behavioral strengths or weaknesses, preferred methods of learning and review, interests or hobbies, and favorite rewards or reinforcers (see Exhibit 5-C, *Student Learning Survey*).

- *Teacher Interview*. The classroom teacher is interviewed about the student. The instructor answers questions about the student's academic skill level and performance, work habits, interactions with peers, and general behaviors.

- *Class and Homework Grades*. Grades from the current year provide a comparison of the student's performance to average class or grade performance. Trends or variations in the target student's grades can also provide insight into underlying academic problems.

- *Attendance/Tardiness Records*. Patterns of absences and tardy arrivals from the current year may suggest evidence of victimization by bullies, work avoidance, school phobia, or other causes. Attendance data across school years may confirm the chronic nature of a student's truancy or tardiness (see Exhibit 5-D, *Measuring Student Attendance/Tardiness: Data Collection Resources*).

- *Office Disciplinary Referrals*. Current disciplinary records show the rate, intensity, and circumstances of behavioral problems as well as patterns of misbehavior. Past years' records may demonstrate a long history of problem behaviors (see Exhibit 5-B, *Student Archival Information Sheet*).

- *Permanent ('Work') Products*. The student is observed completing work independently. The work is then collected and examined. This assessment yields information about the student's independent work habits, ability to use correct problem-solving strategies, and degree of on-task behavior (see Exhibit 5-E, *Permanent Products: Assessing the Completion, Accuracy, and Overall Quality of Student Independent Work*). It allows the user to analyze the student's efficiency and quality in completing seatwork.

- *Curriculum-Based Measurement (CBM).* Short CBM probes have been developed in reading fluency, math computation, writing, spelling, (Shinn, 1989) and phonemic awareness skills (Good & Kaminski, 2000; Kaminski, McConnell., & Carta, 2001). CBM data can be used to compare the target student's performance to that of his peers, and to monitor the student's response to individually tailored interventions. For an in-depth tutorial in the administration and scoring of CBM probes in selected subject areas (see **Appendix B**, *Curriculum-Based Measurement Administration & Scoring Guidelines for Reading, Math, & Writing.* A form designed to collect CBM Reading Fluency data, *Student Record Form: Curriculum-Based Measurement: Oral Reading Fluency*, is to be found as Exhibit 5-F).

- *Daily Behavior Report Cards (DBRCs).* These rating forms can be customized to evaluate specific student behaviors. The teacher uses the DBRC to rate the student on a daily basis, comparing the student's behavior to that of "typical'" peers or to the teacher's behavioral expectations (see Exhibit 5-G, *Daily Behavior Report Cards: A Convenient Behavior Monitoring Tool).* This Exhibit also contains a sample Daily and Weekly Progress Monitoring chart.

- *Structured Behavioral Observations*. Direct observations of student behaviors using a structured recording format provide an estimate of the rate at which problem behaviors occur (DuPaul & Stoner, 1994). The behaviors of "typical" classmates can also be measured to provide a peer comparison (see Exhibit 5-H, *Classroom Behaviors Observation Form (C-BOF): Directions for Use, Scoring, and Interpretation*, and Exhibit 5-I, *Instructional Setting Rating Sheet).*

- *Behavior Logs*. Whenever a behavioral episode occurs, the teacher writes brief notes describing the student's behavior and related information, such as possible triggers and the duration, intensity, and outcome of the episode. The logged information can then be graphed on a behavioral scatterplot. This method of behavioral recording is most useful for tracking significant problem behaviors (e.g., biting an adult) that occur infrequently (see Exhibit 5-J, *Teacher Behavior Log & Student Behavioral Scatterplot*).

## Summative vs. Formative Assessment Data

Data about students can have different qualities. Some sources of student data, referred to as summative data, are most valuable because they provide static, general impressions about how the student is functioning at a moment in time. Other data sources, such as daily behavior report cards, are categorized as *formative* data; they can be collected frequently to provide a stream of information in real time about how the student is responding to various intervention plans.

*Summative data sources*. *Summative* data is static information that provides a fixed snapshot of the student's academic performance or behaviors at a particular point in time. School records are an example of a source of data that is summative in nature. Such information is frequently referred to as archival data. Schools collect and store a large amount of information about students, some of which is saved across multiple school years. Attendance data and office disciplinary referrals are two examples of *archival* records which are comprised of data that is routinely collected on all students. RTI Teams can comb through archival data for useful clues about the student's behavioral or academic problems (for example, whether problems are recent or long standing). Another advantage of archived records is that this information has already been gathered, making it an easy data source for teams to analyze.

In contrast to archival data, b*ackground* information is collected specifically on the target student. Examples of background information are teacher interviews and student interest surveys, each of which can shed light on a student's academic or behavioral strengths and weaknesses. Like archival data, background information is usually summative, providing a measurement of the student at a single point in time. Assessment methods checked off under the column 'Archival/Background' in Exhibit 5-A, *Common Types of Student Assessment & Progress-Monitoring Data*, can be considered examples of summative data.

***Formative data sources***. Formative assessment measures are those that can be administered or collected frequently; for example, on a weekly or even daily basis. These measures provide a flow of regularly updated information about the student's progress in the identified area(s) of academic or behavioral concern. Formative data provide a moving picture of the student; the data unfold through time to tell the story of that student's response to various classroom instructional and behavior management strategies. Examples of measures that provide formative data are Curriculum-Based Measurement probes in oral reading fluency and Daily Behavior Report Cards. Assessment methods checked off under the column "Baseline/Progress-Monitoring" in Exhibit 5-A, *Common Types of Student Assessment & Progress-Monitoring Data*, can be considered examples of formative data.

## Baseline Assessment and Progress-Monitoring

Tracking the student's progress during an intervention is a crucial requirement in RTI. Before a student's response to intervention can be measured, however, the RTI Team must estimate that student's rate of the target behavior prior to the intervention. This step requires the collection of baseline data on the student's performance. (The time period in which baseline information is gathered is known as the *baseline phase*.) Generally, the RTI Team collects at least three to five observations of student behavior during the baseline phase. The middle, or median, baseline observation is typically used as the best estimate of the student's current level of performance prior to starting the intervention phase.

Whenever possible, the methods used to collect baseline data should also be used to collect progress-monitoring data. Schools can employ Curriculum-Based Measurement, for example, to estimate a student's level of oral reading fluency prior to the intervention and also to monitor the child's grown in reading fluency during the intervention period. Daily Behavior Report Cards (DBRCs) are also a measurement method that can be used during both the baseline and progress-monitoring periods. When the intervention phase has begun, the RTI Team frequently monitors the student's progress, as often as once per week. These "pulse" measures provide speedy feedback about whether the student is making adequate progress.

Response to Intervention requires that schools collect data on student progress over time to determine whether an academic or behavioral intervention is working. It is much easier to see the student's overall rate of progress when data are converted to a visual display (Hayes, 1981; Kazdin, 1982). The time-series chart is the type of visual display most commonly used to graph student progress (see Exhibit 5-K, *Setting Up and Interpreting Time-Series Charts*).

## Assessment Data: Information Content vs. Specificity

Educators understand that not all data is of the same value. As an example, a teacher comment made at a child study team meeting that a child is "always disrupting the classroom" provides very different information than frequency counts taken of that same student's out-of-seat and calling-out behaviors during math instruction.

A useful means of understanding the information value of any measure is to be found in the twin concepts of *bandwidth* and *fidelity*. These concepts originated in information theory (Shannon 1949 cited in Cronbach, 1984) and were adopted by Cronbach (1984) to provide an accessible framework for understanding the relationship between breadth and specificity in any method of assessment.

The term *bandwidth* refers to the amount of information or degree of complexity that a message communicates. The term *fidelity* indicates the specificity of that information. An inverse relationship exists between these concepts. That is, as the bandwidth, or amount of information packed into a message, increases (wide-band measures), that greater bandwidth is inevitably accompanied by a decrease in fidelity (that is, the information becomes more general rather than specific). In contrast, as the bandwidth of a message narrows (narrow-band measures), the breadth of information decreases, but the resulting information is more focused and specific.

In applying the concepts of bandwidth and fidelity to the Response to Intervention process, RTI Teams can think of assessment methods as lying along a continuum, whose poles are defined by indirect and direct methods of assessment (Cone,1977).

*Indirect assessment methods*, which include interviews, self-report, and ratings of others' behavior, can be considered wide-band, low fidelity measures. That is, such measures draw upon a large and cumulative knowledge-base with much informational content (e.g., teacher remarks based upon observation of a student across four instructional months), but the information is presented in a general form that does not allow one to predict specific student behaviors with confidence at any single time or in any particular setting.

*Direct methods* are defined by Cone (1978) as direct observations of target student behavior, either in analog (contrived) or natural settings, and are categorized as narrow band, high fidelity. As conditions of behavioral observation more closely approximate the natural conditions in which the treatment or intervention is to be implemented, the bandwidth narrows (that is, the information collected is restricted in its application), but the fidelity increases (one can place increasing confidence in the relevance of the assessment data to the target setting). An RTI assessment is most efficient when it makes use of *multiple measures* of data collection, which vary in bandwidth and level of specificity.

## Integrating Assessment into a School-Wide RTI Process

Schools that successfully integrate student assessment into the RTI process select more than one measure to monitor a targeted student concern, track student progress frequently, and make full use of archival data to create a full assessment picture of the student. The following are recommendations that the RTI Team can use to improve the quality of student data collection:

- *Collect a standard set of background information on each student referred to the RTI Team.* Schools gather and store a great deal of data on their students, and much of this information can be helpful during the RTI process. RTI Teams should develop a standard package of background (archival) information to be collected prior to the initial problem-solving meeting. For each referred student, a Team might elect to gather attendance data, office disciplinary referrals for the current year, and the most recent state assessment results. By taking advantage of a standard package of archival data as one strand in its assessment, the RTI Team makes thrifty use of already-existing information and is able to easily compare target students to a school average in areas that are strong predictors of student success (attendance, disciplinary referrals, test scores, etc.).

- *For each area of concern, select at least two progress-monitoring measures.* RTI Teams can place greater confidence in their progress-monitoring data if they select at least two measures to track any area of student concern (Gresham, 1983), ideally from at least two different sources (e.g., Campbell & Fiske, 1959). With a minimum of two methods in place to monitor a student concern, each measure serves as a check on the other. If the results are in agreement, the Team has greater assurance that it can trust the data. If the measures do not agree with one another, however, the Team can investigate further to determine the reason(s) for the apparent discrepancy.

- *Consider using a mix of direct and indirect measures for progress monitoring.* For example, if a child is a slow and halting reader, the RTI Team may decide to track that student's reading fluency. Using curriculum-based measurement reading probes is an excellent way to monitor progress in reading fluency. As a second reading-related measure, the team might create a customized *Daily Behavior Report Card,* (see Exhibit 5-G) that allows the teacher to rate behaviors that may help or hinder the development of greater reading fluency (e.g., amount of time the student spends in independent reading, the presence or absence of reading-avoidant behaviors, etc.). Alternatively, the team may ask the teacher to keep a cumulative chart recording the number of pages that the student reads independently during the intervention phase, since independent reading is a good fluency building exercise.

- *Monitor student progress frequently.* Progress-monitoring data should reveal in weeks, not months, whether an intervention is working, because no teacher wants to waste time implementing an intervention that is not successful. When progress monitoring is conducted frequently (e.g., weekly), the data can be charted to more quickly reveal whether the student's current intervention plan is effective. When data are collected only infrequently (e.g., monthly), a very long period of time may be required to gather sufficient data to judge the impact of the intervention. Whenever possible, RTI Teams should try to select progress-monitoring measures that allow them to assess the student on at least a weekly basis. Curriculum-based measurement (see Appendix B), *Daily Behavior Report Cards* (see Exhibit 5-G), and *Classroom Behaviors Observations Form* (see Exhibit 5-H) are several assessment methods that can be carried out frequently.

# References

Campbell, D. T., & Fiske, D. W. (1959). Convergent and discriminant validation by the multitraitmultimethod matrix. *Psychological Bulletin, 56*, 81-105.

Cone, J. D. (1977). The relevance of reliability and validity for behavioral assessment. *Behavior Therapy, 8,* 411-426.

Cone, J. D. (1978). The behavioral assessment grid (BAG): A conceptual framework and a taxonomy. *Behavior Therapy, 9*, 882-888.

Cronbach, L. J. (1984). *Essentials of psychological testing* (4th ed.). New York: Harper & Row.

DuPaul, G. J., & Stoner, G. (1994). *ADHD in the schools: Assessment and intervention strategies.* New York: Guilford Press.

Gresham, F. M. (1983). Multitrait-multimethod approach to multifactored assessment: Theoretical rationale and practical application. *School Psychology Review, 12*, 26-34.

Hayes, S.C. (1981). Single case experimental design and empirical clinical practice. *Journal of Consulting and Clinical Psychology*, 49, 193-211.

Kaminski, R., McConnell, S., & Carta, J (February, 2001). *Measuring Growth and Development of Young Children.* NECTAS-OSEP National Meeting. Washington, D.C.

Kazdin, A.E. (1982). *Single-case research designs: Methods for clinical and applied settings.* New York: Oxford Press.

Shinn, M. (1989). *Curriculum-based measurement: Assessing special children.* New York: Guilford.

# Exhibit 5-A
## Common Types of Student Assessment & Progress-Monitoring Data

| Archival/ Background | Baseline/ Progress- Monitoring | Data Sources |
|:---:|:---:|---|
| ✓ | | *Grade Report Cards.* Grades provide evidence of student performance in previous years. Teacher comments describe student academic performance and general behaviors. |
| ✓ | | *Test/Screening Data.* Test records from the student's cumulative folder illustrate academic strengths and weaknesses. Results from group tests and universal screenings given during the current school year give a useful comparison to peer performance. |
| ✓ | | *Student Interview or Self-Completed Interest Survey.* The student can inform adults about perceived academic or behavioral strengths or weaknesses, preferred methods of learning and review, interests or hobbies, and favorite rewards or reinforcers. |
| ✓ | | *Teacher Interview.* The classroom teacher is interviewed about the student. The instructor answers questions about the student's academic skill level and performance, work habits, interactions with peers, and general behaviors. |
| ✓ | ✓ | *Class and Homework Grades.* Grades from the current year provide a comparison of the student to average class or grade performance. Trends or variations in the target student's grades can also provide insight into underlying academic problems. |
| ✓ | ✓ | *Attendance/Tardiness Records.* Patterns of absences and tardy arrivals from the current year may suggest evidence of victimization by bullies, work avoidance, school phobia, or other causes. Attendance data across school years may confirm the chronic nature of the problem. |
| ✓ | ✓ | *Office Disciplinary Referrals.* Current disciplinary records show rate, intensity, and circumstances of behavioral problems as well as patterns of misbehavior. Past years' records may demonstrate a long history of problem behaviors. |

| Archival/ Background | Baseline/ Progress- Monitoring | Data Sources |
|---|---|---|
| | ✓ | *Permanent ('Work') Products.* The student is observed completing independent seatwork. The work is then collected and examined. This assessment yields information about the student's independent work habits, ability to use correct problem-solving strategies, and degree of on-task behavior. |
| | ✓ | *Curriculum-Based Measurement (CBM).* Short CBM probes have been developed in reading fluency, math computation, writing, spelling, and phonemic awareness skills. CBM data can be used to compare the target student to peers and to monitor the student's response to individually tailored interventions. |
| | ✓ | *Daily Behavior Report Cards (DBRCs).* These rating forms can be customized to evaluate specific student behaviors. The teacher uses the DBRC to rate the student on a daily basis, comparing the student's behavior to that of 'typical' peers or to the teacher's behavioral expectations. |
| | ✓ | *Structured Behavioral Observations.* Direct observations of student behaviors using a structured recording format provides an estimate of the rate at which problem behaviors occur, such as out of seat, call-outs, and inattention. The behaviors of 'typical' classmates can also be measured to provide a peer comparison. |
| | ✓ | *Behavior Logs.* Whenever a behavioral episode occurs, the teacher writes brief notes describing the student's behavior and related information, such as possible triggers and the duration, intensity, and outcome of the episode. This method of behavioral recording is most useful for significant problem behaviors (e.g., biting an adult) that occur infrequently. |

# Exhibit 5-B
## Student Archival Information Sheet

Student Name: _____     Current Grade: _____

Person Completing Sheet: _____     Date: _____

**Tests/Screenings**: Note the results of any significant student assessment from the student's records.(e.g., State examinations, District-wide tests, individual screening and/or testing)

| Date | Type/Name of Assessment | Student Score |
|------|------------------------|---------------|
|      |                        |               |
|      |                        |               |
|      |                        |               |
|      |                        |               |

**Report Card Review**: Summarize the student's history of behavior/academic performance as documented on past report cards.

| Grade | School Year | Significant Grades and/or Teacher Comments |
|-------|-------------|--------------------------------------------|
|       |             |                                            |
|       |             |                                            |
|       |             |                                            |
|       |             |                                            |

**Disciplinary Referrals**: List any significant behavioral infractions that resulted in the student receive a disciplinary office referral this year:

| Date | Reason for Referral | Person Referring |
|------|---------------------|------------------|
|      |                     |                  |
|      |                     |                  |
|      |                     |                  |
|      |                     |                  |

Number of days the student was **ABSENT** this year:_____**TARDY** this year:_____

# Exhibit 5-C
## Student Interview: Learning Survey

Student Name: _____Classroom:_____Date:_____

Directions: Please complete this survey to give your teacher information about how you learn best. If you are not sure what to put for an answer, just write down your 'best guess'.

1. What do you prefer to be called by your teacher?_____

2. When is your birthday? _____

3. What is your *most* favorite subject or school activity? _____

4. What is your *least* favorite subject or school activity? _____

5. Do you like working in *groups* or *alone* on projects?  State your reason(s) why:

   _____

   _____

   _____

6. Organizational skills include having all of your work materials on hand in the classroom, using your work time well, and getting work assignments done and handed in on time. On a rating scale from 1 (the lowest rating) to 10 (the highest rating), how would you rate your organizational skills?

   **1    2    3    4    5    6    7    8    9    10**
   **Not organized at all                              Very organized**

7. Describe your idea of the *perfect* classroom.  What would it look like?

   _____

   _____

   _____

8. What are your *favorite* ways to learn? (Pick as many as you like)

___Listening to lectures       ___Working with a friend      ___Working as part of a group
___Listening to a taped book   ___Doing homework          ___Doing research in libraries
___Doing research on the Internet ___Watching an educational video  ___Other:_____

9. Write two words that best describe you:

_____

_____

10. What are your favorite games, activities, sports, hobbies, or other interests?

_____

_____

_____

11. What are your favorite TV shows or movies?

_____

_____

_____

12. Describe how you study or review for a test:

_____

_____

_____

13. Occasionally, students can earn rewards in the class for working hard and turning in completed work. What would be some good rewards or privileges you would like to be able to earn in this classroom?  (Be realistic!):

_____

_____

_____

_____

# Exhibit 5-D
## Measuring Student Attendance/Tardiness:
## Data Collection Resources

Student:_____ Date: _____ Completed by: _____

This section contains three resources for collecting data on student attendance and tardiness.

- *Attendance Records: Calculating Student Attendance/Tardiness.* Using the student's attendance records, a school staff member calculates the rates of absenteeism or tardiness, notes reasons for student non-attendance, and indicates whether each episode of lateness or absence was excused.
- *School Attendance: Teacher Interview Form.* This form is to be completed by the student's teacher. Its questions are designed to provide insight into possible reasons that the student is missing school (e.g., work avoidance, anxiety).
- *School Attendance: Parent Interview Form.* A school staff person administers these interview questions to the parent in a face-to-face or telephone interview.

When your school has collected available information on the student's attendance patterns, your team analyzes the data to develop a 'best guess', or hypothesis, about why the student is chronically absent or late for school. Consult the listing of hypotheses below to select one that best fits or 'explains' the information that you have collected:

| | Hypothesis for Poor Attendance/ Chronic Tardiness | Intervention Ideas |
|---|---|---|
| ☐Y ☐N | The student is experiencing frequent or chronic illness. (Documentation from the student's physician indicates that the student is out of school due to illness.) | • If the student is physically able to complete work when out of school, send work home on days when the student is absent.<br>• Communicate with the student's parents and physician (via school nurse) to explore possible supports that would permit the student to attend school and learn successfully despite the student's illness. |
| ☐Y ☐N | *The student is avoiding work. (Evidence shows a pattern in which the student is more likely to be absent or tardy when specific school learning activities are scheduled.)* | • Adjust the level of difficulty of the academic work that the student is avoiding to ensure greater success.<br>• Make the academic work more engaging by building lessons around topics that the student finds interesting. |

| | Hypothesis for Poor Attendance/ Chronic Tardiness | Intervention Ideas |
|---|---|---|
| ☐Y<br>☐N | *The student is experiencing anxiety toward work or school academic expectations. (The student appears to be anxious about school in general.)* | • Analyze the school setting to determine the specific triggers or conditions that appear to cause the student to become anxious. Sample interventions to address anxiety include:<br>- Changing the manner in which the student demonstrates what he or she has learned (e.g., not being called on in class to answer difficult questions, not requiring that students exchange papers to grade each other's work, etc.)<br>- Working with school or outside mental health professionals and parents to identify triggers to the student's anxiety, and to develop a plan to reduce the student's school anxiety by systematically desensitizing that student's anxiety response. |
| ☐Y<br>☐N | *The student is being picked on or bullied in school.* | • Intervene immediately to stop the bullying or intimidation. |
| ☐Y<br>☐N | The student appears to lack interest in any aspect of his or her school program. | • Explore ideas for changing the student's school program to increase the student's motivation to attend. For example, a student who has no desire to obtain a high school diploma may be motivated to come to school if his or her educational program includes a vocational component that the student finds immediately rewarding. |
| ☐Y<br>☐N | Factors outside the student's control (e.g., transportation issues, family issues) cause the student to be absent or tardy. | • Identify the factor(s) preventing the student from getting to school and develop a school plan to overcome those factors. If necessary, involve outside agencies to intervene to get the student to school. |
| ☐Y<br>☐N | *The school team has identified another reason for the student's absenteeism or tardiness.*<br>Reason: _____<br>_____ | • <br>_____<br>_____<br>_____ |

# Attendance Records: Calculating Student Attendance/Tardiness

Student: _____ Date: _____ Completed by: _____

**Directions:** Review the student's attendance records. For each day when the student was tardy or absent, record the date, attendance status (*absent* or *tardy*), reason for absence or tardiness (if known), and whether the absence/tardy was *excused* (i.e., doctor's note to document student illness).

| Date | Absent/Tardy | Reason (if known) | Excused? | Date | Absent/Tardy | Reason (if known) | Excused? |
|---|---|---|---|---|---|---|---|
| | ☐ Absent<br>☐ Tardy | | ☐ Y<br>☐ N | | ☐ Absent<br>☐ Tardy | | ☐ Y<br>☐ N |
| | ☐ Absent<br>☐ Tardy | | ☐ Y<br>☐ N | | ☐ Absent<br>☐ Tardy | | ☐ Y<br>☐ N |
| | ☐ Absent<br>☐ Tardy | | ☐ Y<br>☐ N | | ☐ Absent<br>☐ Tardy | | ☐ Y<br>☐ N |
| | ☐ Absent<br>☐ Tardy | | ☐ Y<br>☐ N | | ☐ Absent<br>☐ Tardy | | ☐ Y<br>☐ N |
| | ☐ Absent<br>☐ Tardy | | ☐ Y<br>☐ N | | ☐ Absent<br>☐ Tardy | | ☐ Y<br>☐ N |
| | ☐ Absent<br>☐ Tardy | | ☐ Y<br>☐ N | | ☐ Absent<br>☐ Tardy | | ☐ Y<br>☐ N |
| | ☐ Absent<br>☐ Tardy | | ☐ Y<br>☐ N | | ☐ Absent<br>☐ Tardy | | ☐ Y<br>☐ N |
| | ☐ Absent<br>☐ Tardy | | ☐ Y<br>☐ N | | ☐ Absent<br>☐ Tardy | | ☐ Y<br>☐ N |
| | ☐ Absent<br>☐ Tardy | | ☐ Y<br>☐ N | | ☐ Absent<br>☐ Tardy | | ☐ Y<br>☐ N |
| | ☐ Absent<br>☐ Tardy | | ☐ Y<br>☐ N | | ☐ Absent<br>☐ Tardy | | ☐ Y<br>☐ N |

| | | | | | | |
|---|---|---|---|---|---|---|
| ____ TOTAL Days Absent | Divided by | _____ Elapsed School Days | Equals | _____ Absence Rate (decimal) | Times 100 = | _____ Absence Rate (percentage) |
| ____ TOTAL Days Absent | Divided by | _____ Elapsed School Days | Equals | _____ Absence Rate (decimal) | Times 100 = | _____ Absence Rate (percentage) |

## School Attendance: Teacher Interview Form

Student:_____ Date:_____ Completed by: _____

**Teacher Directions:** Please complete the questions below. If you are unsure how to answer a particular item, you are encouraged to indicate your 'best guess' based on your knowledge of the student.

1. What is the student's attitude toward school?

   _____

   _____

2. Does the student talk about feeling anxious or show signs physical symptoms of anxiety relating to school?  _____Y _____ N
   (Examples of physical symptoms that may indicate anxiety include stomachache, trouble sleeping, and loss of appetite.) If *Yes*, please explain.

   _____

   _____

3. Does the student request to leave the classroom (e.g., for bathroom breaks or trips to the nurse's office) more than his or her peers?  _____Y _____ N
   If *Yes,* please explain:

   _____

   _____

4. Does the student complain about being picked on or bullied at school or when traveling to or from school? Or have you observed the student being picked on or bullied?  _____Y _____ N
   If *Yes*, please explain.

   _____

   _____

5. Is the student more likely to miss school or be late for school on certain days of the week or when certain activities are happening at school? _____ Y _____N
   If *Yes*, please explain.

   _____

   _____

# School Attendance: Parent Interview Form

Student: _____ Date: _____Completed by: _____

**Directions:** In a phone or face-to-face interview, ask the student's parent(s) the questions below.

1. What is your child's routine for preparing for school and getting to school each day?

    _____

    _____

2. What is your child's attitude toward school?

    _____

    _____

3. Does your child talk about feeling anxious or experience physical symptoms of anxiety relating to school?    _____Y _____N
    (Examples of physical symptoms that may indicate anxiety include stomachache, trouble sleeping, and loss of appetite.) If *Yes*, please explain.

    _____

    _____

4. Does your child complain about being picked on or bullied at school or when traveling to or from school?  _____Y _____N
    If *Yes*, please explain.

    _____

    _____

5. Is your child more likely to miss school or be late for school on certain days of the week or when certain activities are happening at school? _____ Y_____N
    If *Yes*, please explain.

    _____

    _____

6. What do you believe the school can do to help you to prevent absences and to have your child arrive at school on time?

    _____

    _____

7. What do you believe that you the parent can do to prevent absences and to have your child arrive at school on time?

    _____

    _____

# Exhibit 5-E
## Permanent Products: Assessing the Completion, Accuracy, and Overall Quality of Student Independent Work

Student:_____ Date:_____ Completed by: _____

There are a number of reasons that students might have difficulty in completing independent classroom assignments. School staff can use a 4-step process to collect data about the student's independent work habits, rate of on-task behavior during class assignments, and quality and accuracy of the student's completed work ('permanent products').

**Step 1**: *Collect data on the student's On-Task behavior during independent seatwork.* Visit the student's classroom. Observe the student working independently on a class assignment. Using the *Independent Seatwork Observation Form*, at the end of this Exhibit, track the student's rate of On-Task behavior on the assignment.

Rate of On-Task Behavior:_____%

**Step 2**: *Analyze the student's completed seatwork (permanent product).*

- **Estimate the amount of the assignment completed by the student**. If the assignment contains discrete items (e.g., math computation problems), count up the number of items actually completed by the student. Divide this figure by the total number of items contained in the assignment and then multiply by 100. If the assignment cannot easily be divided into discrete units (e.g., a written essay), estimate the approximate amount of the assignment that the student completed.

  Amount of assignment estimated to have been completed:_____%

- ***Estimate the accuracy or overall quality of the work that the student completed***. *If the assignment contains discrete items (e.g., math computation problems), divide the number of correct items by the number of items the student attempted (including partially completed items), then multiply by 100.*

  *Estimated accuracy of completed work:_____%*
  *OR*
  *If the assignment cannot easily be divided into discrete units (e.g., a written essay), use the simple quality rubric below to judge the overall quality of the work that the student actually completed:*

  *How would you judge the overall quality of the work produced by the student during independent seatwork? Circle your selection:*

| **1** | **2** | **3** | **4** |
|---|---|---|---|
| Significantly below level of peers (rudimentary content, absence of ideas, and/or failure to use key strategies or steps) | Somewhat below level of peers (lacking content, inadequate development of ideas, and/or limited application of key strategies or steps) | At level of peers (e.g., average content, development of ideas, application of key strategies or steps) | Above peers in overall quality (e.g., strong content, ideas developed to an advanced degree, creative application of key strategies or steps) |

**Step 3**: *Compare the student's performance on the assignment to that of a 'typical' classroom peer.* Ask the teacher to select an 'average' student in the class who typically completes independent work at an acceptable level of completion, accuracy and quality. Collect that student's completed seatwork (done during the same work period as that of your target student). Analyze the peer student's seatwork using the same standards used with the target student.

Peer Comparison: Amount of assignment estimated to have been completed:_____%

Peer Comparison: Estimated accuracy of completed work:_____%

Peer Comparison: Quality Rubric Rating: **1      2      3      4**

**Step 4**: *Select interventions that match the 'root cause' of the student's problem with independent work.* Pool the information that you have collected through direct observation of the student, analysis of the student's work products, and a comparison of the student's performance to that of peers. Then generate a hypothesis, or 'best guess', about why the student is having problems with seatwork.

Common reasons for student difficulties with independent work are:

• Carelessness          • Inattention          • Skill deficits          • Lack of motivation

Below are possible scenarios of student problems and sample interventions to consider for each scenario.

| Student Scenarios | Sample Intervention Ideas |
|---|---|
| The student completes independent work quickly with time to spare—but the work contains 'careless' mistakes or is of poor quality. | • Provide the student with incentives to slow down and use the full time allocated to complete the assignment.<br>• Require that the student use a quality checklist or rubric to review work before turning it in. If the student attempts to turn in completed work that does not meet teacher expectations, send the student back to his or her seat to continue to work on the assignment. |
| The student was off-task during much of the work session. The assignment was not completed within the time allocated. | • Use strategies to increase the student's attention to task (e.g., teacher redirection to task, student self-monitoring of work completion). |
| The completed assignment was of poor quality and/or contained many errors. | • Review with the student the skills or strategies required for the assignment.<br>• Give the student correctly completed models similar to what the student must produce for the assignment. Encourage the student to refer to these models whenever he or she is 'stuck'.<br>• Approach the student in a low-key manner periodically during independent seatwork to see if the student requires assistance.<br>• Provide the student an incentive (e.g., five additional minutes of free time) if the student improves the quality or accuracy of the work. |
| *The student did not complete the assignment in the allotted time. However, the student demonstrated a high degree of quality and/or accuracy in his or her work.* | • Boost the student's speed by providing him or her with opportunities to practice the skills or strategies required for the assignment.<br>• Give the student feedback and encouragement as the student increases his or her working speed. |

# Independent Seatwork Observation Form

Student Name:_____ Date:_____

Observer:_____ Location:_____ Start Time:_____ End Time:_____

Description of Activities:_____

_____

This simple observation form is used to determine the amount of time that a student is on-task when completing an independent assignment in the classroom. It can be used for an observation of up to 15 minutes.

**Directions:** Observe the student at a time when the student is scheduled to be engaged in independent seatwork.

*On-Task Behavior* is coded using a momentary time-sampling procedure. At the start of each 15-second interval, the observer glances at the target child for approximately two seconds and determines if the child is on-task or off-task during the brief observation. If the child is found to be on-task (doing his or her assigned seatwork), the interval is marked with an "X." If the child is off-task, the interval remains unmarked. The observer then ignores this behavior category until the onset of the next time interval.

Use Table 1 below ('*Calculate the Rate of On-Task Behavior During the Observation Period*') to calculate the student's *time on task* (engaged academic time).

| | 1 | 2 | 3 | 4 | 5 |
|---|---|---|---|---|---|
| | 0:00 0:15 0:30 0:45 | 1:00 1:15 1:30 1:45 | 2:00 2:15 2:30 2:45 | 3:00 3:15 3:30 3:45 | 4:00 4:15 4:30 4:45 |
| ON-TASK | | | | | |

| | 6 | 7 | 8 | 9 | 10 |
|---|---|---|---|---|---|
| | 5:00 5:15 5:30 5:45 | 6:00 6:15 6:30 6:45 | 7:00 7:15 7:30 7:45 | 8:00 8:15 8:30 8:45 | 9:00 9:15 9:30 9:45 |
| ON-TASK | | | | | |

| | 11 | 12 | 13 | 14 | 15 |
|---|---|---|---|---|---|
| | 10:00 10:15 10:30 10:45 | 11:00 11:15 11:30 11:45 | 12:00 12:15 12:30 12:45 | 13:00 13:15 13:30 13:45 | 14:00 14:15 14:30 14:45 |
| ON-TASK | | | | | |

| Table 1: Calculate the Rate of *On-Task Behavior* During the Observation Period | | | | | | | |
|---|---|---|---|---|---|---|---|
| **Type of Behavior** | Number of intervals in which the On-Task behavior was observed. | | The TOTAL number of intervals in the observation period(s) | | Rate (in decimal form) that the On-Task behavior occurred during the observation. | | Rate (in percentage form) that the On-Task behavior occurred during the observation. |
| **ON-TASK** | | Divided by | | Equals | | Times 100 = | % |

# Exhibit 5-F

## Student Record Form: Curriculum-Based Measurement: Oral Reading Fluency

Student Name: _____ Grade/Classroom: _____

Reading Skill Level: _____ Best Time(s) for CBM Monitoring: _____

**Step 1: Conduct a Survey-Level Assessment:** Use this section to record the student's reading rates in progressively more difficult material.

Date:_____ Book/Reading Level: _____

| | TRW | E | CRW | %CRW |
|---|---|---|---|---|
| A. | ____ | ____ | ____ | ____ |
| B. | ____ | ____ | ____ | ____ |
| C. | ____ | ____ | ____ | ____ |

Date:_____ Book/Reading Level: _____

| | TRW | E | CRW | %CRW |
|---|---|---|---|---|
| A. | ____ | ____ | ____ | ____ |
| B. | ____ | ____ | ____ | ____ |
| C. | ____ | ____ | ____ | ____ |

Date:_____ Book/Reading Level: _____

| | TRW | E | CRW | %CRW |
|---|---|---|---|---|
| A. | ____ | ____ | ____ | ____ |
| B. | ____ | ____ | ____ | ____ |
| C. | ____ | ____ | ____ | ____ |

Date:_____ Book/Reading Level: _____

| | TRW | E | CRW | %CRW |
|---|---|---|---|---|
| A. | ____ | ____ | ____ | ____ |
| B. | ____ | ____ | ____ | ____ |
| C. | ____ | ____ | ____ | ____ |

Date:_____ Book/Reading Level: _____

| | TRW | E | CRW | %CRW |
|---|---|---|---|---|
| A. | ____ | ____ | ____ | ____ |
| B. | ____ | ____ | ____ | ____ |
| C. | ____ | ____ | ____ | ____ |

Date:_____ Book/Reading Level: _____

| | TRW | E | CRW | %CRW |
|---|---|---|---|---|
| A. | ____ | ____ | ____ | ____ |
| B. | ____ | ____ | ____ | ____ |
| C. | ____ | ____ | ____ | ____ |

Date:_____ Book/Reading Level: _____

| | TRW | E | CRW | %CRW |
|---|---|---|---|---|
| A. | ____ | ____ | ____ | ____ |
| B. | ____ | ____ | ____ | ____ |
| C. | ____ | ____ | ____ | ____ |

**Table 1: Sample Estimates of 'Typical' CBM Instructional Reading Levels By Grade**

| Grade | Shapiro (1996) CRW Per Min | Shapiro (1996) Reading Errors | Milwaukee Public Schools (Winter 2000-2001 Local Norms) CRW Per Min for Students in 25th-75th Percentile |
|---|---|---|---|
| 1...... | 40-60 | Fewer than 5 | 22-64 |
| 2...... | 40-60 | Fewer than 5 | 36-78 |
| 3...... | 70-100 | Fewer than 7 | 47-88 |
| 4...... | 70-100 | Fewer than 7 | 60-104 |
| 5...... | 70-100 | Fewer than 7 | 77-121 |
| 6...... | 70-100 | Fewer than 7 | 95-146 |

**Step 2: Compute a Student Reading Goal**

1. At what grade or book level will the student be monitored? (Refer to results of Step 1:*Survey-Level Assessment*)

   _____

2. What is the student's *baseline* reading rate (# correctly read words per min)? _____CRW Per Min

3. When is the *start date* to begin monitoring the student in reading? _____ / _____ / _____

4. When is the *end date* to stop monitoring the student in reading? _____ / _____ / _____

5. How many instructional weeks are there between the start and end dates? (Round to the nearest week if necessary):

   _____ Instructional Weeks

6. What do you *predict* the student's average increase in correctly read words per minute will be for each instructional week of the monitoring period? (See Table 2):

   _____ Weekly Increase in CRW Per Min

7. What will the student's predicted CRW *gain* in reading fluency be at the end of monitoring? (Multiply Item 5 by Item 6): _____

8. What will the student's predicted *reading rate* be at the end of the monitoring period? (Add Items 2 & 7): _____ CRW Per Min

**References**

Fuchs, L.S., Fuchs, D., Hamlett, C.L., Walz, L., & Germann, G. (1993). Formative evaluation of academic progress: How much growth can we expect? *School Psychology Review, 22*, 27-48.

Shapiro, E.S. (1996). *Academic skills problems: Direct assessment and intervention.* New York: Guilford Press.

Student Name: _____    Grade/Classroom: _____

**Step 3: Collect Baseline Data:** Give 3 CBM reading assessments within a one-week period using monitoring-level probes.

**Baseline 1**

Date:_____    Book/Reading Level: _____

| | TRW | E | CRW | %CRW |
|---|---|---|---|---|
| A. | _____ | _____ | _____ | _____ |
| B. | _____ | _____ | _____ | _____ |
| C. | _____ | _____ | _____ | _____ |

**Baseline 2**

Date:_____    Book/Reading Level: _____

| | TRW | E | CRW | %CRW |
|---|---|---|---|---|
| A. | _____ | _____ | _____ | _____ |
| B. | _____ | _____ | _____ | _____ |
| C. | _____ | _____ | _____ | _____ |

**Baseline 3**

Date:_____    Book/Reading Level: _____

| | TRW | E | CRW | %CRW |
|---|---|---|---|---|
| A. | _____ | _____ | _____ | _____ |
| B. | _____ | _____ | _____ | _____ |
| C. | _____ | _____ | _____ | _____ |

**Step 4: Complete CBM Progress-Monitoring Weekly or More Frequently:** Record the results of regular monitoring of the student's progress in reading fluency.

**1.**

Date:_____    Book/Reading Level: _____

| | TRW | E | CRW | %CRW |
|---|---|---|---|---|
| A. | _____ | _____ | _____ | _____ |
| B. | _____ | _____ | _____ | _____ |
| C. | _____ | _____ | _____ | _____ |

**2.**

Date:_____    Book/Reading Level: _____

| | TRW | E | CRW | %CRW |
|---|---|---|---|---|
| A. | _____ | _____ | _____ | _____ |
| B. | _____ | _____ | _____ | _____ |
| C. | _____ | _____ | _____ | _____ |

**3.**

Date:_____    Book/Reading Level: _____

| | TRW | E | CRW | %CRW |
|---|---|---|---|---|
| A. | _____ | _____ | _____ | _____ |
| B. | _____ | _____ | _____ | _____ |
| C. | _____ | _____ | _____ | _____ |

**4.**

Date:_____    Book/Reading Level: _____

| | TRW | E | CRW | %CRW |
|---|---|---|---|---|
| A. | _____ | _____ | _____ | _____ |
| B. | _____ | _____ | _____ | _____ |
| C. | _____ | _____ | _____ | _____ |

**5.**

Date:_____    Book/Reading Level: _____

| | TRW | E | CRW | %CRW |
|---|---|---|---|---|
| A. | _____ | _____ | _____ | _____ |
| B. | _____ | _____ | _____ | _____ |
| C. | _____ | _____ | _____ | _____ |

**6.**

Date:_____    Book/Reading Level: _____

| | TRW | E | CRW | %CRW |
|---|---|---|---|---|
| A. | _____ | _____ | _____ | _____ |
| B. | _____ | _____ | _____ | _____ |
| C. | _____ | _____ | _____ | _____ |

**7.**

Date:_____    Book/Reading Level: _____

| | TRW | E | CRW | %CRW |
|---|---|---|---|---|
| A. | _____ | _____ | _____ | _____ |
| B. | _____ | _____ | _____ | _____ |
| C. | _____ | _____ | _____ | _____ |

**8.**

Date:_____    Book/Reading Level: _____

| | TRW | E | CRW | %CRW |
|---|---|---|---|---|
| A. | _____ | _____ | _____ | _____ |
| B. | _____ | _____ | _____ | _____ |
| C. | _____ | _____ | _____ | _____ |

**9.**

Date:_____    Book/Reading Level: _____

| | TRW | E | CRW | %CRW |
|---|---|---|---|---|
| A. | _____ | _____ | _____ | _____ |
| B. | _____ | _____ | _____ | _____ |
| C. | _____ | _____ | _____ | _____ |

**10.**

Date:_____    Book/Reading Level: _____

| | TRW | E | CRW | %CRW |
|---|---|---|---|---|
| A. | _____ | _____ | _____ | _____ |
| B. | _____ | _____ | _____ | _____ |
| C. | _____ | _____ | _____ | _____ |

**11.**

Date:_____    Book/Reading Level: _____

| | TRW | F | CRW | %CRW |
|---|---|---|---|---|
| A. | _____ | _____ | _____ | _____ |
| B. | _____ | _____ | _____ | _____ |
| C. | _____ | _____ | _____ | _____ |

**12.**

Date:_____    Book/Reading Level: _____

| | TRW | E | CRW | %CRW |
|---|---|---|---|---|
| A. | _____ | _____ | _____ | _____ |
| B. | _____ | _____ | _____ | _____ |
| C. | _____ | _____ | _____ | _____ |

**Table 2: Predictions for Rates of Reading Growth by Grade** (Fuchs, Fuchs, Hamlett, Walz, & Germann, 1993) Increase in Correctly Read Words Per Minute for Each Instructional Week

| Grade Level | Realistic Weekly Goal | Ambitious Weekly Goal |
|---|---|---|
| Grade 1 | 2.0 | 3.0 |
| Grade 2 | 1.5 | 2.0 |
| Grade 3 | 1.0 | 1.5 |
| Grade 4 | 0.85 | 1.1 |
| Grade 5 | 0.5 | 0.8 |
| Grade 6 | 0.3 | 0.65 |

# Case Example: Student Record Form: CBM: Oral Reading Fluency

Student Name: ___Jared M.___     Grade/Classroom: ___Gr. 4/Mrs. Legione___

Reading Skill Level: __Mid-Gr.2 (Tchr Estimate)__     Best Time(s) for CBM Monitoring: __T,Th 12-1:40 pm__

**Step 1: Conduct a Survey-Level Assessment:** Use this section to record the student's reading rates in progressively more difficult material.

Date: _Th 12/5_ Book/Reading Level: _GR 2-Bk 2-P 1_

|     | TRW | E | CRW | %CRW |
|-----|-----|---|-----|------|
| D.  | 93  | 3 | 90  | 97   |
| E.  | 72  | 4 | 68  | 94   |
| F.  | 83  | 1 | (82)| 98   |

Date: _Th 12/5_ Book/Reading Level: _GR 3-Bk 1-P1_

|     | TRW | E | CRW | %CRW |
|-----|-----|---|-----|------|
| D.  | 87  | 2 | (85)| 98   |
| E.  | 94  | 3 | 91  | 97   |
| F.  | 78  | 2 | 76  | 97   |

Date: _Th 12/5_ Book/Reading Level: _GR 3-Bk 2-P1_

|     | TRW | E | CRW | %CRW |
|-----|-----|---|-----|------|
| D.  | 62  | 4 | 58  | 94   |
| E.  | 81  | 4 | 77  | 95   |
| F.  | 73  | 3 | (70)| 96   |

Date: _Th 12/5_ Book/Reading Level: _GR 4-P1_

|     | TRW | E | CRW | %CRW |
|-----|-----|---|-----|------|
| D.  | 58  | 5 | 53  | 91   |
| E.  | 61  | 5 | (56)| 92   |
| F.  | 64  | 6 | 58  | 91   |

Book/Reading Level: _____ Date: _____

|     | TRW | E | CRW | %CRW |
|-----|-----|---|-----|------|
| D.  |     |   |     |      |
| E.  |     |   |     |      |
| F.  |     |   |     |      |

Book/Reading Level: _____ Date: _____

|     | TRW | E | CRW | %CRW |
|-----|-----|---|-----|------|
| D.  |     |   |     |      |
| E.  |     |   |     |      |
| F.  |     |   |     |      |

Book/Reading Level: _____ Date: _____

|     | TRW | E | CRW | %CRW |
|-----|-----|---|-----|------|
| D.  |     |   |     |      |
| E.  |     |   |     |      |
| F.  |     |   |     |      |

**Table 1: Sample Estimates of 'Typical' CBM Instructional Reading Levels By Grade**

| Grade | Shapiro (1996) CRW Per Min | Shapiro (1996) Reading Errors | Milwaukee Public Schools (Winter 2000-2001 Local Norms) CRW Per Min for Students in 25th-75th Percentile |
|-------|------|------|------|
| 1...... | 40-60 | Fewer than 5 | 22-64 |
| 2...... | 40-60 | Fewer than 5 | 36-78 |
| 3...... | 70-100 | Fewer than 7 | 47-88 |
| 4...... | 70-100 | Fewer than 7 | 60-104 |
| 5...... | 70-100 | Fewer than 7 | 77-121 |
| 6...... | 70-100 | Fewer than 7 | 95-146 |

**Step 2: Compute a Student Reading Goal**

9.  At what grade or book level will the student be monitored? (Refer to results of Step 1: *Survey-Level Assessment*)

    __3rd Grade: Book 9 of Silver Burdett & Ginn Rdng Series__

10. What is the student's *baseline* reading rate (# correctly read words per min)? __72__ CRW Per Min

11. When is the *start date* to begin monitoring the student in reading? _1_ / _20_ / _03_

12. When is the *end date* to stop monitoring the student in reading? _3_ / _7_ / _03_

13. How many instructional weeks are there between the start and end dates? (Round to the nearest week if necessary):

    __6__ Instructional Weeks

14. What do you *predict* will be the student's average increase in correctly read words per minute will be for each instructional week of the monitoring period? (See Table 2):

    __1.5__ Weekly Increase in CRW Per Min

15. What will the student's predicted CRW *gain* in reading fluency be at the end of monitoring? (Multiply Item 5 by Item 6): __9 correct words per min__

16. What will the student's predicted *reading rate* be at the end of the monitoring period? (Add Items 2 & 7): _81_ CRW Per Min

**References**

Fuchs, L.S., Fuchs, D., Hamlett, C.L., Walz, L., & Germann, G. (1993). Formative evaluation of academic progress: How much growth can we expect? *School Psychology Review, 22,* 27-48.

Shapiro, E.S. (1996). *Academic skills problems: Direct assessment and intervention.* New York: Guilford Press.

# Case Example

Student Name: _____ Jared M. _____ Grade/Classroom: _____ Gr 4/Mrs. Legione _____

**Step 2: Collect Baseline Data:** Give 3 CBM reading assessments within a one-week period using monitoring-level probes.

**Baseline 1** — Date: T 1/14 — Book/Reading Level: Gr 3: Bk 9

| | TRW | E | CRW | %CRW |
|---|---|---|---|---|
| A. | 79 | 3 | (76) | 96 |
| B. | 76 | 2 | (74) | 97 |
| C. | 66 | 5 | 61 | 92 |

**Baseline 2** — Date: W 1/15 — Book/Reading Level: Gr 3: Bk 9

| | TRW | E | CRW | %CRW |
|---|---|---|---|---|
| A. | 56 | 4 | 52 | 93 |
| B. | 70 | 3 | (67) | 96 |
| C. | 81 | 4 | 77 | 95 |

**Baseline 3** — Date: F 1/17 — Book/Reading Level: Gr 3: Bk 9

| | TRW | E | CRW | %CRW |
|---|---|---|---|---|
| A. | 72 | 3 | (72) | 96 |
| B. | 74 | 2 | 69 | 97 |
| C. | 76 | 2 | 74 | 97 |

**Step 3: Complete CBM Progress-Monitoring Weekly or More Frequently:** Record the results of regular monitoring of the student's progress in reading fluency.

**1.** Date: W 1/22 — Book/Reading Level: 3rd Gr Bk 2-P5

| | TRW | E | CRW | %CRW |
|---|---|---|---|---|
| D. | 89 | 3 | 86 | 97 |
| E. | 75 | 4 | (71) | 95 |
| F. | 74 | 4 | 70 | 95 |

**2.** Date: W 1/29 — Book/Reading Level: "-P6

| | TRW | E | CRW | %CRW |
|---|---|---|---|---|
| D. | 69 | 1 | 68 | 99 |
| E. | 106 | 3 | 103 | 97 |
| F. | 79 | 2 | (77) | 97 |

**3.** Date: M 2/3 — Book/Reading Level: "-P7

| | TRW | E | CRW | %CRW |
|---|---|---|---|---|
| D. | 80 | 3 | 77 | 98 |
| E. | 78 | 3 | (75) | 96 |
| F. | 78 | 4 | 74 | 95 |

**4.** Date: Th 2/13 — Book/Reading Level: "-P8

| | TRW | E | CRW | %CRW |
|---|---|---|---|---|
| A. | 77 | 2 | (75) | 97 |
| B. | 79 | 1 | 78 | 99 |
| C. | 67 | 6 | 61 | 99 |

**5.** Date: Th 2/27 — Book/Reading Level: "-P9

| | TRW | E | CRW | %CRW |
|---|---|---|---|---|
| D. | 75 | 1 | 74 | 99 |
| E. | 80 | 1 | (79) | 99 |
| F. | 81 | 2 | 79 | 98 |

**6.** Date: F 3/7 — Book/Reading Level: "-P10

| | TRW | E | CRW | %CRW |
|---|---|---|---|---|
| D. | 72 | 3 | 69 | 96 |
| E. | 83 | 1 | (82) | 99 |
| F. | 85 | 1 | 84 | 99 |

**7.** Date: M 3/10 — Book/Reading Level: "-P11

| | TRW | E | CRW | %CRW |
|---|---|---|---|---|
| A. | 87 | 2 | 85 | 98 |
| B. | 87 | 3 | (84) | 97 |
| C. | 82 | 4 | 78 | 95 |

**8.** Date: F 3/21 — Book/Reading Level: "-P12

| | TRW | E | CRW | %CRW |
|---|---|---|---|---|
| A. | 89 | 1 | 88 | 99 |
| B. | 86 | 4 | (82) | 95 |
| C. | 82 | 4 | 78 | 95 |

**9.** Date: T 3/25 — Book/Reading Level: "-P13

| | TRW | E | CRW | %CRW |
|---|---|---|---|---|
| D. | 82 | 3 | (79) | 96 |
| E. | 70 | 1 | 69 | 99 |
| F. | 100 | 2 | 98 | 98 |

**10.** Date: W 4/2 — Book/Reading Level: "-P14

| | TRW | E | CRW | %CRW |
|---|---|---|---|---|
| D. | 89 | 3 | (86) | 97 |
| E. | 63 | 3 | 60 | 95 |
| F. | 92 | 3 | 89 | 97 |

**11.** Date: T 4/8 — Book/Reading Level: "-P15

| | TRW | E | CRW | %CRW |
|---|---|---|---|---|
| D. | 93 | 3 | 90 | 97 |
| E. | 88 | 4 | 84 | 95 |
| F. | 89 | 2 | (87) | 98 |

**12.** Date: T 4/15 — Book/Reading Level: "-P16

| | TRW | E | CRW | %CRW |
|---|---|---|---|---|
| D. | 89 | 2 | (87) | 98 |
| E. | 95 | 3 | 92 | 97 |
| F. | 78 | 2 | 76 | 97 |

**Table 2: Predictions for Rates of Reading Growth by Grade**
(Fuchs, Fuchs, Hamlett, Walz, & Germann, 1993)
Increase in Correctly Read Words Per Minute for Each Instructional Week

| Grade Level | Realistic Weekly Goal | Ambitious Weekly Goal |
|---|---|---|
| Grade 1 | 2.0 | 3.0 |
| Grade 2 | 1.5 | 2.0 |
| Grade 3 | 1.0 | 1.5 |
| Grade 4 | 0.85 | 1.1 |
| Grade 5 | 0.5 | 0.8 |
| Grade 6 | 0.3 | 0.65 |

# Exhibit 5-G
## Daily Behavior Report Cards: A Convenient Behavior Monitoring Tool

Daily Behavior Report Cards (DBRCs) are behavior rating forms that teachers use to evaluate the student's global behaviors on a daily basis or even more frequently. An advantage of DBRCs is that these rating forms are quick and convenient for the teacher to complete. This Exhibit contains daily and weekly versions of a generic DBRC, as well as a progress-monitoring chart to record cumulative DBRC ratings.

**Increasing the Reliability of DBRCs.** DBRCs rely heavily on teacher judgment and therefore can present a somewhat subjective view of the student's behavior. When a teacher's ratings on DBRCs are based on subjective opinions, there is a danger that the teacher will apply inconsistent standards each day when rating student behaviors. This inconsistency in assessment can limit the usefulness of report card data. One suggestion that teachers can follow to make it more likely that their report card ratings are consistent and objective over time is to come up with specific guidelines for rating each behavioral goal. For example, one item in the sample DBRC included in this section states that *"The student spoke respectfully and complied with adult requests without argument or complaint."* It is up to the teacher to decide how to translate so general a goal into a rubric of specific, observable criteria that permits the teacher to rate the student on this item according to a 9-point scale. In developing such criteria, the instructor will want to consider:

- *taking into account student developmental considerations.* For example, "Without argument or complaint" may mean "without throwing a tantrum" for a kindergarten student but mean "without loud, defiant talking-back" for a student in middle school.

- *tying Report Card ratings to classroom behavioral norms.* For each behavioral goal, the teacher may want to think of what the typical classroom norm is for this behavior and assign to the classroom norm a specific number rating. The teacher may decide, for instance, that the target student will earn a rating of 7 ('Usually/Always') each day that the student's compliance with adult requests closely matches that of the 'average' child in the classroom.

- *developing numerical criteria when appropriate.* For some items, the teacher may be able to translate certain more general Report Card goals into specific numeric ratings. If a DBRC item rates a student's compliance with adult requests, for example, the teacher may decide that the student is eligible to earn a rating of 7 or higher on this item on days during which instructional staff had to approach the student no more than once about noncompliance.

**Charting Report Card Ratings.** Daily Behavior Report Card ratings can be charted over time to provide a visual display of the student's progress toward behavioral goals. The sample DBRC (daily and weekly versions) included in this section has its own progress-monitoring chart, which permits the teacher to graph student behavior for up to 4 school weeks. The instructor simply fills in the bubble each day that matches the numerical rating that he or she assigned to the student for the specific behavioral goal. As multiple points are filled in on the graph, the instructor connects those points to create a time-series progress graph. (Figure 1 contains an example of a completed progress-monitoring chart.) When enough data points have been charted, the behavior graph can be used to judge the relative effectiveness of any strategies put in place to improve the student's behavior.

**Using DBRCs as a Self-Monitoring Intervention.** DBRCs are primarily used as a behavior-monitoring tool. However, teachers may also choose to use DBRCs as part of a student self-monitoring program, in which the student rates their own behaviors each day. If teachers decide to use student behavior report cards for self-monitoring, they should first identify and demonstrate for the student the behaviors that the student is to monitor and show the student how to complete the behavior report card. Since it is important that the student learn the teacher's behavioral expectations, the instructor should meet with the student daily, ask the student to rate their own behaviors, and then share with the student the *teacher's* ratings of those same behaviors. The teacher and student can use this time to discuss any discrepancies in rating between their two forms. (If report card ratings points are to be applied toward a student reward program, the teacher might consider allowing points earned on a particular card item to count toward a reward *only* if the student's ratings fall within a point of the teacher's, to encourage the student to be accurate in their ratings.)

---

## Figure 1: Example of completed DBRC progress-monitoring form

*During instructional periods, the student focused his or her attention on teacher instructions, classroom lessons and assigned work.*

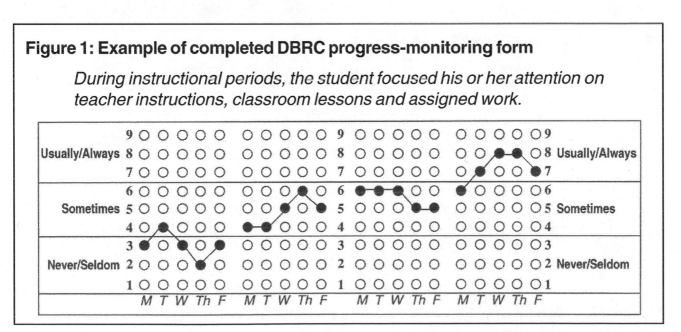

# Daily Classroom Behavior Report Card

Student: _____        Date: _____

Teacher: _____        Classroom: _____

Directions: Review each of the Behavior Report Card items below. For each item, rate the degree to which the student showed the behavior or met the behavior goal.

## During instructional periods, the student focused his or her attention on teacher instructions, classroom lessons and assigned work.

Circle the degree to which the student met the behavioral goal:

1........2........3....|....4........5........6....|....7........8........9

Never/Seldom            Sometimes                   Usually/Always

## The student interacted with classmates appropriately and respectfully.

Circle the degree to which the student met the behavioral goal:

1........2........3....|....4........5........6....|....7........8........9

Never/Seldom            Sometimes                   Usually/Always

## The student completed and turned in his or her assigned class work on time.

Circle the degree to which the student met the behavioral goal:

1........2........3....|....4........5........6....|....7........8........9

Never/Seldom            Sometimes                   Usually/Always

## The student spoke respectfully and complied with adult requests without argument or complaint.

Circle the degree to which the student met the behavioral goal:

1........2........3....|....4........5........6....|....7........8........9

Never/Seldom            Sometimes                   Usually/Always

# Weekly Classroom Behavior Report Card

Student:

_____

Teacher: _____    Classroom: _____

Directions: Review each of the Behavior Report Card items below. For each item, rate the degree to which the student showed the behavior or met the behavior goal.

| Date | __/__/__ | __/__/__ | __/__/__ | __/__/__ | __/__/__ |
|---|---|---|---|---|---|
| **Behavioral Target** | **M** | **T** | **W** | **Th** | **F** |
| ***During instructional periods, the student focused his or her attention on teacher instructions, classroom lessons and assigned work.***<br><br>Select the degree to which the goal was met:<br>1...2...3...\|...4...5...6...\|...7...8...9<br>Never/Seldom  Sometimes  Usually/Always | ____ Pts | ____ Pts | ____ Pts | ____ Pts | ____ Pts |
| ***The student interacted with classmates appropriately and respectfully.***<br><br>Select the degree to which the goal was met:<br>1...2...3...\|...4...5...6...\|...7...8...9<br>Never/Seldom  Sometimes  Usually/Always | ____ Pts | ____ Pts | ____ Pts | ____ Pts | ____ Pts |
| ***The student completed and turned in his or her assigned class work on time.***<br><br>Select the degree to which the goal was met:<br>1...2...3...\|...4...5...6...\|...7...8...9<br>Never/Seldom  Sometimes  Usually/Always | ____ Pts | ____ Pts | ____ Pts | ____ Pts | ____ Pts |
| ***The student spoke respectfully and complied with adult requests without argument or complaint.***<br><br>Select the degree to which the goal was met:<br>1...2...3...\|...4...5...6...\|...7...8...9<br>Never/Seldom  Sometimes  Usually/Always | ____ Pts | ____ Pts | ____ Pts | ____ Pts | ____ Pts |

# Classroom Behavior Report Card
# Progress-Monitoring Chart

**Student Name:** _____

**Start Date:** Wk 1: __ / __ / __     Wk 2: __ / __ / __     Wk 3: __ / __ / __     Wk 4: __ / __ / __
               M T W Th F        M T W Th F            M T W Th F        M T W Th F

*During instructional periods, the student focused his or her attention on teacher instructions, classroom lessons and assigned work.*

*The student interacted with classmates appropriately and respectfully.*

# Classroom Behavior Report Card
# Progress-Monitoring Chart

**Student Name:** _____

**Start Date:** Wk 1: ___ / ___ / ___   Wk 2: ___ / ___ / ___   Wk 3: ___ / ___ / ___   Wk 4: ___ / ___ / ___
                M  T  W  Th  F      M  T  W  Th  F         M  T  W  Th  F      M  T  W  Th  F

## The student completed and turned in his or her assigned class work on time.

|  | | M T W Th F | M T W Th F | | M T W Th F | M T W Th F | | |
|---|---|---|---|---|---|---|---|---|
| Usually/Always | 9 | ○○○○○ | ○○○○○ | 9 | ○○○○○ | ○○○○○ | 9 | Usually/Always |
| | 8 | ○○○○○ | ○○○○○ | 8 | ○○○○○ | ○○○○○ | 8 | |
| | 7 | ○○○○○ | ○○○○○ | 7 | ○○○○○ | ○○○○○ | 7 | |
| Sometimes | 6 | ○○○○○ | ○○○○○ | 6 | ○○○○○ | ○○○○○ | 6 | Sometimes |
| | 5 | ○○○○○ | ○○○○○ | 5 | ○○○○○ | ○○○○○ | 5 | |
| | 4 | ○○○○○ | ○○○○○ | 4 | ○○○○○ | ○○○○○ | 4 | |
| Never/Seldom | 3 | ○○○○○ | ○○○○○ | 3 | ○○○○○ | ○○○○○ | 3 | Never/Seldom |
| | 2 | ○○○○○ | ○○○○○ | 2 | ○○○○○ | ○○○○○ | 2 | |
| | 1 | ○○○○○ | ○○○○○ | 1 | ○○○○○ | ○○○○○ | 1 | |

M T W Th F   M T W Th F   M T W Th F   M T W Th F

## The student spoke respectfully and complied with adult requests without argument or complaint.

|  | | M T W Th F | M T W Th F | | M T W Th F | M T W Th F | | |
|---|---|---|---|---|---|---|---|---|
| Usually/Always | 9 | ○○○○○ | ○○○○○ | 9 | ○○○○○ | ○○○○○ | 9 | Usually/Always |
| | 8 | ○○○○○ | ○○○○○ | 8 | ○○○○○ | ○○○○○ | 8 | |
| | 7 | ○○○○○ | ○○○○○ | 7 | ○○○○○ | ○○○○○ | 7 | |
| Sometimes | 6 | ○○○○○ | ○○○○○ | 6 | ○○○○○ | ○○○○○ | 6 | Sometimes |
| | 5 | ○○○○○ | ○○○○○ | 5 | ○○○○○ | ○○○○○ | 5 | |
| | 4 | ○○○○○ | ○○○○○ | 4 | ○○○○○ | ○○○○○ | 4 | |
| Never/Seldom | 3 | ○○○○○ | ○○○○○ | 3 | ○○○○○ | ○○○○○ | 3 | Never/Seldom |
| | 2 | ○○○○○ | ○○○○○ | 2 | ○○○○○ | ○○○○○ | 2 | |
| | 1 | ○○○○○ | ○○○○○ | 1 | ○○○○○ | ○○○○○ | 1 | |

M T W Th F   M T W Th F   M T W Th F   M T W Th F

# Exhibit 5-H
## Classroom Behaviors Observation Form (C-BOF):
## Directions for Use, Scoring, and Interpretation
(Adapted from Wright, 1995)

The Classroom Behaviors Observation Form (C-BOF) is a direct method for observing and recording student behaviors associated with off-task and disruptive student classroom behaviors. It can be used to collect direct observation data about the student's rates of on-task and disruptive or distracting classroom behaviors.

The C-BOF is adapted from a similar rating instrument created by Wright (1995). This rating form incorporates the findings of Platzman et al. (1992), who conducted a comprehensive survey of ADHD observation systems and discovered that three general classes of behavior were most effective in distinguishing children with ADHD from those who lacked the disorder. The three most "diagnostic" behaviors for ADHD are inappropriate calling out or verbalizations, excessive motor activity, and rates of off-task behavior. The C-BOF allows the observer to record these diagnostic 'ADHD' behaviors, as well the rate of interactions that peers and the teacher have with the target student.

### Conducting Observations With the C-BOF
Conduct a series of brief (10-15 minute) observations in the location(s) and during instructional or learning activities when the student typically displays problem behaviors. Because student behavior can vary considerably over time, it is recommended that you conduct at least three classroom observations of the student during both the baseline and intervention phases of the RTI plan.

*Number of Observations.* Because student behaviors can vary considerably across days, observations should be conducted with the C-BOF on at least two (and preferably three) different school days, with each observation lasting at least 10-15 minutes. Multiple observations are required to determine the degree that the behaviors of the target student vary from day to day. In many cases, however, more than two observations may be required to collect adequate behavioral data. For example, if a teacher reports that the child appears off-task and overactive in the reading group, yet pays close attention during math, the observer will probably need to observe at least two reading and two math sessions to establish the variability of student behavior both across days and across academic subjects.

*Behavioral Definitions and Directions.* Here are definitions of the C-BOF target behaviors:

- **Schoolwork (SW)** —This category encompasses any formal learning activity that the student has been assigned to complete or is expected to take part in. For example, if the entire class has been assigned a worksheet to complete independently at their desks, Schoolwork is defined as the student sitting at his or her desk, completing the worksheet. In a large group setting in which the teacher is presenting a lesson to the class and asking them questions about the instructional content, Schoolwork is defined as obvious attending, with the student watching the teacher and responding as appropriate. Schoolwork is not scored if the child is doing something other than the assigned work (e.g., daydreaming, talking with a friend about non-school subjects). If the observer is at all unsure if the student is engaged in an allowable and educationally related activity, the teacher should be approached unobtrusively during or soon after the observation and asked if the student's activities fell within the instructor's definition of acceptable academic engagement that qualifies as Schoolwork.

- **Out of Seat (OS)** — Any observed instance in which the student has left his or her seat during instructional time is scored as Out of Seat. This category includes those situations in which the student obtains permission to leave his or her seat (e.g., to run an errand for the teacher, take a bathroom break, etc.), as well as those in which the student has left his or her seat without permission.

- **Playing with Objects/Motor Activity (PLO/MO)** — Two related kinds of behavior are collapsed into the single category. Any instance in which the child plays for 2 seconds or more with an object (e.g., a small toy, eraser, piece of paper) is scored. Additionally, this category is scored for instances in which the child displays repetitive, "restless" motor movement (e.g., rapping a desktop, rocking a tipped chair back and forth, tapping a foot) for 2 seconds or more. On the other hand, if the child were rummaging through her or his desk apparently looking for something, the observer would not score the behavior as PLO/MO because the behavior is presumed to be purposeful and to lack the aimless or repetitive quality that defines the category.

- **Calling Out/Verbalization (CO)** — The basic unit for the category is any verbalization by the target child during an instructional period that is considered inappropriate because the child failed to use accepted procedures for gaining permission to speak or is making noises that fall outside accepted academic discourse. Examples of Calling out/Verbalizations might include a student shouting out an answer without raising his hand, a child humming loudly during a math test, or a student who makes "nonsense" noises while another child is reading aloud to the group. Whispering is considered an example of CO/Verb if audible to the recorder. Direct communication between the target child and another individual is not coded as CO/Verb but instead is noted as a "Peer Interaction" or "Teacher Interaction."

- **Peer Interaction (PI)** — Verbal exchanges between the target child and classmates are recorded, regardless of which party initiated the interaction.

- **Teacher Interaction (TI)** — Verbal exchanges between the target child and the instructor are recorded.

*Recording Behaviors With the C-BOF.* Target behaviors are scored on the C-BOF as follows:

- **Schoolwork (SW)**: The SW category is coded using a momentary time-sampling procedure. At the start of each 15-second interval, the observer glances at the target child for approximately two seconds and determines if the child is on-task or off-task during the brief observation. If the child is found to be on-task (doing schoolwork), the interval is marked with an "X." If the child is off-task, the interval remains unmarked. The observer then ignores this behavior category until the onset of the next time interval.

- **Out of Seat (OS)**: Incidents of OS are recorded as whole -interval events; that is, if any incident of OS is observed during an interval, the entire interval is marked with a single "X." If a single episode of OS continues uninterrupted across intervals, each successive interval in which the student remains out of seat is coded as OS. Multiple episodes of OS during a single interval are not separately noted but instead are simply coded with a single "X" for that interval.

- **Playing with Objects/Motor Activity (PLO/MO)**. PLO/MO behavior is recorded using the whole-interval method. When any incident of PLO/MO is observed during an interval, the entire interval is marked with a single "X." If a single episode of PLO/MO continues uninterrupted across intervals, each successive interval in which the student remains out of seat is coded as PLO/MO. Multiple episodes of PLO/MO during a single interval are not separately noted but instead are simply coded with a single "X" for that interval.

- **Calling Out/Verbalization (CO)**. CO behavior is recorded using the whole-interval method. When any incident of CO/Verb is observed during an interval, the entire interval is marked with a single "X." Multiple episodes of CO/Verb during a single interval are not separately noted but instead are simply coded with a single "X" for that interval.

- **Peer Interaction (PI)**. PI behavior is recorded using the whole-interval method. When any incident of PI is observed during an interval, the entire interval is marked with a single "X." Multiple episodes of PI during a single interval are not separately noted but instead are simply coded with a single "X" for that interval.

- **Teacher Interaction (TI)**. Teacher Interactions are recorded using the whole-interval method. When any incident of TI is observed during an interval, the entire interval is marked with a single "X." Multiple episodes of TI during a single interval are not separately noted but instead are simply coded with a single "X" for that interval. Record a (+) to signify positive or neutral teacher-student interactions and a (-) to denote negative teacher-student interactions.

*Scoring and Summarizing C-BOF Results.* When the C-BOF has been completed for a single session, the observer calculates the probabilities that each of the target behaviors would appear. These probabilities are calculated as *the number of intervals in which the behavior was observed divided by all intervals that elapsed during the observation period.*

The answer (quotient) from this division operation is then multiplied by 100 to yield an approximate percentage of time that which the target behavior was displayed during the observation.

For example, if the observation period lasted for 60 intervals and the child was found to be doing Schoolwork during 42 of those intervals, an estimate of time on-task would be calculated as follows:

- 42 intervals observed as Schoolwork (SW) divided by the total of 60 intervals = 0.7

- 0.7 x 100 = 70 % of observed intervals coded as SW

Reference: Wright, J. (1995). *ADHD: A school-based evaluation manual.* Retrieved July 23, 2006, from http://www.jimwrightonline.com/pdfdocs/adhdManual.PDF

# Classroom Behaviors Observation Form (C-BOF)

Student Name: _____   Date: _____

Observer: _____   Location: _____   Start Time: _____   End Time: _____

Description of Activities: _____

_____

### 1

| | 0:00 | 0:15 | 0:30 | 0:45 |
|---|---|---|---|---|
| SW | | | | |
| OS | | | | |
| PLO / MO | | | | |
| CO | | | | |
| PI | | | | |
| TI | | | | |

### 2

| | 1:00 | 1:15 | 1:30 | 1:45 |
|---|---|---|---|---|
| SW | | | | |
| OS | | | | |
| PLO / MO | | | | |
| CO | | | | |
| PI | | | | |
| TI | | | | |

### 3

| | 2:00 | 2:15 | 2:30 | 2:45 |
|---|---|---|---|---|
| SW | | | | |
| OS | | | | |
| PLO / MO | | | | |
| CO | | | | |
| PI | | | | |
| TI | | | | |

### 4

| | 3:00 | 3:15 | 3:30 | 3:45 |
|---|---|---|---|---|
| SW | | | | |
| OS | | | | |
| PLO / MO | | | | |
| CO | | | | |
| PI | | | | |
| TI | | | | |

### 5

| | 4:00 | 4:15 | 4:30 | 4:45 |
|---|---|---|---|---|
| SW | | | | |
| OS | | | | |
| PLO / MO | | | | |
| CO | | | | |
| PI | | | | |
| TI | | | | |

### 6

| | 5:00 | 5:15 | 5:30 | 5:45 |
|---|---|---|---|---|
| SW | | | | |
| OS | | | | |
| PLO / MO | | | | |
| CO | | | | |
| PI | | | | |
| TI | | | | |

### 7

| | 6:00 | 6:15 | 6:30 | 6:45 |
|---|---|---|---|---|
| SW | | | | |
| OS | | | | |
| PLO / MO | | | | |
| CO | | | | |
| PI | | | | |
| TI | | | | |

### 8

| | 7:00 | 7:15 | 7:30 | 7:45 |
|---|---|---|---|---|
| SW | | | | |
| OS | | | | |
| PLO / MO | | | | |
| CO | | | | |
| PI | | | | |
| TI | | | | |

### 9

| | 8:00 | 8:15 | 8:30 | 8:45 |
|---|---|---|---|---|
| SW | | | | |
| OS | | | | |
| PLO / MO | | | | |
| CO | | | | |
| PI | | | | |
| TI | | | | |

### 10

| | 9:00 | 9:15 | 9:30 | 9:45 |
|---|---|---|---|---|
| SW | | | | |
| OS | | | | |
| PLO / MO | | | | |
| CO | | | | |
| PI | | | | |
| TI | | | | |

### 11

| | 10:00 | 10:15 | 10:30 | 10:45 |
|---|---|---|---|---|
| SW | | | | |
| OS | | | | |
| PLO / MO | | | | |
| CO | | | | |
| PI | | | | |
| TI | | | | |

### 12

| | 11:00 | 11:15 | 11:30 | 11:45 |
|---|---|---|---|---|
| SW | | | | |
| OS | | | | |
| PLO / MO | | | | |
| CO | | | | |
| PI | | | | |
| TI | | | | |

### 13

| | 12:00 | 12:15 | 12:30 | 12:45 |
|---|---|---|---|---|
| SW | | | | |
| OS | | | | |
| PLO / MO | | | | |
| CO | | | | |
| PI | | | | |
| TI | | | | |

### 14

| | 13:00 | 13:15 | 13:30 | 13:45 |
|---|---|---|---|---|
| SW | | | | |
| OS | | | | |
| PLO / MO | | | | |
| CO | | | | |
| PI | | | | |
| TI | | | | |

### 15

| | 14:00 | 14:15 | 14:30 | 14:45 |
|---|---|---|---|---|
| SW | | | | |
| OS | | | | |
| PLO / MO | | | | |
| CO | | | | |
| PI | | | | |
| TI | | | | |

## Behavior Rating Codes

**SW**=*Schoolwork*: Student is engaged in the expected instructional activity when observed at the start of each observation interval.

**OS**=*Out of Seat*: The student leaves his or her assigned seat (e.g., to stand, sharpen a pencil, or approach the teacher).

**PLO / MO**=*Playing With Objects/Motor Activity*: The student plays with an object (e.g., pencil) or displays repetitive, "restless" motor movement (e.g., rapping a desktop, rocking a tipped chair back and forth, tapping a foot). The behavior is scored only if it lasts for 2 seconds or longer.

**CO** =*Call-Out/Verbalization*: The student calls out without using accepted procedures for gaining permission to speak or makes noises that fall outside accepted academic discourse (e.g., 'nonsense' noises).

**PI**= *Peer Interaction*. Verbal exchanges between the target child and classmates are recorded, regardless of which party initiated the interaction.

**TI**= *Teacher Interaction*. Verbal exchanges between the target child and the instructor are recorded. Record a (+) to signify positive or neutral interactions and a (-) to denote negative interactions.

Student Name: _____  Date: _____ / _____ / _____  Observer: _____

## Directions for Scoring and Summarizing C-BOF Results

- Column B. Count up the number of intervals in which the target behavior was observed and write them into this column.

- Column D: Count up the TOTAL number of intervals that made up the monitoring period (e.g., 60). Write them into this column.

- Column F: For each row, divide the figure in Column B by the figure in Column D. Write the answer (quotient) into Column F. In **decimal form**, this is the rate that the behavior occurred during the observation.

- Column H: Multiply the figure in Column F by 100. In **percentage form**, this is the rate that the behavior occurred during the observation.

### Table 1: Calculate the Rate that Target Behaviors Occurred during the Observation Period

| Column A | Column B | Column C | Column D | Column E | Column F | Column G | Column H |
|---|---|---|---|---|---|---|---|
| **Type of Behavior** | Number of intervals in which the behavior was observed. | | The TOTAL number of intervals in the observation period(s) | | Rate (in decimal form) that the behavior occurred during the observation. | | Rate (in percentage form) that the behavior occurred during the observation. |
| **SW:** School Work | | *Divided by* | | *Equals* | | *Times 100 =* | % |
| **OS:** Out of Seat | | *Divided by* | | *Equals* | | *Times 100 =* | % |
| **PLO / MO:** Playing With Objects / Motor Behavior | | *Divided by* | | *Equals* | | *Times 100 =* | % |
| **CO:** Call-Outs / Verbalizations | | *Divided by* | | *Equals* | | *Times 100 =* | % |
| **PI:** Poor Interactions | | *Divided by* | | *Equals* | | *Times 100 =* | % |
| **TI+:** Positive or Neutral Teacher Interactions | | *Divided by* | | *Equals* | | *Times 100 =* | % |
| **TI-:** Negative Teacher Interactions | | *Divided by* | | *Equals* | | *Times 100 =* | % |

### Table 2: Chart the Student's Behavior Profile

## C-BOF Behavior Profile

Date: _____ / _____ / _____
Setting:/Activity:
_____

Percentage / Observed Intervals: 100, 90, 80, 70, 60, 50, 40, 30, 20, 10, 0

Columns: SW  OS  PLO/MO  CO  PI  TI+  TI-

| SW = | CO = |
| OS = | PI = |
| PLO/MO = | TI+ =   TI - = |

# Classroom Behaviors Observation Form Data Summary: Student:_____

**Directions:** Use this form to record and compare observations completed across multiple days with the C-BOF. Enter each day's observation results into one of the 'Obsv' charts. First, check whether a specific observation was conducted during the 'Baseline' or 'Intervention' phase. For each Baseline or Intervention observation, write the percentage of intervals during which the target behaviors were observed. Then draw lines to connect the plotted values for the undesirable behaviors OS, PLO/MO, CO, and PI to create a connected series. (Note that the charted values for SW, TI+, and TI- are separated from the other observed behaviors by solid lines and should *not* be connected to them because Schoolwork and Teacher Interactions are not considered 'undesirable student behaviors'.) Compare the patterns of the completed observation charts to one another, noting any significant variations or changes in the patterns of recorded behaviors over time (e.g., increase in Schoolwork, decrease in Call-Outs or Peer Interactions).

**Obsv 1:** __ Baseline __ Intervention
Date: ____/____/____
Setting:/Activity: _____

Percentage / Observed Intervals

| SW | OS | PLO/MO | CO | PI | TI+ | TI- |
|----|----|--------|----|----|-----|-----|

SW =    CO =
OS =    PI =
PLO/MO =    TI+ =    TI - =

**Obsv 2:** __ Baseline __ Intervention
Date: ____/____/____
Setting:/Activity: _____

Percentage / Observed Intervals

| SW | OS | PLO/MO | CO | PI | TI+ | TI- |
|----|----|--------|----|----|-----|-----|

SW =    CO =
OS =    PI =
PLO/MO =    TI+ =    TI - =

**Obsv 3:** __ Baseline __ Intervention
Date: ____/____/____
Setting:/Activity: _____

Percentage / Observed Intervals

| SW | OS | PLO/MO | CO | PI | TI+ | TI- |
|----|----|--------|----|----|-----|-----|

SW =    CO =
OS =    PI =
PLO/MO =    TI+ =    TI - =

**Obsv 4:** __ Baseline __ Intervention
Date: ____/____/____
Setting:/Activity: _____

Percentage / Observed Intervals

| SW | OS | PLO/MO | CO | PI | TI+ | TI- |
|----|----|--------|----|----|-----|-----|

SW =    CO =
OS =    PI =
PLO/MO =    TI+ =    TI - =

**Obsv 5:** __ Baseline __ Intervention
Date: ____/____/____
Setting:/Activity: _____

Percentage / Observed Intervals

| SW | OS | PLO/MO | CO | PI | TI+ | TI- |
|----|----|--------|----|----|-----|-----|

SW =    CO =
OS =    PI =
PLO/MO =    TI+ =    TI - =

**Obsv 6:** __ Baseline __ Intervention
Date: ____/____/____
Setting:/Activity: _____

Percentage / Observed Intervals

| SW | OS | PLO/MO | CO | PI | TI+ | TI- |
|----|----|--------|----|----|-----|-----|

SW =    CO =
OS =    PI =
PLO/MO =    TI+ =    TI - =

# Classroom Behaviors Observation Form (C-BOF): Case Example

**Case Background.** Ricky was a 3rd-grade student referred to his school's Intervention Team because he had been doing poorly in both reading and writing. During the time that Ricky was being monitored by the Intervention Team, a total of six direct observations were completed, all during whole-group instruction scheduled for Ricky's English/Language Arts period. Three observations were completed prior to the initial Intervention Team meeting (Baseline Phase) and three additional observations were conducted after the intervention had been put into place (Intervention Phase).

**Individual C-BOF Observation.** Figure 1 shows an example of a completed C-BOF form representing one behavioral observation period of 15 minutes. This observation was completed during the Baseline phase, before the Intervention Team had met to create an intervention plan.

Figure 2 displays the scored and summarized results of the single C-BOF observation. The student showed a low rate of on-task behavior, with intervals in which Ricky was engaged in Schoolwork falling at only 48 percent of the total observed intervals. Ricky also displayed relatively high rates of the following undesirable behaviors: Call-Outs (25 percent), Playing With Objects/Motor Behaviors (37 percent), and Peer Interactions (23 percent). Interestingly, his teacher interacted with Ricky during a quarter (25 percent) of observed intervals, a high rate for any instructor to engage a student! Of those interactions, however, the teacher approached Ricky four times more often (20 percent of intervals) for 'negative' reasons such as to reprimand him for misbehavior or redirect Ricky to task than she did for 'positive' reasons (5 percent of intervals) such as to praise Ricky or call on him to contribute to the class discussion.

**Charted Summary of Several Baseline and Intervention Observations Using the C-BOF.** A completed example of the C-BOF Data Summary Form that appears in Figure 3 shows the charted results of Ricky's six classroom observations that were carried out over several weeks. Three of the observations were completed during the Baseline Phase and three took place during the Intervention Phase.

It is apparent that Ricky showed significant improvements in behaviors during the Intervention Phase (Observations 4, 5, & 6). His on-task behavior—represented by the Schoolwork category—jumped significantly when the intervention was in effect. Also, Ricky's undesirable behaviors (Call-Outs, Playing With Objects/Motor Behavior, and Peer Interactions) dropped as a result of the intervention.

The data from this form reveal another noteworthy change: during the Baseline Phase, Ricky's teacher was overwhelmingly likely to approach him for 'negative' reasons. After the intervention was put into place, she approached him just as frequently as before—but now was much more likely to have positive interactions with Ricky, such as praising or calling on him. At the follow-up Intervention Team meeting, the team and teacher agreed that her decision to consciously engage Ricky in positive interactions appeared to contribute to his improved classroom attention and lower level of problem behaviors.

# Case Example: Classroom Behaviors Observation Form (C-BOF)

Student Name: _____Ricky Smith_____  Date: ____Feb 6, 2006____

Observer: ____Mr. Wright____  Location: ____3rd Grade Classroom____  Start Time: __10:22__  End Time: ____10"37____

Description of Activities: Mrs. Conroy, classroom teacher, reviewed upcoming reading vocabulary, asked students higher-level comprehension questions from a story that they had read on the prior day, and introduced a writing assignment.

## 1

| | 0:00 | 0:15 | 0:30 | 0:45 |
|---|---|---|---|---|
| SW | | | ✓ | ✓ |
| OS | | | | |
| PLO / MO | | | | |
| CO | | ✓ | ✓ | |
| PI | | | ✓ | |
| TI | | | | + |

## 2

| | 1:00 | 1:15 | 1:30 | 1:45 |
|---|---|---|---|---|
| SW | | ✓ | ✓ | |
| OS | | ✓ | | |
| PLO / MO | | | | |
| CO | | ✓ | | |
| PI | | | | ✓ |
| TI | | | | − |

## 3

| | 2:00 | 2:15 | 2:30 | 2:45 |
|---|---|---|---|---|
| SW | | ✓ | ✓ | ✓ |
| OS | | | | |
| PLO / MO | | | ✓ | ✓ |
| CO | | | ✓ | |
| PI | | | ✓ | |
| TI | | | | + |

## 4

| | 3:00 | 3:15 | 3:30 | 3:45 |
|---|---|---|---|---|
| SW | | | ✓ | |
| OS | ✓ | | | |
| PLO / MO | ✓ | | | |
| CO | | ✓ | | |
| PI | ✓ | ✓ | ✓ | |
| TI | | | − | |

## 5

| | 4:00 | 4:15 | 4:30 | 4:45 |
|---|---|---|---|---|
| SW | | | | |
| OS | | | | |
| PLO / MO | | | | |
| CO | | | | |
| PI | | | | |
| TI | | | | |

## 6

| | 5:00 | 5:15 | 5:30 | 5:45 |
|---|---|---|---|---|
| SW | | ✓ | | ✓ |
| OS | | | | |
| PLO / MO | | | | |
| CO | | | ✓ | |
| PI | | ✓ | | |
| TI | | | | − |

## 7

| | 6:00 | 6:15 | 6:30 | 6:45 |
|---|---|---|---|---|
| SW | | ✓ | ✓ | ✓ |
| OS | | | | |
| PLO / MO | | ✓ | | |
| CO | | | | |
| PI | | | ✓ | ✓ |
| TI | | | − | |

## 8

| | 7:00 | 7:15 | 7:30 | 7:45 |
|---|---|---|---|---|
| SW | ✓ | | ✓ | |
| OS | | | | |
| PLO / MO | | | ✓ | ✓ |
| CO | | ✓ | | |
| PI | | ✓ | | |
| TI | | | − | − |

## 9

| | 8:00 | 8:15 | 8:30 | 8:45 |
|---|---|---|---|---|
| SW | | ✓ | ✓ | ✓ |
| OS | | | | |
| PLO / MO | | ✓ | | |
| CO | | | ✓ | |
| PI | ✓ | | | |
| TI | | | − | |

## 10

| | 9:00 | 9:15 | 9:30 | 9:45 |
|---|---|---|---|---|
| SW | | | | |
| OS | ✓ | | | |
| PLO / MO | | | | |
| CO | ✓ | ✓ | | ✓ |
| PI | | | | |
| TI | | | | |

## 11

| | 10:00 | 10:15 | 10:30 | 10:45 |
|---|---|---|---|---|
| SW | | | | |
| OS | | | | |
| PLO / MO | | ✓ | ✓ | |
| CO | | | ✓ | ✓ |
| PI | | | | |
| TI | | | | − |

## 12

| | 11:00 | 11:15 | 11:30 | 11:45 |
|---|---|---|---|---|
| SW | | | ✓ | ✓ |
| OS | | | | |
| PLO / MO | | ✓ | ✓ | ✓ |
| CO | | ✓ | | |
| PI | | | | |
| TI | | | − | − |

## 13

| | 12:00 | 12:15 | 12:30 | 12:45 |
|---|---|---|---|---|
| SW | ✓ | | | |
| OS | | | | |
| PLO / MO | | | | |
| CO | | ✓ | ✓ | ✓ |
| PI | | | | |
| TI | | | − | |

## 14

| | 13:00 | 13:15 | 13:30 | 13:45 |
|---|---|---|---|---|
| SW | ✓ | | ✓ | |
| OS | | | | |
| PLO / MO | | | | |
| CO | | ✓ | ✓ | |
| PI | | | | |
| TI | | + | | |

## 15

| | 14:00 | 14:15 | 14:30 | 14:45 |
|---|---|---|---|---|
| SW | | ✓ | ✓ | ✓ |
| OS | | | | |
| PLO / MO | | | ✓ | |
| CO | | | ✓ | ✓ |
| PI | | | ✓ | ✓ |
| TI | | | | − |

## Behavior Rating Codes

**SW**=*Schoolwork:* Student is engaged in the expected instructional activity when observed at the start of each observation interval.

**OS**=*Out of Seat:* The student leaves his or her assigned seat (e.g., to stand, sharpen a pencil, or approach the teacher).

**PLO / MO**=*Playing With Objects/Motor Activity:* The student plays with an object (e.g., pencil) or displays repetitive, "restless" motor movement (e.g., rapping a desktop, rocking a tipped chair back and forth, tapping a foot). The behavior is scored only if it lasts for 2 seconds or longer.

**CO** =*Call-Out/Verbalization:* The student calls out without using accepted procedures for gaining permission to speak or makes noises that fall outside accepted academic discourse (e.g., 'nonsense' noises).

**PI**= *Peer Interaction.* Verbal exchanges between the target child and classmates are recorded, regardless of which party initiated the interaction.

**TI**= *Teacher Interaction.* Verbal exchanges between the target child and the instructor are recorded. Record a (+) to signify positive or neutral interactions and a (-) to denote negative interactions.

# Case Example

Student Name: _____Ricky Smith_____  Date: ____Feb 6, 2006____  Observer: _____Mr. Wright_____

## Directions for Scoring and Summarizing C-BOF Results

- Column B. Count up the number of intervals in which the target behavior was observed and write them into this column.

- Column D: Count up the TOTAL number of intervals that made up the monitoring period (e.g., 60). Write them into this column.

- Column F: For each row, divide the figure in Column B by the figure in Column D. Write the answer (quotient) into Column F. In **decimal form**, this is the rate that the behavior occurred during the observation.

- Column H: Multiply the figure in Column F by 100. In **percentage form**, this is the rate that the behavior occurred during the observation.

### Table 1: Calculate the Rate that Target Behaviors Occurred during the Observation Period

| Column A | Column B | Column C | Column D | Column E | Column F | Column G | Column H |
|---|---|---|---|---|---|---|---|
| **Type of Behavior** | Number of intervals in which the behavior was observed. | | The TOTAL number of intervals in the observation period(s) | | Rate (in decimal form) that the behavior occurred during the observation. | | Rate (in percentage form) that the behavior occurred during the observation. |
| **SW:** School Work | 29 | Divided by | 60 | Equals | 0.48 | Times 100 = | 48 % |
| **OS:** Out of Seat | 3 | Divided by | 60 | Equals | 0.05 | Times 100 = | 5 % |
| **PLO / MO:** Playing With Objects / Motor Behavior | 15 | Divided by | 60 | Equals | 0.25 | Times 100 = | 25 % |
| **CO:** Call-Outs / Verbalizations | 22 | Divided by | 60 | Equals | 0.37 | Times 100 = | 37 % |
| **PI:** Peer Interactions | 14 | Divided by | 60 | Equals | 0.23 | Times 100 = | 23 % |
| **TI+:** Positive or Neutral Teacher Interactions | 3 | Divided by | 60 | Equals | 0.05 | Times 100 = | 5 % |
| **TI-:** Negative Teacher Interactions | 12 | Divided by | 60 | Equals | 0.20 | Times 100 = | 20 % |

### Table 2: Chart the Student's Behavior Profile

**C-BOF Behavior Profile**

Date: __2__/__6__/06__
Setting:/Activity: _English/Language Arts____

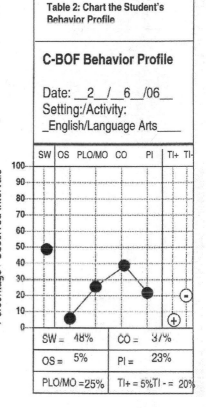

| | |
|---|---|
| SW = 48% | CO = 37% |
| OS = 5% | PI = 23% |
| PLO/MO =25% | TI+ = 5% TI - = 20% |

# Case Example
## Classroom Behaviors Observation Form Data Summary: Student:_____Ricky Smith_____

**Directions:** Use this form to record and compare observations completed across multiple days with the C-BOF. Enter each day's observation results into one of the 'Obsv' charts. First, check whether a specific observation was conducted during the 'Baseline' or 'Intervention' phase. For each Baseline or Intervention observation, write the percentage of intervals during which the target behaviors were observed. Then draw lines to connect the plotted values for the undesirable behaviors OS, PLO/MO, CO, and PI to create a connected series. (Note that the charted values for SW, TI+, and TI- are separated from the other observed behaviors by solid lines and should *not* be connected to them because Schoolwork and Teacher Interactions are not considered 'undesirable student behaviors'.) Compare the patterns of the completed observation charts to one another, noting any significant variations or changes in the patterns of recorded behaviors over time (e.g., increase in Schoolwork, decrease in Call-Outs or Peer Interactions).

**Obsv 1:** _X_ Baseline
___ Intervention
Date: ___2_/__6__/_06_
Setting:/Activity:
_English/Language Arts____

| SW = | 48% | CO = | 37% |
| OS = | 5% | PI = | 23% |
| PLO/MO = | 25% | TI+ = 5% | TI - = 20% |

**Obsv 2:** _X_ Baseline
___ Intervention
Date: __2__/_14__/_06_
Setting:/Activity:
_English/Language Arts____

| SW = | 63% | CO = | 40% |
| OS = | 12% | PI = | 28% |
| PLO/MO = | 42% | TI+ = 8% | TI - = 23% |

**Obsv 3:** _X_ Baseline
___ Intervention
Date: _2___/_17__/_06_
Setting:/Activity:
_English/Language Arts____

| SW = | 52% | CO = | 30% |
| OS = | 3% | PI = | 42% |
| PLO/MO = | 30% | TI+ = 7% | TI - = 13% |

**Obsv 4:** __ Baseline
_X_ Intervention
Date: __3_/_13__/_06_
Setting:/Activity:
_English/Language Arts____

| SW = | 82% | CO = | 8% |
| OS = | 5% | PI = | 13% |
| PLO/MO = | 20% | TI+ = 20% | TI - = 5% |

**Obsv 5:** __ Baseline
_X_ Intervention
Date: __3_/_22__/_06_
Setting:/Activity:
_English/Language Arts____

| SW = | 73% | CO = | 12% |
| OS = | 5% | PI = | 10% |
| PLO/MO = | 15% | TI+ = 23% | TI - = 10% |

**Obsv 6:** __ Baseline
_X_ Intervention
Date: __3_/_28__/_06_
Setting:/Activity:
_English/Language Arts____

| SW = | 87% | CO = | 5% |
| OS = | 8% | PI = | 20% |
| PLO/MO = | 18% | TI+ = 30% | TI - = 3% |

**156 RTI Toolkit: A Practical Guide for Schools**

# Exhibit 5-I
## Instructional Setting Rating Sheet

Student:_____ Completed by: _____

Date___ /____/____ Time___:___ to ___:___ Teacher_____

Directions: Rate the items below evaluating the instructional environment during your observation of the student. For each item, circle the response that best fits your observation. Add comments, particularly to explain items that receive low ratings.

1. The teacher made sure that the student was paying attention before giving instructions, directions, or asking questions:

| 1 | 2 | 3 | 4 |
|---|---|---|---|
| Not at all | Occasionally | Frequently | Nearly all of the time |

2. The teacher monitored to be sure that the student understood the material being taught:

| 1 | 2 | 3 | 4 |
|---|---|---|---|
| Not at all | Occasionally | Frequently | Nearly all of the time |

3. Classroom disruptions were handled immediately or prevented:

| 1 | 2 | 3 | 4 |
|---|---|---|---|
| Not at all | Occasionally | Frequently | Nearly all of the time |

4. The teacher engaged the student in the lesson by asking questions that the student could answer:

| 1 | 2 | 3 | 4 |
|---|---|---|---|
| Not at all | Occasionally | Frequently | Nearly all of the time |

5. Expectations for appropriate student behavior were clear (e.g., follow classroom rules, work carefully):

| 1 | 2 | 3 | 4 |
|---|---|---|---|
| Not at all | Occasionally | Frequently | Nearly all of the time |

6. Interactions between the student and classmates were positive:

| 1 | 2 | 3 | 4 |
|---|---|---|---|
| Not at all | Occasionally | Frequently | Nearly all of the time |

7. Interactions between the student and teacher were positive:

| 1 | 2 | 3 | 4 |
|---|---|---|---|
| Not at all | Occasionally | Frequently | Nearly all of the time |

8. The student received immediate, specific, positive feedback about her or his behavior or academic performance:

| 1 | 2 | 3 | 4 |
|---|---|---|---|
| Not at all | Occasionally | Frequently | Nearly all of the time |

9. The general noise level and behavior of other students in the classroom were conducive to group instruction or independent seatwork:

| 1 | 2 | 3 | 4 |
|---|---|---|---|
| Not at all | Occasionally | Frequently | Nearly all of the time |

10. The student appeared to be placed in work that was instructionally appropriate:

    YES    NO

Comments:_____

# Exhibit 5-J
## Teacher Behavior Log & Student Behavioral Scatterplot

Directions: Record each incident of problem student behavior in the behavior log below.

---

Student Name:_____ Observer: _____

- - - - - - - - - - - - - - - - - - - - - - - - - - - - - - - - - - - - - - - - -

Time:___:___a.m./p.m.  Date: ___ / ___ / ___ Location: _____

Brief narrative of incident (including persons involved, scheduled activity, triggering event(s), outcome(s));

_____

_____

_____

How long did this incident last? _____ mins

How severe was the behavior in the incident?

| **1** | **2** | **3** |
|---|---|---|
| **Not Severe** | **Somewhat Severe** | **Very Severe** |

---

Student Name:_____ Observer: _____

- - - - - - - - - - - - - - - - - - - - - - - - - - - - - - - - - - - - - - - - -

Time:___:___a.m./p.m.  Date: ___ / ___ / ___ Location: _____

Brief narrative of incident (including persons involved, scheduled activity, triggering event(s), outcome(s));

_____

_____

_____

How long did this incident last? _____ mins

How severe was the behavior in the incident?

| **1** | **2** | **3** |
|---|---|---|
| **Not Severe** | **Somewhat Severe** | **Very Severe** |

# Behavioral Scatterplot

Student:_____ Date:_____ Completed by _____

**Directions:** Write the student's general daily schedule in the column labeled 'Activity/Class Schedule'. For each day during which target problems behaviors were monitored in the student's *behavioral log*, mark an 'X' in the appropriate date column at the time when the problem behavior occurred. When all behaviors have been plotted at the correct date and time of their occurrence, look for possible explanatory patterns between the activities scheduled and the behaviors observed --e.g., due to physical setting variables, academic task demands, presence or absence of adult supervision, etc.

| Time | Activity / Class Schedule | Date/Day _____ | Date/Day _____ | Date/Day _____ | Date/Day _____ | Date/Day _____ |
|------|------|------|------|------|------|------|
| 7:30-7:45 | | | | | | |
| 7:45-8:00 | | | | | | |
| 8:00-8:15 | | | | | | |
| 8:15-8:30 | | | | | | |
| 8:30-8:45 | | | | | | |
| 8:45-9:00 | | | | | | |
| 9:00-9:15 | | | | | | |
| 9:15-9:30 | | | | | | |
| 9:30-9:45 | | | | | | |
| 9:45-10:00 | | | | | | |
| 10:00-10:15 | | | | | | |
| 10:15-10:30 | | | | | | |
| 10:30-10:45 | | | | | | |
| 10:45-11:00 | | | | | | |
| 11:00-11:15 | | | | | | |
| 11:15-11:30 | | | | | | |
| 11:30-11:45 | | | | | | |
| 11:45-12:00 | | | | | | |
| 12:00-12:15 | | | | | | |
| 12:15-12:30 | | | | | | |
| 12:30-12:45 | | | | | | |
| 12:45-1:00 | | | | | | |
| 1:00-1:15 | | | | | | |
| 1:15-1:30 | | | | | | |
| 1:30-1:45 | | | | | | |
| 1:45-2:00 | | | | | | |
| 2:00-2:15 | | | | | | |
| 2:15-2:30 | | | | | | |
| 2:30-2:45 | | | | | | |
| 2:45-3:00 | | | | | | |
| 3:00-3:15 | | | | | | |
| 3:15-3:30 | | | | | | |
| 3:30-3:45 | | | | | | |
| 3:45-4:00 | | | | | | |
| 4:00-4:15 | | | | | | |
| 4:15-4:30 | | | | | | |

# Exhibit 5-K
## Setting Up and Interpreting Time-Series Charts

Response to Intervention requires that schools collect data on student progress over time to demonstrate whether an academic or behavioral intervention is working. It is much easier to see the student's overall rate of progress when data are converted to a visual display. The *time-series chart* is the type of visual display most commonly used to graph student progress. This brief tutorial will provide guidelines for setting up a time-series chart and interpreting plotted data (Hayes, 1981; Kazdin,1982).

### Components of the time-series chart

Time-series charts are structured in a standardized manner to help viewers to better understand the data that they display. Some of the charting conventions described below (labeling of the chart axes, separation of data phases) are standard elements of time-series charts. Other conventions, such as use of aimlines, are most commonly used when charting Curriculum-Based Measurement data.

- *Labels of Vertical ('Y') and Horizontal ('X') Axes*. The vertical axis of the chart is labeled with the 'behavior' that is being measured. In the chart displayed in Figure 1, the behavior to be plotted is 'Correctly Read Words Per Minute'. The horizontal axis of the chart displays the timespan during which progress-monitoring took place. Our sample chart shows that the student was monitored from the dates of January 28 through April 8.

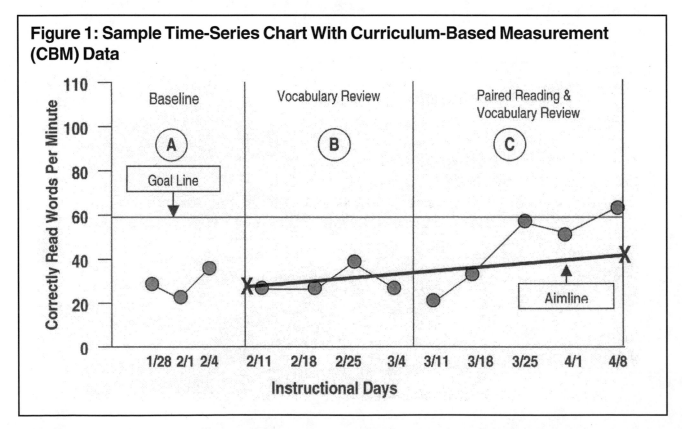

**Figure 1: Sample Time-Series Chart With Curriculum-Based Measurement (CBM) Data**

- *Phase Changes.* The chart is divided into *phases*, with each phase representing a time period in which data are collected under similar conditions. Phases are visually separated on the chart with vertical lines. Each phase is also typically labeled to indicate the intervention condition in effect during that phase (e.g., 'Baseline: Teacher whole-group math instruction'). Data collected within a phase are plotted as a series of connected data points. However, there is always a break in the plotted data between phases to indicate that the conditions under which data were collected differed in each phase. In Figure 1, sections A, B, and C of the chart represent different phases.

- *Baseline Data.* RTI Teams will often collect *baseline* data to determine a student's starting point before an intervention is begun. Baseline data provides a snapshot of the student's level of academic or behavioral functioning before an individualized intervention is put into place. Phase A of the chart in Figure 1 shows an example of baseline data points. It is generally recommended that a minimum of 3-5 data points be collected during the baseline phase. If a visual inspection reveals that the overall trend of the baseline data is relatively flat or moving in the direction opposite that desired by school staff, the RTI Team concludes the baseline phase and implements the intervention. However, if the baseline phase shows a strong *positive* trend (moves strongly in the desired direction), the team should delay putting the intervention in place and continue to monitor student progress, since the instructional or behavioral strategies being used during the baseline phase are clearly benefiting the child.

- *Progress-Monitoring Data.* Once an individualized academic or behavioral intervention has been put into place for a student, the RTI Team then monitors the intervention frequently (e.g., weekly) to track that student's *response* to the intervention. Sections B and C of the chart in Figure 1 display progress-monitoring data collected during two intervention phases.

- *Plotting Goal Line and Aimline.* When charting student progress, it is helpful to include visual indicators that show the *goal* that the student is striving to reach as well as the *expected rate of progress* that the student is predicted to make.

The *goal line* is drawn on the chart as a vertical line that represents a successful level of performance. In Figure 2, the goal line for correctly read words is set at 59 words per minute, the typical skill level in the classroom of the student being monitored. The *aimline* is a sloping line that shows the rate at which the student is predicted to make progress if the intervention is successful. The aimline in Figure 2 shows an expected increase of about 1.5 words per week in reading fluency. By plotting both goal line and aimline on the progress-monitoring chart, the RTI Team can visually compare the student's actual performance on a given day to his or her expected rate of progress (aimline) and eventual goal for improvement (goal line).

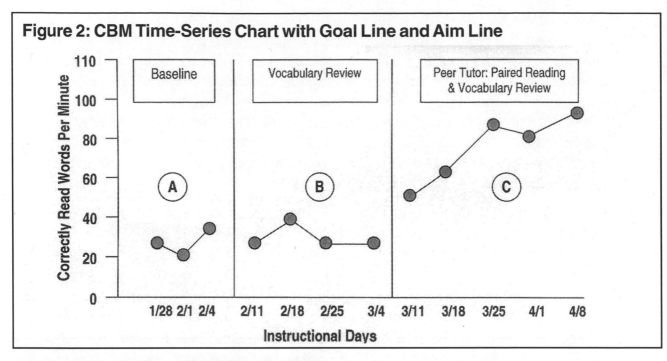

Figure 2: CBM Time-Series Chart with Goal Line and Aim Line

## Visual interpretation of time-series data

When data points are plotted on a time-series chart, the observer can use techniques of visual analysis to uncover meaningful patterns in the data. Trend, variability, and level of data points can all yield significant clues to help in data interpretation.

- *Trend.* Trend is the slope of increase or decrease visible in charted data. A strong trend in the desired direction during an intervention phase would indicate that the intervention is having the predicted positive impact. The data series in section B of Figure 3 shows a much stronger upward trend than that in section A.

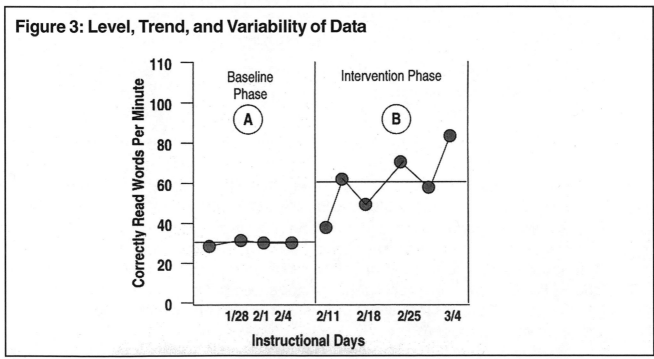

Figure 3: Level, Trend, and Variability of Data

- *Variability.* The amount of variability, or fluctuation, of data in each phase can have an impact on progress monitoring. When data in a series show little variability, RTI Teams may need to collect only a small amount of data to show a clear trend. When there is considerable variability, though, RTI Teams may be required to collect more data to discern the underlying trend. The data series charted in Phase B of Figure 3 shows much more variability than the series in Phase A.

- *Level.* The level of a data series is the average, or mean, of the data within that series. For example, in a data series with four values (45, 58, 62, 47), the level (mean) is 53. The level can be a useful method for summarizing the average for each data phase, particularly when there is a considerable amount of variability in the data. On a time-series chart, the level of a data series is usually plotted as a horizontal line corresponding to the mean of the phase. In Figure 3, the level of Phase B (60 correctly read words per minute) is considerably greater than that of Phase A (34 correctly read words per minute).

## Plotting trendlines to determine the underlying 'trend' of charted data

Data points plotted on a time-series chart often have considerable fluctuation, or variability, making it difficult to 'see' the underlying trend of the data with any precision. Trendlines are straight lines superimposed on charted data to show a simplified 'best estimate' of the student's actual rate of progress. This section presents an easy method for plotting a trendline by hand.

*Plotting trendlines with the Tukey method.* To plot the trendline using the Tukey method, the observer first counts up the data-points on the graph and draws two vertical lines that divide the data-points evenly into 3 groupings. (If the number of data-points does not exactly divide into 3 parts, the groupings should be approximately equal. For example, if the chart contains 11 data-points, they can be divided into groups of 4, 3, and 4 data-points.)

Next, the observer concentrates on the first and third sections of the graph, ignoring the middle section. In each of the two selected sections, the observer finds the median point on the X (horizontal) and Y (vertical) axes and marks an "X" on the graph at the place where those points intersect. To locate the median time (e.g., instructional week) on the horizontal axis of a section, the observer looks at the span of weeks in which data was collected. For example, if data-points appear for weeks 1- 5 in the first section, the observer considers the middle, or median, point to be week 3.

## Figure 4: Plotting a trendline with the Tukey Method

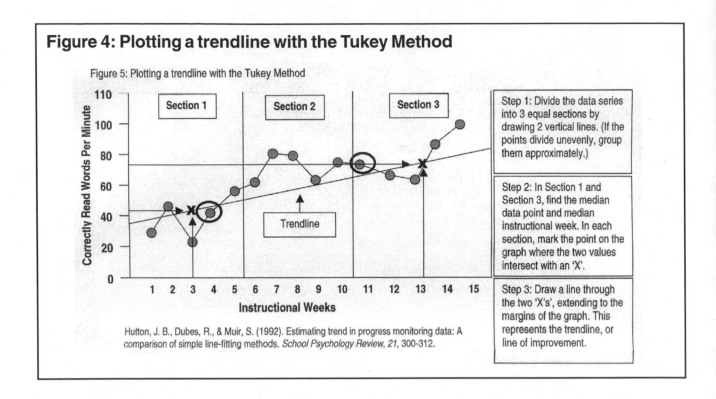

Figure 5: Plotting a trendline with the Tukey Method

**Step 1:** Divide the data series into 3 equal sections by drawing 2 vertical lines. (If the points divide unevenly, group them approximately.)

**Step 2:** In Section 1 and Section 3, find the median data point and median instructional week. In each section, mark the point on the graph where the two values intersect with an 'X'.

**Step 3:** Draw a line through the two 'X's', extending to the margins of the graph. This represents the trendline, or line of improvement.

Hutton, J. B., Dubes, R., & Muir, S. (1992). Estimating trend in progress monitoring data: A comparison of simple line-fitting methods. *School Psychology Review, 21*, 300-312.

To locate the median number of observed behaviors on the vertical axis, the observer examines the data-points in the graph-section, selecting the median or middle, value from among the range of points. For example, if data-points for weeks 1- 5 in the first section are 30, 49, 23, 41, and 59, the median (middle) value is 41. When the observer has found and marked the point of intersect of median X and Y values in both the first and third sections, a line is then drawn through the two points, extending from the left to the right margins of the graph. By drawing a line through the 2 X's plotted on the graph, the observer creates a trendline that provides a reasonably accurate visual summary of progress.

### References

Hayes, S.C. (1981). Single case experimental design and empirical clinical practice. Journal of Consulting and Clinical Psychology, 49, 193-211.

Kazdin, A.E. (1982). Single-case research designs: Methods for clinical and applied settings. New York: Oxford Press.

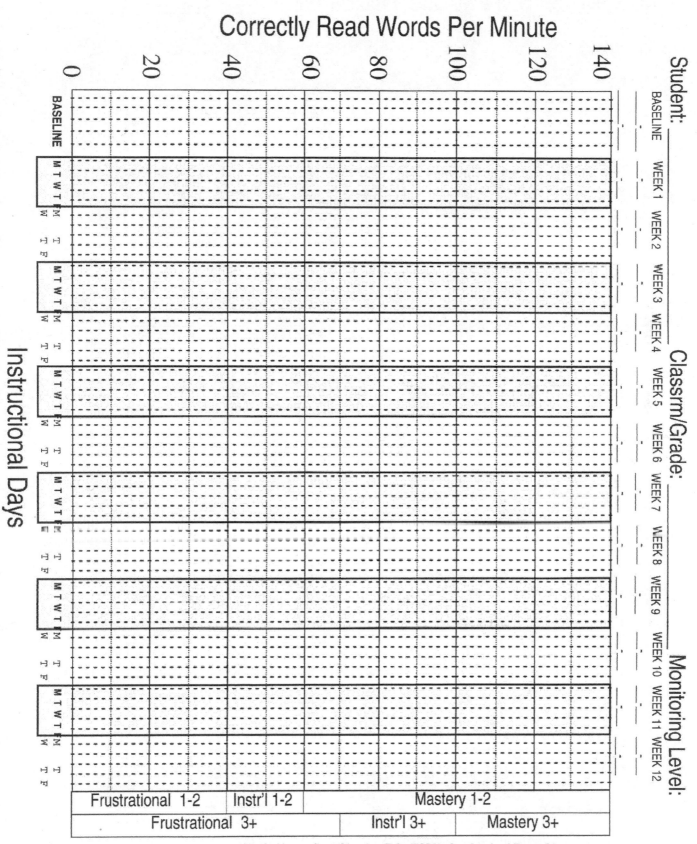

**Correctly Read Words Per Minute**

Student: _____

Classrm/Grade: _____

Monitoring Level: _____

BASELINE | WEEK 1 | WEEK 2 | WEEK 3 | WEEK 4 | WEEK 5 | WEEK 6 | WEEK 7 | WEEK 8 | WEEK 9 | WEEK 10 | WEEK 11 | WEEK 12

0    20    40    60    80    100    120    140

**Instructional Days**

BASELINE

| Frustrational 1-2 | Instr'l 1-2 | Mastery 1-2 |
| Frustrational 3+ | Instr'l 3+ | Mastery 3+ |

*(Grade Norms from Shapiro, E.S. (1996). Academic skills problems: Direct assessment and intervention (2nd ed.) New York: Guilford*

# Correct Digits Per 2 Minutes: Problem Type(s):_____

Student:

Classrm/Grade:

Monitoring Level:

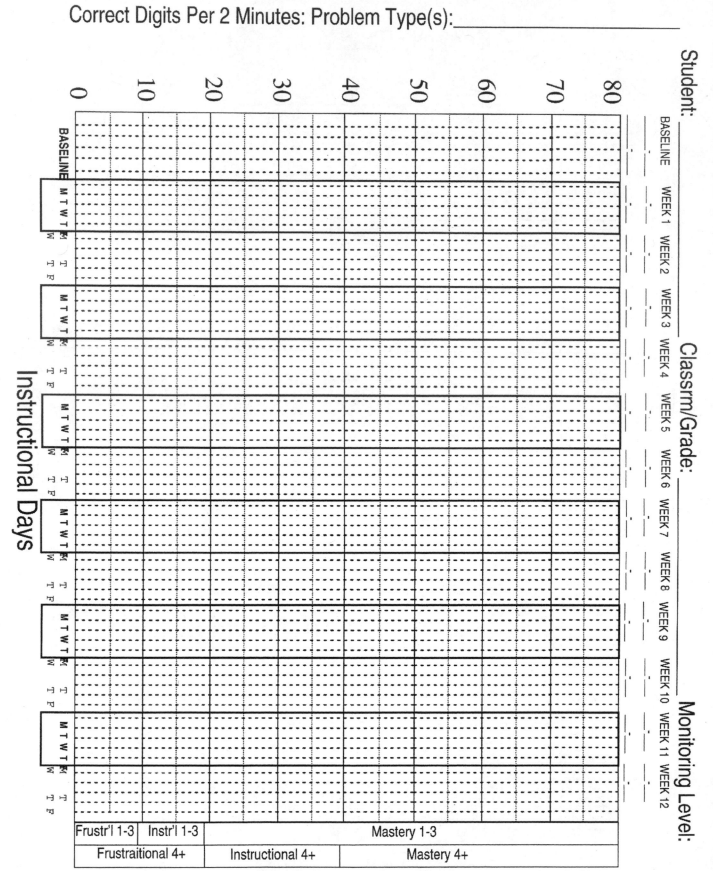

(Grade Norms from Shapiro, E.S. (1996). *Academic skills problems: Direct assessment and intervention* (2nd ed.) New York: Guildord

Writing Sample Per 3 Minutes: ___Total Words ___#Correctly Spelled Words ___# Correct Writing Sequences ___ #Correct Punctuation

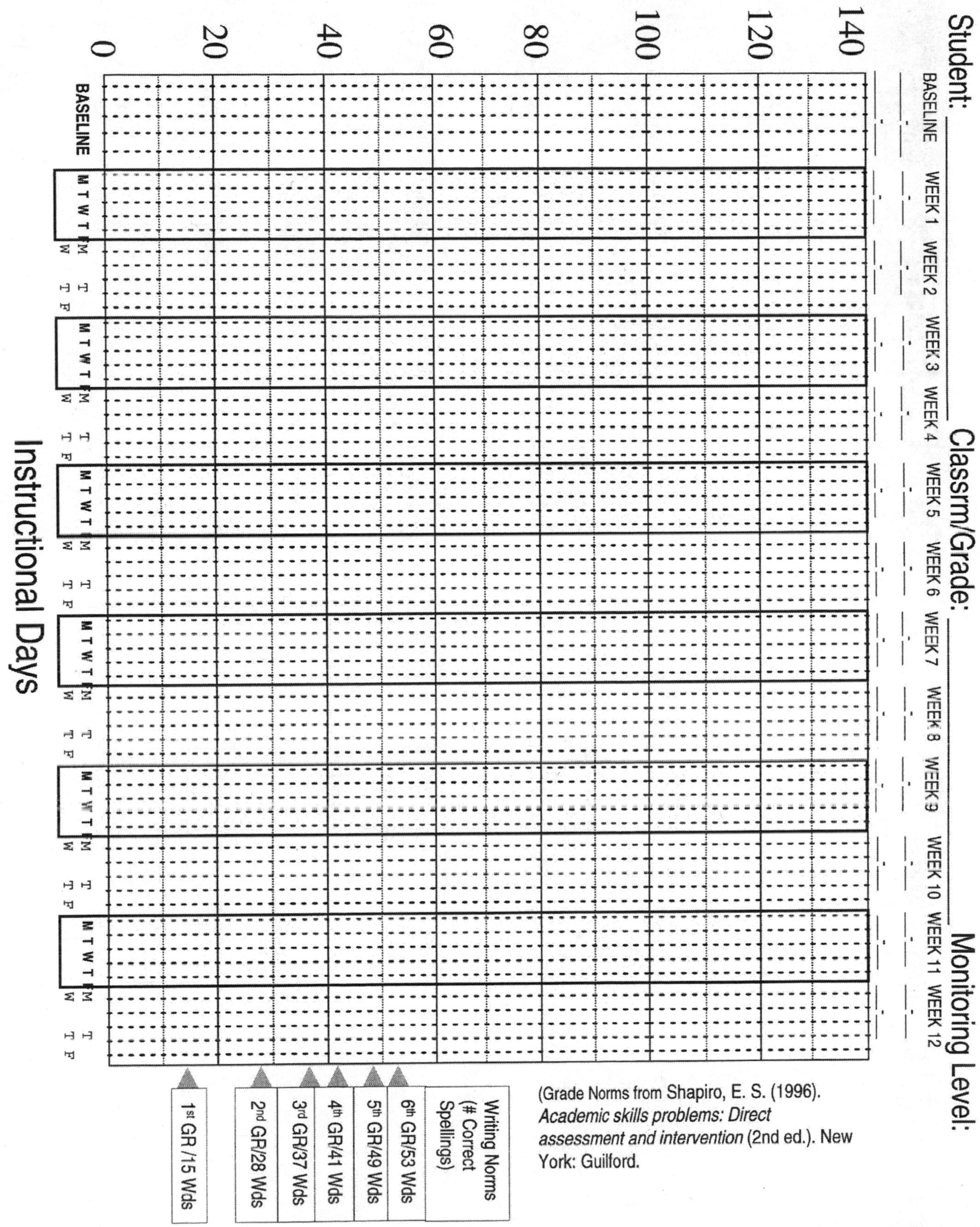
Student:
Classrm/Grade:
Monitoring Level:
BASELINE
WEEK 1
WEEK 2
WEEK 3
WEEK 4
WEEK 5
WEEK 6
WEEK 7
WEEK 8
WEEK 9
WEEK 10
WEEK 11
WEEK 12
0
20
40
60
80
100
120
140
M T W T F
Instructional Days
Writing Norms (# Correct Spellings)
1st GR /15 Wds
2nd GR/28 Wds
3rd GR/37 Wds
4th GR/41 Wds
5th GR/49 Wds
6th GR/53 Wds

(Grade Norms from Shapiro, E. S. (1996). *Academic skills problems: Direct assessment and intervention* (2nd ed.). New York: Guilford.

Behavior/Skill to Measure: _____

Student: _____  Classrm/Grade: _____  Monitoring Level: _____

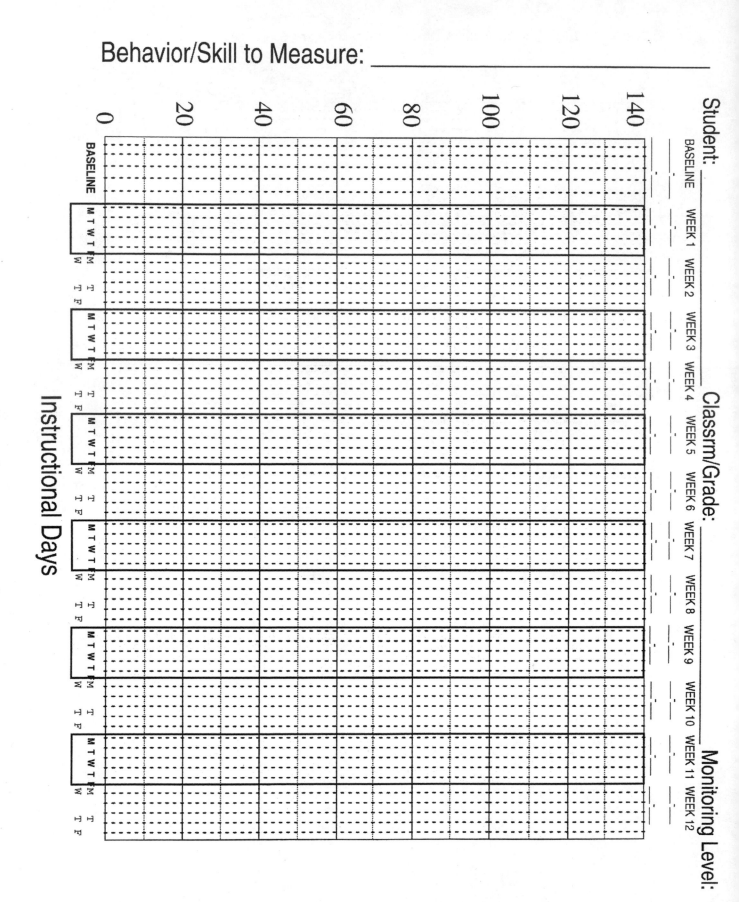

Instructional Days

# Chapter 6

## Is the Intervention Working?
### Guidelines for Goal-Setting and Decision-Making

The Response to Intervention model requires that educators make an ongoing series of decisions about a struggling learner. Think of a motorist with a map driving through unfamiliar country to reach a destination. At each intersection or fork in the road, the traveler consults the map to note the remaining distance to the destination. If the motorist has gotten lost, he or she will change direction or alter the route to get back on track toward reaching the destination. Like that traveler, RTI Teams are regularly checking a student's progress in the RTI model and making decisions about how to proceed. RTI Teams must answer such common questions as:

- How much of an academic skill or performance gap should a student have before being referred to the RTI Team?

- How ambitious should RTI Team goals for student improvement?

- How many intervention plans should be attempted with the student before the student is referred to special education?

In an ideal world, RTI Teams would be able to consult a set of ironclad decision-rules that would infallibly guide them through each decision point in the RTI process. In reality, however, teams must often use their best judgment in ambiguous circumstances when deciding the best course of action for a student. RTI decision-rules are not like a mathematical algorithm in which the user follows a well-defined set of instructions to always arrive at the same immutable answer. Instead, many idiosyncratic variables influence an RTI Team's decisions about a student, such as the nature and severity of that student's presenting problem(s), the level of cooperation and competence of the referring teacher, intervention resources available within the school, support and backing from the school administrator, parent concerns about the student, state mandates regarding the RTI process, and so on.

Additionally, the RTI model is still in the process of development (e.g., Barnett, Daly, Jones, & Lentz, 2004; Fuchs, 2003; Fuchs & Fuchs, 2006), and experts have yet to reach agreement about the nature or sequence of decision rules that should be used during the problem-solving process. Nonetheless, Fuchs (2003) has outlined an RTI-friendly 'dual discrepancy' model for identifying learning disabilities that is becoming widely accepted. The first discrepancy of Fuchs' model is documented when a student displays a significant academic delay relative to grade-peers (skill gap). This discrepancy in academic skills or performance triggers a referral to the RTI Team, which meets to create one or more intervention plans to help the student close the academic skill gap. If the student fails to catch up with peers despite the RTI Team's best efforts, this lack of expected progress represents a second discrepancy (improvement gap). According to the dual discrepancy model, a student would be referred to special education only when both skill and improvement gaps have been documented. The present manual adopts the dual discrepancy approach to determining when a student should be considered for special education services.

In this chapter, RTI Teams will find common-sense guidelines, or decision rules, that they can use effectively to evaluate students' response to Tier II interventions. In summary, it is recommended that RTI Teams:

- Accept referrals for any student with significant academic delays who has not responded to classroom (Tier I) attempts at remediation;

- Select a means (local norms, research norms, criterion-referenced benchmarks, etc.) for determining "expected level' of student performance;

- Document the student's failure to respond to at least two (and preferably three or more) intervention plans before referring to special education.

The rest of the chapter is devoted to a general discussion of RTI decision rules, including those that deal with goal setting and monitoring student progress. For specific guidelines for goal setting in the context of RTI Team meetings, the reader is referred to Chapter 3. A detailed presentation of methods for monitoring student progress is to be found in Chapter 5.

## Methods to Determine a Student's Expected Level of Achievement

When deciding whether a student has significant academic delays in comparison to peers (Discrepancy I in Fuchs (2003) Dual Discrepancy model), RTI Teams must first decide how they will determine "average" or "expected" levels of academic achievement. Three widely used methods for calculating the academic level at which a target student should be operating are *local norms, research norms,* and *criterion-referenced benchmarks.* Teams should be prepared to use any one of these methods depending on the nature of the student concern and the availability of school resources or research data.

- *Local Norms.* One method for determining the skill level required for school success is to sample the academic abilities of "typical" students at specific grade levels in a school or district. The resulting data can be compiled into *local norms.* The collection of local norms is most closely associated with curriculum-based measurement (CBM), a technique for assessing basic academic skills. For example, a school may decide to use CBM to assess the oral reading fluency level of a representative sample of students in grades one through six at three points during the year: fall, winter, and spring. (Local norms are collected at several-month intervals to adjust for expected growth of academic skills among students throughout the school year (Shinn, 1989). For each grade level, data from each of these local norms can be analyzed and condensed into a five-number summary (Moore & McCabe, 2005) that includes the lowest reading score, the reading rate of the student at the 25th percentile, the median reading rate, the reading rate of the student at the 75th percentile, and the highest reading score. If a particular student is found to be struggling in reading, the RTI Team can compare that student's reading fluency rate to the local norms for his or her grade level to calculate the reading skill gap between that student and peers. Detailed guidelines for creating local norms in CBM can be found in Shinn (1989) or Wright (n.d.).

An advantage of local norms is that they will show with precision the skill gap between a struggling student and his or her classmates. A potential drawback of local norms, however, is that these norms can vary substantially across districts and even across schools within districts. In a large urban district, for example, a school with high rates of poverty in one part of the city may produce local norms that are significantly lower than local norms from another school located in a more affluent neighborhood. If these building-wide norms are used as a key indicator for identifying students who need individualized interventions, their variability across schools may result in inconsistencies in how children are identified for referral to RTI Teams. Districts can take certain steps (e.g., aggregating local norms from across the district to create district norms) to adjust for differences in average academic performance between schools. However, those steps can only minimize—not eliminate—the potential for significant differences in average performance between schools.

- *Research Norms*. Some research studies have collected data on typical rates of academic performance or other instructionally relevant behavior from samples of students and published that data in the form of *research norms*. RTI Teams find such pre-existing research norms to be convenient to use. While research norms can be a helpful starting point in estimating expected levels of student performance, they should generally be used cautiously. One limitation to some research norms, for example, is that they are based on small samples of students and therefore may not reflect a true picture of average student performance across the nation. Another possible drawback of research norms is that the groups of students used in these studies are not representative of the racial and ethnic diversity of student populations in specific school districts, thereby limiting the usefulness of those norms.

Nonetheless, some research norms are particularly robust, drawn from an impressive amount of data from a broad sampling of students. Both the reading fluency norms prepared by Tindal, Hasbrouck & Jones (2005) and the school attendance norms published by the National Center for Education Statistics (2005) are based on the records of thousands of students across a number of states. Examples of research norms in oral reading fluency, math computation, writing, and student attendance can be found in Exhibit 6-A, *Selected Research-Based Norms for Academic Skills and Related Behaviors.*

- *Criterion-Referenced Benchmarks.* Local and research norms can be developed for those academic skills or behaviors, such as math computation and oral reading fluency, that can be easily quantified and reliably measured. However, there will be many occasions when RTI Teams will ponder specific concerns of a struggling student for which no formal norms exist. Homework completion, reading comprehension, and knowledge of higher-level math operations are just three examples of academic competencies for which schools are unlikely to have norms.

When faced with a lack of clear-cut norms, the RTI Team can work with the referring teacher to set a *criterion-referenced benchmark*—that is, an assessment that compares a student's performance on an academic task or behavior to a pre-selected standard of mastery (e.g., Fuchs & Fuchs, 2006). For example, a teacher may refer a student to the RTI Team because she often does not turn in homework. Based on the grading formula for the course, the teacher estimates that the student will receive a passing grade if she manages to turn in at least 80 percent of assigned homework. So the RTI Team and teacher adopt this homework completion goal of 80 percent as a criterion-referenced benchmark and intervention goal.

A disadvantage of criterion-referenced benchmarks is that they can be somewhat arbitrary, often based largely on teacher judgment. An advantage of such benchmarks, however, is that they can be applied flexibly to a very wide range of student academic skills and behaviors for which formal peer norms are unavailable. Also, because teachers must ultimately decide whether a student is sufficiently successful in a classroom to pass the course or advance to the next grade, those instructors are the logical experts in judging what a struggling student's threshold of academic performance (criterion-referenced benchmark) should be to demonstrate that the student has successfully responded to intervention.

## Closing the Gap: Calculating Expected Rates of Student Progress

Students who fail to close the academic gap with peers (Discrepancy II in Fuchs (2003) Dual Discrepancy Model) may have a learning disability. The RTI Team cannot determine whether the student in fact is adequately responding to intervention and catching up with peers unless the team first sets a goal for student improvement and then monitors the student to document whether he or she actually attains that goal. The team problem-solving forms in Chapter 3 provide a framework for calculating student academic and behavioral goals. This section presents several general methods that teams can use to calculate expected rates of student progress in response to intervention plans.

- *Growth Norms Based on Research.* While scarce, some research articles have been published that track average rates of student progress in basic academic skills over time. For example, one study that tracked student growth across grades in oral reading fluency (Fuchs, Fuchs, Hamlett, Walz, & Germann, 1993) found that students in grade one increased reading fluency an average of two words per minute during each instructional week while grade six students increased reading fluency an average of 0.3 words per minute each week (see Table 2 in Exhibit 5-F for the full set of reading norms from this study). Research-based norms are convenient but may be based on small sample sizes. Still, when available, they can be helpful starting points for calculating expected student rates of growth.

- *Growth Estimates Based on Distance Between Target Student Performance and Local Norms.* If a school or district has compiled its own local norms (for example, in curriculum-based measurement oral reading fluency), the grade norms of a student with academic delays represent the goal toward which that student will work. For example, if a school's local norms indicate that the typical reading rate in 4th grade text is 73 words per minute in that building, then this figure may be used as the ultimate goal for a 4th grade student who has deficits in reading fluency. The RTI Team would calculate a rate of weekly improvement that the student must achieve to allow him ultimately to catch up with his or her peers. Directions for calculating rates of student growth using local norms in curriculum-based measurement can be found in Shinn (1989).

- *Growth Rates Based on Criterion-Referenced Benchmarks.* If criterion-referenced benchmarks are set as goals for student performance, then these benchmarks become the goal toward which the student works. The RTI Team and referring teacher would set weekly rates of student improvement sufficiently ambitious to help the student to achieve the benchmark within a reasonable period of time.

## Frequently Asked Questions About Decision-Making Under the RTI Model

The most frequent questions regarding RTI decision rules seek guidelines for applying those rules to the RTI Team process:

- *How large an academic skill gap does a student need to exhibit to be referred to the RTI Team for a Tier II intervention?* Schools have a great deal of latitude in determining when and for what reasons a child should be referred to the RTI Team. Certainly, the school system continues to have a "child-find" responsibility to discover those students at risk for chronic academic failure. Once identified, these students should be referred to the RTI Team in as speedy a manner as possible. But schools should also encourage teachers to refer students to the RTI Team proactively, *before* those students learning-related problems become ingrained, to give these struggling students the best chance of closing the skill gap with peers. Successful RTI schools generally set the expectation that, as soon as teachers note that a student is falling behind in academics, these instructors will try a series of feasible Tier I, universal strategies that target the student's area(s) of difficulty and will document those efforts. However, if the student fails to make acceptable progress within a reasonable amount of time with these classroom strategies in place and is at serious risk of academic failure, teachers should then refer the student to the RTI Team.

- *How long should an intervention plan be in place before a decision can be made about whether the student should be referred to special education?* Federal regulations that define the role of RTI in the special education identification process state that, in order to establish that a child has a learning disability, the school must first show that "[t]he child does not make sufficient progress to meet age or State approved grade-level standards" in one of several possible academic and language domains (34 C.F.R. § 300.309(a)(2)(i)). However, there is not yet consensus in the research community about specific details of the RTI model (Barnett, Daly, Jones, & Lentz, 2004), including the question of what criteria to use in deciding whether a child has made "sufficient progress." In the absence of firm decision rules, RTI Teams should consider the following informal guidelines:

1.  The RTI Team should implement and monitor the student through at least two (and preferably three or more) intervention plans before deciding whether the student should be referred for special education evaluation. If the student fails to respond to a series of several well-implemented, research-based intervention attempts, the school has greater assurance that instructional factors do not adequately explain the student's lack of academic success, indicating that the child may in fact have an educational disability.

2.  The RTI Team must determine the minimum level of progress that signifies a successful intervention. If, for example, a student comes very close to meeting his intervention goal to increase reading fluency but falls just short, despite three successive intervention plans, should the team refer the student to special education or continue to modify the intervention plan and monitor student progress? There are no firm score cut-offs in such cases; teams must decide whether that student's progress is adequate through ongoing discussion with the referring teacher about the student's classroom performance, as well as through consideration of the magnitude of the skill gap that remains between the referred student and typical peers. A sample form that can help schools apply decision rules to judge the success or failure of student intervention plans can be found in Exhibit 6-B, *Evaluating the Intervention Plan of the 'Non-Responding' Student: A Guide.*

•   *When should a student be referred directly for a special education evaluation rather than to an RTI Team?* The federal regulations that define RTI (34 C.F.R. 300 & 301, 2006) link it explicitly to the process of diagnosing learning disabilities. In those cases in which a learning disability is suspected, therefore, schools should first refer students to the RTI Team to document their response to Tier II interventions. Indeed, because at least half of all students who eventually require special education services become classified as Learning Disabled (Office of Special Education Programs, 2005), the RTI Team should expect to review the majority of initial teacher referrals to help to establish or to rule out the diagnosis of LD. If there is strong evidence, however, that the student has a type of special education disability *other* than LD (e.g., speech or Language Impairment, Traumatic Brain Injury), the school should consider bypassing the RTI Team and referring the student *directly* for a special education evaluation.

# References

34 C.F.R. 300 & 301 (2006). *Assistance to States for the Education of Children With Disabilities and Preschool Grants for Children With Disabilities.*

Barnett, D. W., Daly, E. J., Jones, K. M., & Lentz, F.E. (2004). Response to intervention: Empirically based special service decisions from single-case designs of increasing and decreasing intensity. *Journal of Special Education, 38,* 66-79.

Fuchs, L. (2003). Assessing intervention responsiveness: Conceptual and technical issues. *Learning Disabilities Research & Practice, 18(3),* 172-186.

Fuchs, D., & Fuchs, L. S. (2006). Introduction to Response to Intervention: What, why, and how valid is it? *Reading Research Quarterly, 41,* 93-99.

Fuchs, L.S., Fuchs, D., Hamlett, C.L., Walz, L., & Germann, G. (1993). Formative evaluation of academic progress: How much growth can we expect? *School Psychology Review, 22,* 27-48.

Moore, D. S., & McCabe, G. P. (2005). *Introduction to the practice of statistics* (5th ed.). New York: W. H. Freeman.

National Center for Education Statistics. (2005). Student effort and academic progress. Retrieved December 18, 2006, from http://nces.ed.gov/programs/coe/2006/section3/indicator24.asp#info

Office of Special Education Programs. (2005). *26th annual (2004) report to Congress on the implementation of the Individuals with Disabilities Education Act.* Retrieved December 15, 2006, from http://www.ed.gov/about/reports/annual/osep/2004/26th-vol-1.pdf

Shinn, M. R. (1989). *Curriculum-based measurement: assessing special children*. New York: Guilford Press.

Tindal, G., Hasbrouck, J., & Jones, C. (2005). *Technical report #33: Oral reading fluency: 90 years of measurement*. Behavioral Research and Teaching ,University of Oregon, College of Education. Retrieved December 28, 2006, from http://brt.uoregon.edu/techreports/ORF_90Yrs_Intro_TechRpt33.pdf

Wright, J. (n.d.). *Curriculum-based measurement: A manual for teachers*. Retrieved September 23, 2006, from http://www.jimwrightonline.com/pdfdocs/cbaManual.pdf

# Exhibit 6-A
## Selected Research-Based Norms for Academic Skills and Related Behaviors

The research norms below are drawn from a range of published sources. RTI Teams consulting these norms should consider the source and quality of the data when using them to calculate 'typical' rates of student performance.

| Curriculum-Based Measurement: Oral Reading Fluency (Tindal, Hasbrouck, & Jones, 2005) | | | |
|---|---|---|---|
| **Correctly Read Words Per Minute** | | | |
| **Grade** | *Fall* | *Winter* | *Spring* |
| 1 | NA | 23 | 53 |
| 2 | 51 | 72 | 89 |
| 3 | 71 | 92 | 107 |
| 4 | 94 | 112 | 123 |
| 5 | 110 | 127 | 139 |
| 6 | 127 | 140 | 150 |
| 7 | 128 | 136 | 150 |
| 8 | 133 | 146 | 151 |

Comments: These multi-state norms are based on a large sample size and are among the best research norms available for oral reading fluency.

| Curriculum-Based Measurement: Math Computation (Adapted from Deno & Mirkin, 1977) | | |
|---|---|---|
| **Grade** | **Digits Correct in 2 Minutes** | **Digits Incorrect in 2 Minutes** |
| 1-3 | 20-38 | 6-14 |
| 4 & Up | 40-78 | 6-14 |

Comments: These math computation norms are still widely referenced. However, the norms were collected nearly 30 years ago and may not be widely representative because they were drawn from a relatively small sample of students. Additionally, the norms make no distinction between easy and more challenging math computation problem types. Because of these limitations, these norms are best regarded as a rough indicator of 'typical' student math computation skills.

| Curriculum-Based Measurement: Writing (Mirkin, Deno, Fuchs, Wesson, Tindal, Marston, & Kuehnle, 1981) | |
|---|---|
| **Grade** | **Total Words Written in 3 Minutes** |
| 1 | 15 |
| 2 | 28 |
| 3 | 37 |
| 4 | 41 |
| 5 | 49 |
| 6 | 53 |

Comments: These research norms in writing are still among the few that have been published. While they can be useful as a general starting point for estimating 'typical' writing skills, these norms also have limitations: they are somewhat dated, were based on a relatively small sample size, and apply only to one area of CBM writing— 'total words written'.

| School Attendance: Rates of Absenteeism (National Center for Educational Statistics, 2005) | |
|---|---|
| **Grade** | **Days of School Missed Per Month** |
| All Grades (K-12) | 80% of students in a large national sample missed *no more than* 2 days of school per month. |

Comments: These attendance norms were compiled from a large data set. They are a reliable yardstick for estimating 'typical' rates of student attendance.

| Time on Task (Anderson, 1976; Gettinger, 1985) | |
|---|---|
| **Grade** | **Time on Task** |
| All Grades (K-12) | 80% or more (estimated) |

Comments: There are few reliable norms for the amount of 'on-task' behavior a student must show in the classroom to have an optimal chance for success. The issue is further complicated because existing studies of typical rates of 'time on task' often fail to distinguish between passive academic engagement (student simply looking at the teacher) and student active academic engagement (student actively showing what they have learned through involvement in observable activities). There is little disagreement, though, that students need to attend to instruction in order to learn. Therefore, RTI Teams are encouraged to set a goal of at least 80% on task (counting both passive and active student engagement).

## References

Anderson, L. (1976). An empirical investigation of individual Differences in time to learn. *Journal of Educational Psychology*, 68, 226-233.

Deno, S.L., & Mirkin, P.K. (1977). Data-based program modification: A manual. Reston, VA: Council for Exceptional Children.

Gettinger, M. (1985). Time allocated and time spent relative to time needed for learning as determinants of achievement. *Journal of Educational Psychology*, 77(1), 3-11.

Mirkin,P.K., Deno, S.L., Fuchs, L., Wesson, C.,Tindal, G., Marston, D., & Kuehnle, K. (1981). Procedures to develop and monitor progress on IEP goals. Minneapolis: University of Minnesota, Institute for Research on Learning Disabilities.

National Center for Education Statistics. (2005). Student effort and academic progress. Retrieved December 18, 2006, from http://nces.ed.gov/programs/coe/2006/section3/indicator24.asp#info

Tindal, G., Hasbrouck, J., & Jones, C. (2005). Technical report #33: Oral reading fluency: 90 years of measurement. Behavioral Research and Teaching ,University of Oregon, College of Education. Retreived December 28, 2006, from http://brt.uoregon.edu/techreports/ORF_90Yrs_Intro_TechRpt33.pdf

# Exhibit 6-B
## Evaluating the Intervention Plan of the 'Non-Responding' Student: A Guide

**Directions**: If your RTI Team has a student who is not adequately responding to intervention, use the form below as an organizing tool to evaluate the quality and outcome of the intervention plan(s) attempted. If the student meets all criteria outlined below (see 'Recommendation' sections) and continues to show significant school-based problems, your team should consider referring him or her for a special education evaluation.

- - - - - - - - - - - - - - - - - - - - - - - - - - - - - - - - - - - - - - - - - - - - - - - - - -

1. *Target Problems.* The student was initially found to have skill or performance gaps relative to peers that significantly affected his or her chances for school success in the following area(s):

Problem definition 1: _____

Problem definition 2: _____

Your team agreed that these problem definitions were stated in clear, measurable, observable terms. _____Y _____ N
[Recommendation: If '**No**', refer the student back to the RTI Team and define more precisely the problem area(s).]

- - - - - - - - - - - - - - - - - - - - - - - - - - - - - - - - - - - - - - - - - - - - - - - - - -

2. *Intervention Plan Elements.*
   - Interventions used with the student were research-based.           __Y__N
   - All interventions were carried out as designed with a high level of quality __Y__N ('intervention follow-through').
   [Recommendation: If '**No**' to either of the items, put research-based interventions in place and monitor them closely to ensure quality of intervention follow-through]

- - - - - - - - - - - - - - - - - - - - - - - - - - - - - - - - - - - - - - - - - - - - - - - - - -

3. *Number of Intervention Plans Tried and Time-Lines.* A minimum of 2 or more intervention plans was attempted. Each plan was implemented for a long enough period of time to demonstrate whether it was effective. _____Y_____N

   - Plan 1: Start Date:__/__/__ End Date:__/__/__ Number of Instructional Weeks:_____
   
   Comments:_____

   - Plan 2: Start Date:__/__/__ End Date:__/__/__ Number of Instructional Weeks:_____
   
   Comments:_____

• Plan 3: Start Date: __/__/__ End Date: __/__/__ Number of Instructional Weeks: ____

Comments: _____

• Plan 4: Start Date: __/__/__ End Date: __/__/__ Number of Instructional Weeks: ____

Comments: _____

[Recommendation: If fewer than **2** intervention plans have been attempted, continue to monitor the student through the RTI Team and try additional interventions as needed. If any of the plans were implemented **for too short a time** to show progress, consider employing the same intervention plan again and monitor long enough to judge its effectiveness.]

- - - - - - - - - - - - - - - - - - - - - - - - - - - - - - - - - - - - - - - - - - - - - - - - - - -

4. *Progress Monitoring.* The student's progress was monitored regularly in each of the problem areas identified in Section 1. At least two measures were used to track student progress in each problem area. ____Y____N

**Problem definition #___:** Measurement method used:_____

Goal set for student:_____ Final student level :_____ Goal met? __Y__N

**Problem definition #___:** Measurement method used:_____

Goal set for student:_____ Final student level :_____ Goal met? __Y__N

**Problem definition #___:** Measurement method used:_____

Goal set for student:_____ Final student level :_____ Goal met? __Y__N

**Problem definition #___:** Measurement method used:_____

Goal set for student:_____ Final student level :_____ Goal met? __Y__N

[Recommendation: If fewer than **2 methods** were used to monitor a problem area, select additional monitoring methods and continue the intervention for several more weeks before making a decision about the student's response to intervention. If the student met **most or all** monitoring goals, consider maintaining the current intervention plan, raising the student's goals, and continuing to monitor the student's progress.]

# Chapter 7

## Future Developments in RTI:
### Preparing for RTI 2.0

Schools that follow the guidelines presented in this book and make full use of its resources will be well on their way to establishing a strong RTI process in their buildings. As was noted in the Chapter 1, however, RTI is still a model under construction (Barnett, Daly, Jones & Lentz, 2004; Gresham, 2001). The fact that RTI continues to undergo substantial development and revision should come as no surprise. It is a young initiative; the national push to bring RTI to schools began only with the recent reauthorization of the Individuals with Disabilities Education Improvement Act (IDEIA) in 2004.

## RTI 2.0: The Next Generation of Response to Intervention

Educators committed to RTI as a means for improving the services for difficult-to-teach students must take on the challenge of introducing a model that for now is promising but incomplete—a work in progress. Indeed, schools currently taking on RTI initiatives are to be forgiven if they feel a bit like the pilot who was directed to build a plane while flying it! The encouraging news, though, is that a research effort is picking up momentum to carry out RTI effectiveness studies, develop definitive decision rules to guide RTI Teams, fill in gaps in the "research-based intervention" literature, document ways that schools can scale up the RTI process in a cost-effective manner to meet the needs of large numbers of struggling students, and clarify the role of RTI within the continuum of legal due process protections guaranteed under special education legislation. Even as schools work in the present to put a fledgling RTI process into place, hints are emerging to suggest what the next, more advanced phase of RTI will look like.

This book adopts the term "Response to Intervention 2.0" to describe this coming phase of RTI innovation. While somewhat speculative, the following predictions about future improvements to the model are based on existing, cutting-edge developments in the field of RTI:

- *Consensus on decision rules.* In the RTI process, students advance to higher levels of individualized academic support as they demonstrate ongoing need for that support. To reliably judge when students require more intensive levels of service, however, schools must be able to implement firm decision rules. Expect that, over time, schools will adopt more uniform sets of research-based interventions and methods of progress monitoring. As this occurs, schools should also be able to apply standardized decision rules to determine student success.

  To cite one current example of a research-based measure with its own decision-rules, many schools across the nation now use the criterion-referenced benchmarks from the DIBELS (Dynamic Indicators of Basic Early Literacy Skills) both to screen students who might require Tier I (universal) interventions and to monitor the reading progress of students referred for Tier II (individualized) interventions (Good & Kaminski, 2001). It is expected that, in the future, additional methods will also become available to monitor other academic referral concerns. In addition, as identical methods of intervention and assessment come to be used across school districts, corresponding decision rules are likely to be created and widely shared for making key RTI decisions at the Tier I and Tier II levels, such as recommended length of intervention trials and the number of intervention attempts required prior to a special education referral. (See Vaughn, Linan-Thompson, & Hickman, 2003 as one exemplar of research into length and intensity of reading interventions.)

- *Growing collection of RTI scalability and cost effectiveness studies.* As districts of all sizes implement versions of RTI, published case studies detailing the resources required, methods used, and resulting student outcomes in selected districts will start to appear. As the collection of published RTI case studies continues to grow, researchers will analyze this knowledge database to formulate general guidelines for implementing RTI that will enhance districts' chances for success. (Pioneering RTI case studies from two very different educational agencies can already be found in Grimes & Kurns, 2003 and Marston, Muyskens, Lau & Canter, 2003. Also, see Fuchs & Fuchs, 2006 for a framework for building RTI capacity that might be used as a starting point for evaluating districts' implementation of the model.)

- *"Standardized" State-Level RTI Packages.* As states promote RTI in their districts, educators can expect that many state education departments will develop their own versions of RTI models and mandate that schools adopt them. For example, the Mississippi Department of Education (2006) and the New Mexico Public Education Department (n.d.) have developed specific guidelines for setting up RTI Intervention Teams. A number of other states are also in the process of assembling RTI guidelines.

- *Free online banks of intervention resources.* Federal regulations define the "child's response to scientific, research-based intervention" as central to RTI (34 C.F.R. 300 & 301, 2006; p. 46786). It is clear, then, that RTI will only be as effective as the quality of the interventions that is selected for struggling learners. A feature of RTI 2.0 will be the establishment of expansive collections of online banks of scientific, research-based intervention resources that schools will be able to access for free or at a nominal cost. A current example of a free bank of school-based intervention resources can be found at the web site Intervention Central (*www.interventioncentral.org*). Also, visit the U.S. Department of Education 'What Works Clearinghouse' (*http://www.whatworks.ed.gov/*), an impartial site that rates the effectiveness of intervention packages in Beginning Reading, Early Childhood Education, Elementary

School Math, Middle School Math Curricula, and Dropout Prevention.

- *"One-stop" Internet progress-monitoring sites.* A major focus of RTI is the collection of academic data to track student progress during interventions. In coming years, schools will be able to log on to web sites that contain extensive collections of student assessment materials. These sites will also have the capability to generate visual displays of student progress, school norms, etc.

  At present, two web sites bundle advanced academic assessment, progress-monitoring, and charting tools in innovative ways that provide a glimpse of how schools are likely to formatively evaluate students under RTI 2.0. The DIBELS (Dynamic Indicators of Basic Early Literacy Skills) site (*http://dibels.uoregon.edu/*) has early reading and oral reading probes and a number of charting options. AIMSWEB (*http://www.aimsweb.com/*) has a full range of Curriculum-Based Measurement (CBM) monitoring probes in reading, math, writing, spelling, and early literacy and early numeracy. It also offers full charting capabilities for visual analysis of data.

## Marching Toward RTI 2.0: How Schools Can Stay Current With the Evolving Response to Intervention Model

The task of building and maintaining an RTI process of high quality represents a moving target. As the RTI model advances, schools should keep abreast of changes to guarantee that they continue to operate most efficiently and follow best practices in RTI. Below are several suggestions that schools can implement to ensure they remain current as the present RTI model evolves toward RTI 2.0:

- *Collaborate with other schools or districts in the area.* Starting an RTI initiative is hard work. But schools can ease that workload a bit by regularly networking with other schools in the region and pooling their best ideas to make RTI a reality. Whether the school network communicates via face-to-face meetings, on an listserv, or by some other means, it can highlight individual school's innovative strategies for promoting the concept of Response to Intervention among stakeholders, running effective RTI Intervention Teams, monitoring student progress, identifying useful intervention ideas for common student referral concerns, and successfully confronting other potentially thorny RTI challenges.

- *Communicate with the state education department about RTI projects or directives.* There is a high probability that the education department in each state will be actively promoting the concept of RTI, for example, rolling out pilot RTI projects, making funds available to schools for RTI grants, or issuing directives on mandated RTI requirements. Each school or district should establish contact with the chief state education department representative who oversees RTI to stay informed of upcoming RTI initiatives. By proactively tracking state efforts, a school is in a better position to identify RTI grants for which it is eligible or gain additional lead-time to modify the building's RTI process to conform to any new state-driven RTI mandates.

- *Tie school professional development activities to RTI.* Schools frequently offer professional development opportunities to staff; workshops can be designed to build the school's RTI readiness. On a yearly basis, inventory your school's capacity to implement the key elements of the RTI model. (Exhibit 2-B, *Response-to-Intervention School Readiness Survey, can help to conduct* this annual inventory.) Then, offer workshops that selectively develop your staff's skills in those RTI elements that need strengthening. In this manner, staff development continuously builds your school's RTI capacity.

- *Make use of online RTI resources.* Schools that take advantage of RTI resources on the Internet can gain an edge in successfully establishing RTI. The World Wide Web contains advanced tutorials in the RTI model, as well as intervention, progress monitoring, and graphing tools. As an added incentive, schools that routinely troll the

Internet for RTI materials and technical assistance are likely to stay more fully informed of advances in the RTI model itself, and are thus better able to adapt their RTI procedures to match those improvements. (See Exhibit 7-A, *Response to Intervention 2.0: Selected Internet Resources*, for a sampling of web resources that can help schools to implement RTI.)

## RTI: A Promise Fulfilled

This book opened with the folktale, *Stone Soup*. That story's message of sharing and collaboration embodies the potential of RTI to energize the school community to work together so that struggling learners can achieve success. This process of transforming a school's culture to fully conform to and reflect the RTI model will take several years of hard work. However, RTI can offer real benefits to a school from its very inception. As staff members become familiar with the RTI model and adopt a common language to discuss the needs of all students, they work more efficiently to identify intervention and monitoring plans that are effective. Instead of the frustration that ensues when students experience chronic failure before receiving help, teachers feel more supported because of the RTI Team's targeted involvement and assistance. A school's intervention resources are no longer fragmented and compartmentalized. Instead, schools coordinate and enhance these supports to match the unique needs of its student population.

Author Ursula LeGuin has written, "It is good to have an end to journey toward; but it is the journey that matters, in the end." This book provides guidelines for beginning the RTI process. But schools must have the courage to take that first step and embark on the exciting journey of Response to Intervention. Those that do will discover that RTI expands the school's capacity to help the full range of student learners, making for more successful students and more effective teachers. Through implementation of RTI there is potential of benefit for all stakeholders of the teaching-learning process: students, staff, parents and the community as a whole.

# References

34 C.F.R. 300 & 301 (2006). Assistance to States for the Education of Children With Disabilities and Preschool Grants for Children With Disabilities.

Barnett, D. W., Daly, E. J., Jones, K. M., & Lentz, F.E. (2004). Response to intervention: Empirically based special service decisions from single-case designs of increasing and decreasing intensity. *Journal of Special Education, 38,* 66-79.

Fuchs, L. S., & Fuchs, D. (2006). A framework for building capacity for responsiveness to intervention. *School Psychology Review, 35,* 621-626.

Good, R. H., & Kaminski, R. A. (2001). *Dynamic indicators of basic early literacy skills* (6th ed.). Eugene, OR: Institute for the Development of Educational Achievement.

Gresham, F. M. (2001). *Responsiveness to intervention: An alternative approach to the identification of learning disabilities.* Paper presented at the Learning Disabilities Summit, Washington DC.

Grimes J. & Kurns, S. (2003, December). *An intervention-based system for addressing NCLB and IDEA expectations: A multiple tiered model to ensure every child learns.* Paper presented at the National Research Center on Learning Disabilities Responsiveness-to-Intervention Symposium, Kansas City, MO.

Marston, D., Muyskens, P., Lau, M., & Canter, A. (2003). Problem-Solving model for decision making with high-incidence disabilities: The Minneapolis experience. *Learning Disabilities Research & Practice, 18(3)*, 187–200.

Mississippi Department of Education (2006). *Three tier instructional model: Teacher Support Team.* Retrieved January 9, 2007, from http://www.mde.k12.ms.us/acad1/programs/tst/faqtst.doc

New Mexico Public Education Department (n.d.). *Student Assistance Team manual.* Retrieved January 8, 2007, from http://www.sde.state.nm.us/resources/downloads/sat.manual.html

Vaughn, S., Linan-Thompson, S., & Hickman, P. (2003). Response to instruction as a means of identifying students with reading/learning disabilities. *Exceptional Children, 69,* 391-409.

# Exhibit 7-A
## Response to Intervention 2.0: Selected Internet Resources
(adapted from Wright (n.d.))

These Internet sites are examples of cutting-edge information and resources that can help schools improve their current RTI model and to transform it into 'RTI 2.0':

### 1. Understanding the RTI Model
*NRCLD Responsiveness-to-Intervention Symposium.* The National Research Center on Learning Disabilities held a symposium on RTI in December 2003. This web page contains papers, PowerPoint presentations, and brief video clips of nationally prominent RTI researchers. Speakers at the conference considered such issues as the basic feasibility of RTI in schools, operationalizing the concept of 'response to intervention', the number of 'Tiers' or levels of intervention that should be in place in the RTI model to identify and program for children at risk, and what methods other than RTI might be considered for identifying Learning Disabilities in children. Still the best collection of RTI 'concept' articles on the Internet!
• Web address: http://www.nrcld.org/symposium2003/index.html

### 2. Creating an RTI Intervention Team
*School-Based Intervention Teams* . The School-Based Intervention Team (SBIT) project was successfully piloted in Syracuse, NY, and has been adopted by a number of other districts around the country. This page contains all of the team meeting forms and other helpful problem-solving resources.
• Web address: http://www.interventioncentral.org/htmdocs/interventions/sbit.php

*STEEP (System to Enhance Educational Performance).* Dr. Joe Witt of Louisiana State University created the STEEP problem-solving process, which is now used in schools across the nation. Districts that sign up for STEEP training can access training, intervention, and assessment tools on the Internet.
• Web address: http://www.isteep.com

### 3. Selecting the Right RTI Intervention
*Dr. Mac's Amazing Behavior Management Advice Site.* Students with academic delays may also show behavioral problems. This site serves up research-based behavior management strategies with a healthy dose of humor. But the site's creator, Dr. Tom McIntyre, knows what he is talking about! He is a professor of special education at Hunter College of the City University of New York and a former public-school teacher.
• Web address: http://www.behavioradvisor.com/

*Intervention Central.* Go to this site to browse through many classroom management and instructional ideas that are drawn from current research on effective interventions.
• Web address: http://www.interventioncentral.org/

*What Works.* The U.S. Department of Education 'What Works Clearinghouse' is an impartial site that rates the effectiveness of intervention packages in such areas as Beginning Reading, Early Childhood Education, Elementary School Math, Middle School Math Curricula, and Dropout Prevention. The site is periodically updated with information on new intervention topics.
• Web address: http://www.whatworks.ed.gov/

### 4. Monitoring Student Progress Under RTI

*AIMSweb.* This is the most comprehensive site for Curriculum-Based Measurement (CBM) resources on the Internet. It contains student progress-monitoring probes in oral reading fluency (English and Spanish), spelling, written expression, math computation, early literacy, early numeracy, and more. The site also contains CBM training materials and performance norms. Schools that subscribe to AIMSweb can upload and store their CBM data—as well as create charts to track the student's progress, compare the student to school norms, etc.
• Web address: http://www.aimsweb.com/measures/

*CBM Warehouse.* Curriculum-Based Measurement (CBM) is the gold standard for measuring academic progress through RTI. This webpage is a directory of CBM resources available on the Internet. CBM Warehouse has links to CBM training materials, manuals that explain the administration, scoring, and interpretation of CBM probes, progress-monitoring materials, and more.
• Web address: http://www.interventioncentral.org/htmdocs/interventions/cbmwarehouse.php

*Daily Behavior Report Cards.* The Behavior Reporter is a free online application that allows educators to create and print customized Daily Behavior Report Cards within minutes. The site contains a library of common behavior goals organized by type of presenting problem (e.g., Inattention, Aggressive Behaviors, Work Completion) that users can edit to meet their needs.
• Web address: http://www.jimwrightonline.com/php/tbrc/tbrc.php

*DIBELS.* The DIBELS (Dynamic Indicators of Basic Early Literacy Skills) site has early reading and oral reading probes. The site also allows districts to upload and store progress-monitoring data and has a number of options for creating student charts and graphs. The DIBELS performance benchmarks have become something of a 'gold standard' for RTI Teams to measure student reading-fluency and foundation literacy skills.
• Web address: http://dibels.uoregon.edu/

## 5. Graphing RTI Data for Visual Analysis

*ChartDog.* An online charting solution is ChartDog, an Internet application that allows RTI Teams to enter data into a web form, then transform that data into a fully formatted, printable time-series chart with a single click of a button. The application is free, can plot trendlines, and has other data analysis tools as well.

• Web address: http://www.jimwrightonline.com/php/chartdog_2_0/chartdog.php

## References

Wright (n.d.) *RTI_Wire.* Retrieved January 4, 2007, from http://www.jimwrightonline.com/php/rti/rti_wire.php

# Appendix A

## *School-Wide Strategies for Managing...*

### READING

The ability to read allows individuals access to the full range of a culture's artistic and scientific knowledge. Reading is a complex act. Good readers are able to fluently decode the words on a page, to organize and recall important facts in a text, to distill from a reading the author's opinions and attitudes, and to relate the content of an individual text to a web of other texts previously read. The foundation that reading rests upon is the ability to decode. Emergent readers require the support of more accomplished readers to teach them basic vocabulary, demonstrate word attack strategies, model fluent reading, and provide corrective feedback and encouragement. Newly established readers must build fluency and be pushed to exercise their reading skills across the widest possible range of settings and situations. As the act of decoding becomes more effortless and automatic, the developing reader is able to devote a greater portion of cognitive energy to understanding the meaning of the text.

Reading comprehension is not a single skill, but consists of a cluster of competencies that range from elementary strategies for identifying and recalling factual content to highly sophisticated techniques for inferring an author's opinions and attitudes. As researcher Michael Pressley points out, reading comprehension skills can be thought of as unfolding along a timeline. Before beginning to read a particular selection, the skilled student reader must engage prior knowledge, predict what the author will say about the topic, and set specific reading goals. While reading, the good reader self-monitors his or her understanding of the text, rereads sentences and longer passages that are unclear, and updates predictions about the text based on what he or she has just read. After completing a text, the good reader summarizes its main points (perhaps writing them down), looks back in the text to clarify any points that are unclear, and continues to think about the text and its implications for a period of time.

It is also possible to think of reading comprehension as a bundle of interdependent skills that range from basic to more advanced. Teachers should ensure that students understand and appropriately use simple comprehension strategies (such as looking back in a text to clarify factual information) before teaching advanced comprehension strategies such as SQ3R ('Survey, Question, Read, Recite, Review'). Ultimately, reading is a competency that is continually honed and improved over a lifetime. The teacher's goal is to build students into independent readers whose skills improve with self-guided practice. Below are a number of instructional strategies to promote word decoding, reading decoding, and reading comprehension.

**Independent Practice: Set Up Reading Centers** *(Florida Center for Reading Research, 2005)*. When students have mastered a reading skill, they can work independently at reading centers to practice and become more fluent in that skill under the watchful eye of the teacher. The reading center is set up with fun and engaging activities designed to extend and reinforce literacy content presented by the teacher. Students work on independent reading-related activities individually or in pairs or groups. As examples of reading center choices, students may listen to taped books, read alone or to each other, use magnetic letters to spell a specified list of words, or create storyboards or comic strips that incorporate pictures and words. Each reading center activity is tied to specific student literacy goals. The activities in reading centers may change often to give children a chance to practice new skills and to keep the content of these centers fresh and engaging.

**Reading Comprehension: Activating Prior Knowledge** *(Hansen, & Pearson, 1983)*. The instructor demonstrates to students how they can access their prior knowledge about a topic to improve comprehension of an article or story. The instructor first explains the benefit of using prior knowledge. The instructor tells students that recalling their prior experiences ("their own life") can help them to understand the content of their reading—because new facts make sense only when we connect them to what we already know. Next, the instructor demonstrates the text prediction strategy to the class by selecting a sample passage (displayed as an overhead) and using a "think-aloud" approach to illustrate the strategy steps:

- *Think about what and why*: The teacher connects the article to be read with the instructor's own prior knowledge about the topic. The teacher might say, for example, "I am about to read a short article about [topic]. Before I read the article, though, I should think about my life experiences and what they might tell me about [topic]. By thinking about my own life, I will better understand the article."

- *Select main ideas from the article to pos prior knowledge and prediction questions*: The teacher chooses up to 3 main ideas that appear in the article or story. For each key idea, the instructor poses one question requiring that readers tap their own prior knowledge of the idea (e.g., "What are your own attitudes and experiences about [idea]?") and another that prompts them to predict how the article or story might deal with the idea (e.g., "What do you think the article will say about [idea]?").

- *Have students read the article independently*: Once the teacher has primed students' prior knowledge by having them respond to the series of prior-knowledge and prediction questions, students read the selection independently.

**Reading Comprehension: Anticipation Reading Guide** *(Duffelmeyer, 1994; Merkley, 1996)*. To activate their prior knowledge of a topic, students complete a brief questionnaire on which they must express agreement or disagreement with opinion questions tied to the selection to be read; students then engage in a class discussion of their responses. The instructor first constructs the questionnaire. Each item on the questionnaire is linked to the content of the article or story that the students will read. All questionnaire items use a forced-choice format in which the student must simply agree or disagree with the item. After students have completed the questionnaire, the teacher reviews responses with the class, allowing students an opportunity to explain their rationale for their answers. Finally, students read the article or story.

**Reading Comprehension: Building Comprehension of Textbook Readings Through SQ3R** *(Robinson, 1946)*. Students grasp a greater amount of content from their textbook readings when they use the highly structured SQ3R (Survey, Question, Read, Recite, Review) process.

1. *Survey:* Prior to reading a section of the textbook, the reader surveys the selection by examining charts, tables, or pictures, looking over chapter headings and subheadings, and reading any individual words or blocks of text highlighted by the publisher.

2. *Question:* In preparation for reading, the reader generates and writes down a series of key questions about the content based on the material that he or she has surveyed.

3. *Read:* As the reader reads through the selection, he or she seeks answers to the questions posed.

4. *Recite:* After finishing the selection, the reader attempts to recite from memory the answers to the questions posed. If stuck on a question, the reader scans the text to find the answer.

5. *Review:* At the end of a study session, the reader reviews the list of key questions and again recites the answers. If the reader is unable to recall an answer, he or she goes back to the text to find it.

**Reading Comprehension: Conversing With the Writer Through Text Annotation** *(Harris, 1990; Sarkisian, Toscano, Tomkins-Tinch, & Casey, 2003)*. Students are likely to increase their retention of information when they interact actively with their reading by jotting comments in the margin of the text. Students are taught to engage in an ongoing "conversation" with the writer by recording a running series of brief comments in the margins of the text. Students may write annotations to record their opinions of points raised by the writer, questions triggered by the reading, or vocabulary words that the reader does not know and must look up. NOTE: Because this strategy requires that students write in the margins of a book or periodical, text annotation is suitable for courses in which students have either purchased the textbook or have photocopies of the reading available on which to write.

**Reading Comprehension: Mining Information from the Text Book** *(Garner, Hare, Alexander, Haynes, & Vinograd, 1984)*. With "text lookback" the student increases recall of information by skimming previously read material in the text in a structured manner to look that information up. First, define for the student the difference between "lookback" and "think" questions. "Lookback" questions are those for which the answer can be found right in the article, while "think" questions are those that ask you to give your own opinion, belief, or ideas. When faced with a "lookback" question, readers may need to look back in the article to find the information that they need. But readers can save time by first skimming the article to get to the general section where the answer to the question is probably located. To skim efficiently, the student should:

1. Read the "lookback" question in the text carefully and highlight the section that tells the reader what to look for (e.g., "What does the article say are the FIVE MOST ENDANGERED SPECIES of whales today?").

2. Look for titles, headings, or illustrations in the article that might tell the reader where the information that he or she is looking for is probably located.

3. Read the beginning and end sentences in individual paragraphs to see if that paragraph might contain the desired information.

**Reading Comprehension: Previewing the Chapter** *(Gleason, Archer, & Colvin, 2002)*. The student who systematically previews the contents of a chapter before reading it increases comprehension, by creating a mental map of its contents, activating prior knowledge about the topic, and actively forming predictions about what he or she is about to read. In the previewing technique, the student browses the chapter headings and subheadings. The reader also studies any important graphics and looks over review questions at the conclusion of the chapter. Only then does the student begin reading the selection.

**Reading Comprehension: "Question-Answer Relationships" (QAR)** *(Raphael, 1982; Raphael, 1986)*. Students are taught to identify "question-answer relationships", matching the appropriate strategy to comprehension questions based on whether a question is based on fact, requires inferential thinking, or draws upon the reader's own experience. Students learn that answers to RIGHT THERE questions are fact-based and can be found in a single sentence, often accompanied by clue words that also appear in the question. Students are informed that they will also find answers to THINK AND SEARCH questions in the text, but they must piece those answers together by scanning the text and making connections between different pieces of factual information. AUTHOR AND YOU questions require that students take information or opinions that appear in the text and combine them with their own experiences or opinions to formulate an answer. ON MY OWN questions are based on the students' own experiences and do not require knowledge of the text to answer. Students are taught to identify question-answer relationships in class discussion and demonstration. They are then given specific questions and directed to identify the question type and to use the appropriate strategy to answer.

**Reading Comprehension: Reading Actively** *(Gleason, Archer, & Colvin, 2002).* By reading, recalling, and reviewing the contents of every paragraph, the student improves comprehension of the longer passage. The instructor teaches students to first read through the paragraph, paying particular attention to the topic and important details and facts. The instructor then directs students to cover the paragraph and state (or silently recall) the key details of the passage from memory. Finally, the instructor prompts students to uncover the passage and read it again to see how much of the information in the paragraph the student had been able to accurately recall. This process is repeated with all paragraphs in the passage.

**Reading Fluency: Listening, Reading, And Receiving Corrective Feedback** *(Rose & Sherry, 1984; Van Don, Boksebeld, Font Freide, & Van den Hurk, J.M., 1991).* The student rehearses a text by first following along silently as a more accomplished reader (tutor) reads a passage aloud; then the student reads the same passage aloud while receiving corrective feedback as needed. The student and tutor sit side-by-side at a table with a book between them. The tutor begins by reading aloud from the book for about 2 minutes while the student reads silently. If necessary, the tutor tracks his or her progress across the page with an index finger to help the student to keep up. At the end of the 2 minutes, the tutor stops reading and asks the student to read aloud. If the student commits a reading error or hesitates for longer than 3-5 seconds, the tutor tells the student the correct word and has the student continue reading. For each new passage, the tutor first reads the passage aloud before having the student read aloud.

**Reading Fluency: Paired Reading** *(Topping, 1987).* The student builds fluency and confidence as a reader by first reading aloud in unison with an accomplished reader, then signaling that he or she is ready to read on alone with corrective feedback. The more accomplished reader (tutor) and student sit in a quiet location with a book positioned between them. The tutor says to the student, "Now we are going to read aloud together for a little while. Whenever you want to read alone, just tap the back of my hand like this [demonstrate] and I will stop reading. If you come to a word you don't know, I will tell you the word and begin reading with you again." Tutor and student begin reading aloud together. If the student misreads a word, the tutor points to the word and pronounces it. Then the student repeats the word. When the student reads the word correctly, tutor and student resume reading through the passage. When the child delivers the appropriate signal (a hand tap) to read independently, the tutor stops reading aloud and instead follows along silently as the student continues with oral reading. The tutor occasionally praises the student in specific terms for good reading (e.g., "That was a hard word. You did a nice job sounding it out!"). If, while reading alone, the child either commits a reading error or hesitates for longer than 5 seconds, the tutor points to the error-word and pronounces it. Then the tutor tells the student to say the word. When the student pronounces the error-word correctly, tutor and student resume reading aloud in unison. This tandem reading continues until the student again signals to read alone.

**Reading Fluency: Repeated Reading** *(Herman, 1985; Rashotte & Torgesen, 1985; Rasinski, 1990)*. The student increases fluency in decoding by repeatedly reading the same passage while receiving help with reading errors. A more accomplished reader (tutor) sits with the student in a quiet location with a book positioned between them. The tutor selects a passage in the book of about 100 to 200 words in length. The tutor directs the student to read the passage aloud. If the student misreads a word or hesitates for longer than 5 seconds, the tutor reads the word aloud and has the student repeat the word correctly before continuing through the passage. If the student asks for help with any word, the tutor reads the word aloud. If the student requests a word definition, the tutor gives the definition. When the student has completed the passage, the tutor directs the student to read the passage again. The tutor directs the student to continue rereading the same passage until either the student has read the passage a total of 4 times or the student reads the passage at the rate of at least 85 to 100 words per minute. Then tutor and student select a new passage and repeat the process.

**Word Decoding: Drilling Error Words** *(Jenkins & Larson, 1979)*. When students practice, drill, and receive corrective feedback on words that they misread, they can rapidly improve their vocabulary and achieve gains in reading fluency. Here are steps that the teacher or tutor will follow in the Error Word Drill:

1. When the student misreads a word during a reading session, write down the error word and date in a separate "Error Word Log".

2. At the end of the reading session, write out all error words from the reading session onto index cards. If the student has misread more than 20 different

words during the session, use just the first 20 words from your error-word list. If the student has misread fewer than 20 words, consult your "Error Word Log" and select enough additional error words from past sessions to build the review list to 20 words.

3. Review the index cards with the student. Whenever the student pronounces a word correctly, remove that card from the deck and set it aside. A word is considered correct if it is read correctly within 5 seconds. Self-corrected words are counted as correct if they are made within the 5-second period. Words read correctly after the 5-second period expires are counted as incorrect.

4. When the student misses a word, pronounce the word for the student and have the student repeat the word. Then say, "What word?" and direct the student to repeat the word once more. Place the card with the missed word at the bottom of the deck.

5. Error words in the deck are presented until all have been read correctly. All word cards are then gathered together, reshuffled, and presented again to the student. The drill continues until either time runs out or the student has progressed through the deck without an error on two consecutive cards.

**Word Decoding: Tackling Multi-Syllabic Words** *(Gleason, Archer, & Colvin, 2002)*. The student uses affixes (suffixes and prefixes) and decodable chunks to decode multi-syllabic words. The instructor teaches students to identify the most common prefixes and suffixes present in multi-syllable words, and trains students to readily locate and circle those affixes. The instructor also trains students to segment the remainder of unknown words into chunks, stressing that readers do not need to divide these words into dictionary-perfect syllables. Rather, readers informally break up the word into graphemes (any grouping of letters including one or more vowels that represents a basic sound unit, or grapheme, in English). Readers then decode the mystery word by reading all affixes and graphemes in the order that they appear in that word.

**Word Decoding: Teach a Hierarchy of Strategies** *(Haring, Lovitt, Eaton & Hansen, 1978)*. The student has a much greater chance of successfully decoding a difficult word when he or she uses a "'Word Attack Hierarchy" which is a coordinated set of strategies that move from simple to more complex. The student uses successive strategies until solving the word.

1. When the student realizes that he or she has misread a word, the student first attempts to decode the word again.

2. Next, the student reads the entire sentence, using the context of that sentence to try to figure out the word's meaning and pronunciation.

3. The student breaks the word into parts, pronouncing each one.

4. If still unsuccessful, the student uses an index card to cover sections of the word, each time pronouncing only the part that is visible. The student asks, "What sound does ___ make?" using phonics information to sound out the word.

5. If still unsuccessful, the student asks a more accomplished reader to read the word.

## References

Duffelmeyer, F.A. (1994). Effective anticipation guide statements for learning from expository prose. *Journal of Reading*, 37, 452 - 457.

Florida Center for Reading Research (2005). *Student center activities: Teacher resource guide*. Retrieved August 20, 2006, from http://www.fcrr.org/Curriculum/pdf/TRG_Final_Part1.pdf

Garner, R., Hare, V.C., Alexander, P., Haynes, J., & Vinograd, P. (1984). Inducing use of a text lookback strategy among unsuccessful readers. *American Educational Research Journal*, 21, 789-798.

Gleason, M. M., Archer, A. L., & Colvin, G. (2002). Interventions for improving study skills. In M. A. Shinn, H. M. Walker & G. Stoner (Eds*.), Interventions for academic and behavior problems II: Preventive and remedial approaches* (pp.651-680). Bethesda, MD: National Association of School Psychologists.

Hansen, J. & Pearson, P.D. (1983). An instructional study: Improving the inferential comprehension of good and poor fourth-grade readers. *Journal of Educational Psychology*, 75, 821-829.

Haring, N.G., Lovitt, T.C., Eaton, M.D., & Hansen, C.L. (1978). *The fourth R: Research in the classroom*. Columbus, OH: Charles E. Merrill Publishing.

Harris, Jane (1990). *Text annotation and underlining as metacognitive strategies to improve comprehension and retention of expository text.* Paper presented at the Annual Meeting of the National Reading Conference (Miami).

Herman, P.A. (1985). The effects of repeated readings on reading rate, speech pauses, and word recognition accuracy. *Reading Research Quarterly,* 20, 553-565.

Jenkins, J. & Larsen, D. (1979). Evaluation of error-correction procedures for oral reading. *Journal of Special Education*, 13, 145-156.

Merkley, D.J. (1996). Modified anticipation guide. *The Reading Teacher*, 50, 365-368.

Raphael, T. (1982). Question-answering strategies for children. *The Reading Teacher*, 36, 186-190.

Raphael, T. (1986). Teaching question answer relationships, revisited. The Reading Teacher, 39, 516-522.

Rashotte, C.A. & Torgesen, J.K. (1985). Repeated reading and reading fluency in learning disabled children. *Reading Research Quarterly*, 20, 180-188.

Rasinski, T.V. (1990). Effects of repeated reading and listening-while-reading on reading fluency. *Journal of Educational Research,* 83(3), 147-150.

Robinson, F. P. (1946). Effective study. New York: Harper & Row.

Rose, T.L., & Sherry, L. (1984). Relative effects of two previewing procedures on LD adolescents' oral reading performance. *Learning Disabilities Quarterly*, 7, 39-44.

Sarkisian V., Toscano, M., Tomkins-Tinch, K., & Casey, K. (2003). *Reading strategies and critical thinking*. Retrieved October 15, 2006, from http://www.academic.marist.edu/alcuin/ssk/stratthink.html

Topping, K. (1987). Paired reading: A powerful technique for parent use. *The Reading Teacher*, 40, 608-614.

Van Bon, W.H.J., Boksebeld, L.M., Font Freide, T.A.M., & Van den Hurk, J.M. (1991). A comparison of three methods of reading-while-listening. *Journal of Learning Disabilities*, 24, 471-476.

## WRITING

The act of writing contains its own inner tensions. Writers must abide by a host of rules that govern the mechanics and conventions of writing yet are also expected— within the constraints of those rules— to formulate original, even creative, thoughts. It is no wonder that many students find writing to be a baffling exercise and have little sense of how to break larger writing assignments into predictable, achievable subtasks. But, of course, writing can be taught and writing can be mastered. The best writing instruction places the process of written expression on a timeline: Good writers first plan their writing. Then they write. Once a draft has been created, good writers review and revise their work. While the stages of the writing process are generally sequential, good writers also find themselves jumping frequently between these stages (for example, collecting additional notes and writing new sections of a paper as part of the revision process). Depending upon their stage of development as writers, struggling student writers may benefit from the following strategies:

**Content: Memorize a Story Grammar Checklist** *(Reid & Lienemann, 2006)*. Students write lengthier stories that include greater detail when they use a memorized strategy to judge their writing-in-progress. These young writers are taught a simple mnemonic device with 7 elements: "WWW, What=2, How = 2". This mnemonic translates into a story grammar checklist:

- WHO the main character is;

- WHERE the story takes place;

- WHEN the story occurs;

- WHAT the main character(s) do or plan to do;

- WHAT happens next;

- HOW the story concludes; and

- HOW the character(s) feel about their experiences.

Students are taught this strategy through teacher demonstration, discussion, teacher modeling; and student use of the strategy with gradually fading teacher support. When students use the 'WWW, What=2, How = 2' tactic independently, they may still need occasional prompting to use it in their writing. NOTE: Teachers can apply this intervention idea to any genre of writing (e.g., persuasive essay), distilling its essential elements into a similar short, easily memorized checklist to teach to students.

**Fluency: Have Students Write Every Day** *(Graham, Harris & Larsen, 2001)*. Short daily writing assignments can build student writing fluency and make writing a more motivating activity. For struggling writers, formal writing can feel much like a foreign language, with its own set of obscure grammatical rules and intimidating vocabulary. Just as people learn another language more quickly and gain confidence when they use it frequently, however, poor writers gradually develop into better writers when they are prompted to write daily, and receive rapid feedback and encouragement about that writing. The teacher can encourage daily writing by giving short writing assignments, allowing time for students to journal about their learning activities, requiring that they correspond daily with pen pals via email, or even posting a question on the board as a bell-ringer activity that students can respond to in writing for extra credit. Short daily writing tasks have the potential to lower students' aversion to writing and boost their confidence in using the written word.

**Fluency: Self-Monitor and Graph Results to Increase Writing Fluency**
*(Rathvon, 1999).* Students gain motivation to write through daily monitoring and charting of their own and classwide rates of writing fluency. At least several times per week, assign your students timed periods of "freewriting" when they write in their personal journals. "Freewriting" periods are the same amount of time each day. After each "freewriting" period, direct each student to count up the number of words he or she has written in the daily journal entry (whether spelled correctly or not). Next, tell students to record their personal writing-fluency score in their journal and also chart the score on their own time-series graph for visual feedback. Then collect the day's writing-fluency scores of all students in the class, sum those scores, and chart the results on a large time-series graph posted at the front of the room. At the start of each week, calculate that week's goal of increasing total class words written, by taking last week's score and increasing by five percent. At the end of each week, review the class score and praise students if they have shown good effort.

**Instruction: Essentials of Good Teaching Benefit Struggling Writers**
*(Gersten, Baker, & Edwards, 1999).* Teachers are most successful in reaching students with writing delays when their instruction emphasizes the full writing process, provides strategy sheets, offers lots of models of good writing, and gives students timely editorial feedback. Good instructors build their written expression lessons around the three stages of writing –planning, writing, and revision— and make those stages clear and explicit. Skilled instructors also provide students with "think sheets" that outline step-by-step strategies for tackle the different phases of a writing assignment (e.g., taking concise notes from research material; building an outline; proofreading a draft). Students become stronger writers when exposed to different kinds of expressive text, such as persuasive, narrative, and expository writing. Teachers can make students more confident and self-sufficient as writers when they give them access to plentiful examples of good prose models that the student can review when completing a writing assignment. Finally, strong writing teachers provide supportive and timely feedback to students about their writing. When teachers or classmates offer writing feedback to the student, they are honest but also maintain an encouraging tone.

**Motivation: Stimulate Interest With an Autobiography Assignment** *(Bos & Vaughn, 2002).* Assigning the class to write their own autobiographies can motivate hard-to-reach students who seem uninterested in most writing assignments. Have students read a series of autobiographies of people who interest them. Discuss these biographies with the class. Then assign students to write their own autobiographies. (With the class, create a short questionnaire that students can use to interview their parents and other family members to collect information about their past.) Allow students to read their finished autobiographies for the class.

**Organization: Build an Outline by Talking Through the Topic** *(The Writing Center, University of North Carolina at Chapel Hill, n.d./23 December 2006)*. Students who struggle to organize their notes into a coherent outline can tell others what they know about the topic, and then capture the informal logical structure of that conversation to create a working outline. The student studies notes from the topic and describes what he or she knows about the topic and its significance to a listener. (The student may want to audio-record this conversation for later playback.) After the conversation, the student jots down an outline from memory to capture the structure and main ideas of the discussion. This outline 'kernel' can then be expanded and refined into the framework for a paper.

**Organization: "Reverse Outline" the Draft** *(The Writing Center, University of North Carolina at Chapel Hill, n.d./23 December 2006)*. Students can improve the internal flow of their compositions through "reverse outlining". The student writes a draft of the composition. Next, the student reads through the draft, jotting notes in the margins that signify the main idea of each paragraph or section. Then the student organizes the margin notes into an outline to reveal the organizational structure of the paper. This 'reverse outline' allows the student to note whether sections of the draft are repetitious, are out of order, or do not logically connect with one another.

**Planning: Brainstorm to Break the 'Idea' Logjam** *(The Writing Center, University of North Carolina at Chapel Hill, n.d./28 December 2006)*. Brainstorming is a time-tested method that can help students to generate motivating topics for writing assignments and uncover new ideas to expand and improve their compositions. Here are four brainstorming strategies to teach to students:

- *Freewriting*: The student sets a time limit (e.g., 15 minutes) or length limit (e.g., one hand-written page) and spontaneously writes until the limit is reached. The writer does not judge the writing but simply writes as rapidly as possible, capturing any thought that comes to mind on the topic. Later, the student reviews the freewriting to pick out any ideas, terms, or phrasing that might be incorporated into the writing assignment.

- *Listing:* The student selects a topic based on an idea or key term related to the writing assignment. The writer then rapidly brainstorms a list of any items that might possibly relate to the topic. Finally, the writer reviews the list to select items that might be useful in the assigned composition or trigger additional writing ideas.

- *Similes:* The student selects a series of key terms or concepts linked to the writing assignment. The student brainstorms, using the framework of a simile: " _1_ is like _2_." The student plugs a key term into the first blank and then generates as many similes as possible (e.g., "A SHIP is like a CITY ON THE SEA.").

- *References:* The student jots down key ideas or terms from the writing assignment. He or she then browses through various reference works (dictionaries, encyclopedias, specialized reference works on specific subjects) looking randomly for entries that trigger useful ideas. Writers might try a variation of this strategy by typing assignment-related search terms into GOOGLE or another online search engine.

**Proofreading: Teach A Memory Strategy** *(Bos & Vaughn, 2002).* When students regularly use a simple, portable, easily memorized plan for proofreading, the quality of their writing can improve significantly. Create a poster to be put up in the classroom summarizing the SCOPE proofreading elements:

- **S**pelling: Are my words spelled correctly?

- **C**apitalization: Have I capitalized all appropriate words, including first words of sentences, proper nouns, and proper names?

- **O**rder of words: Is my word order (syntax) correct?

- **P**unctuation: Did I use end punctuation and other punctuation marks appropriately?

- **E**xpression of complete thoughts: Do all of my sentences contain a noun and verb to convey a complete thought?

Review the SCOPE proofreading steps by copying a first-draft writing sample onto an overhead and evaluating the sample with the class using each item from the SCOPE poster. Then direct students to pair off and together evaluate their own writing samples using SCOPE. When students appear to understand the use of the SCOPE plan, require that they use this strategy to proofread all written assignments before turning them in.

**Proofreading: Use Selective Proofreading With Highlighting of Errors** *(Frus, n.d./18 November 2006).* To prevent struggling writers from becoming overwhelmed by teacher proofreading corrections, focus on only one or two proofreading areas when correcting a writing assignment. Create a student writing skills checklist that inventories key writing competencies (e.g., grammar/syntax, spelling, vocabulary, etc.). For each writing assignment, announce to students that you will grade the assignment for overall content but will make proofreading corrections on only 1-2 areas chosen from the writing skills checklist. Select different proofreading targets for each assignment and match these to common writing weaknesses in your classroom. Also, to prevent cluttering the student's paper with potentially discouraging teacher comments and editing marks, underline problems in the student' text with a highlighter and number the highlighted errors sequentially at the left margin of the student paper. Then, if necessary, write teacher comments on a separate feedback sheet to explain the writing errors. (Identify each comment with the matching error-number from the left margin of the student's worksheet.) With fewer proofreading comments, the student can better attend to the teacher feedback. Also, even a heavily edited student assignment looks neat and tidy when teachers use the highlighting/numbering technique, preventing students from becoming disheartened at the site of an assignment scribbled over with corrective comments.

**Spelling: Leverage the Power of Memory Through Cover-Copy-Compare** *(Murphy, Hern, Williams, & McLaughlin, 1990)*. Students increase their spelling knowledge by copying a spelling word from a correct model and then recopying the same word from memory. Give students a list of 10-20 spelling words, an index card, and a blank sheet of paper. For each word on the spelling list, the student:

1. Copies the spelling list item onto a sheet of paper;

2. Covers the newly copied word with the index card;

3. Writes the spelling word again on the sheet, spelling it from memory; and

4. Uncovers the copied word and checks to ensure that the word copied from memory is spelled correctly.

If that word is spelled incorrectly, the student repeats the sequence above until the word copied from memory is spelled correctly, then moves to the next word on the spelling list.

### References

Bos, C.S. & Vaughn, S. (2002). *Strategies for teaching students with learning and behavior problems*. Boston: Allyn and Bacon.

Frus, P. (n.d./18 November 2006). *Commenting effectively on student writing*. Retrieved November 18, 2006, from http://www.crlt.umich.edu/crlttext/P7_2text.html

Gersten, R., Baker, S., & Edwards, L. (1999). *Teaching expressive writing to students with learning disabilities: A meta-analysis*. New York: National Center for Learning Disabilities.

Graham, S., Harris, K. R., & Larsen, L. (2001). Prevention and intervention of writing difficulties for students with learning disabilities. *Learning Disabilities Research & Practice*, 16, 74-84.

Murphy, J., Hern, C., Williams, R., & McLaughlin, T. (1990). The effects of the copy, cover, and compare approach in increasing spelling accuracy with learning disabled students. *Contemporary Educational Psychology*, 15, 378-386.

Rathvon, N. (1999). *Effective school interventions*. New York: Guilford Press.

Reid, R. & Lienemann, T.O. (2006). Self-regulated strategy development for written expression with students with attention deficit/hyperactivity disorder. *Exceptional Children*, 73, 53-68.

The Writing Center, University of North Carolina at Chapel Hill (n.d.). *Brainstorming*. Retrieved December 28, 2006, from http://www.unc.edu/depts/wcweb/handouts/brainstorming.html

The Writing Center, University of North Carolina at Chapel Hill (n.d.). *Reorganizing your draft*. Retrieved December 23, 2006, from http://www.unc.edu/depts/wcweb/handouts/organization.html

# Appendix B
## Curriculum-Based Measurement Administration & Scoring Guidelines

This guide to the administration and scoring of CBM Reading, Math, and Writing measures is taken from the online manual *Curriculum-based measurement: A manual for teachers* (Wright, n.d.). The reader who would like to review a more comprehensive overview of CBM can download that manual at no cost from: *http://www.jimwrightonline.com/pdfdocs/cbaManual.pdf*

## Introduction

In contrast to less formal methods of monitoring classroom academic skills, the hallmark of Curriculum-Based Measurement is that it follows standardized procedures of administration and scoring. Because CBM does make use of a standardized format, the instructor can have confidence that the information provided by this direct-assessment approach will serve as a reliable and valid indicator of school skills. In effect, results obtained from CBM probes are replicable (that is, separate adults independently giving similar CBM probes to the same child within a short span of time can be expected to come up with closely matching results).

Before moving to specific instructions for giving and scoring CBM probes, however, it is useful to examine two more general decisions to be made by an instructor who wishes to use CBM in the classroom. First, of course, the teacher must select one or more areas of basic academic skills that the instructor wishes to assess through CBM. Well-researched CBM procedures are presently in place for reading, mathematics, spelling, writing, and phonemic awareness. Next, the teacher will need to define a measurement pool of items to be included in CBM probes. As Figure 1 illustrates, the term measurement pool simply refers to the specific range of instructional materials from which the instructor has decided to draw the content of CBM probes:

---

**Figure 1: Examples of measurement pools to be used in creating CBM probes in basic-skill areas:**
- **Reading**: Passages drawn at random from a single basal reading text.
- **Math:** Addition problems with single-digit terms and sums no greater than 18..
- **Writing:** Story-starters suitable for a specific grade-level.

---

A few examples may help to give a clearer idea of the concept of the measurement pool. If a teacher wishes to assess a younger child's reading fluency, he might choose to track her progress using CBM passage-probes taken at random from a 2nd grade reader. The measurement pool in this case would be the range of suitable passages contained in a single reading book. Similarly, a 5th grade instructor may decide to collect classroom

CBM spelling norms on a regular basis. If she is using a specific spelling curriculum in her class (e.g., Scott Foresman spelling text), she could list all of the words to be taught from that book during the school year. Random CBM spelling probes could then be drawn repeatedly from this measurement pool of collected words.

Once the instructor has established a pool of items to be randomly selected for basic-skill probes, that teacher is ready to prepare, administer, and score CBM probes according to standardized procedures. The important elements of CBM probes that are standardized include the following: **materials, directions for administration, time limit,** and **scoring rules**. The remainder of this section will review the standardized procedures for CBM in reading, mathematics, and writing.

## CBM ORAL READING FLUENCY
### Description
To complete a CBM reading fluency probe, the examiner sits down individually with the child and has the student read aloud for 1 minute from each of 3 separate reading passages. During the student's reading, the examiner makes note of any reading errors in each passage. Then the examiner calculates the number of words correctly read in the passage. Next, the examiner ranks in ascending order the word-totals correctly read for the 3 passages and chooses the middle, or median, score as the best indicator of the student's "true" reading rate in the selected reading material.

**Creating a measurement pool for reading-fluency probes**
If a teacher's classroom reading program is based upon a basal reading series, the instructor can treat the sum of passages contained within each basal text as a separate measurement pool. When creating probes, the instructor would simply select passages at random from a designated basal text.

If a reading program makes use of other materials instead (e.g., novels or short stories drawn from a number of sources), the instructor may choose one of two approaches. First, the teacher may still select passages from a basal reading series to use as CBM probes for reading fluency. In essence, the teacher would be using the basal series as a reading-fluency measurement tool—a common collection of passages of graded difficulty in which to monitor the reading progress of students participating in an independent reading program. This approach is convenient because the passages within a single basal are presumed to be of a similar level of difficulty, a necessary consideration for the instructor who plans to create standardized reading probes. Instructors who have put together their own reading programs can also assume that students in any effective reading program should show generalized growth in reading fluency—growth that will be apparent even when tracked in basal reading passages.

Alternatively, the teacher who follows a non-basal reading program may decide to apply one of several readability formulas (e.g., Fry's Readability Index) to the reading materials used in the classroom. In this manner, the instructor should be able to group novels of similar difficulty together into several successive levels. These levels would resemble separate "basal" reading texts. When preparing CBM reading probes, the instructor can simply draw passages randomly from those novels grouped at the desired level of difficulty and use those passages to track the child's reading progress.

## Preparing CBM reading-fluency probes

When assessing the fluency skills of students placed in a basal reading series, the instructor chooses 3 passages at random from the basal text chosen for assessment. For children in the 1st and 2nd grades, each passage should be approximately 150 words long, while passages of about 250 words should be prepared for older students. Passages selected should not contain too much dialog and should avoid an excessive number of foreign words or phrases. In addition, only prose passages should be used in CBM assessments. Poetry and drama should be avoided because they tend to vary considerably and do not represent the kind of text typically encountered by students.

---

**Figure 2: Example of CBM Oral Reading Fluency Probe**

**Examiner Copy**

| | |
|---|---|
| Summertime! How lovely it was in the country, with | 9 |
| the wheat standing yellow, the oats green, and the hay all | 20 |
| stacked down in the grassy meadows! And there went the stork | 31 |
| on his long red legs, chattering away in Egyptian, for | 41 |
| he had learned that language from his mother. The fields and | 52 |

**Student Copy**

Summertime! How lovely it was in the country, with
the wheat standing yellow, the oats green, and the hay all
stacked down in the grassy meadows! And there went the stork
on his long red legs, chattering away in Egyptian, for
he had learned that language from his mother. The fields and

---

For ease of administration, the instructor will want to prepare examiner and student copies of each passage. Ideally, reading passages should be free of illustrations that may help a child to interpret the content of the text. While the teacher may type out copies of a passage, another often-used method is to photocopy a selection from the basal and to cut-and-paste a version of the passage that omits any illustrations but retains the letter-size and font found in the original story. The examiner copy should have a cumulative word total listed along the right margin of the passage for ease of scoring (see Figure 2 above).

## Materials needed for giving CBM reading probes
- Numbered and unnumbered copies of reading passage
- Stopwatch
- Pencil or marker

## Administration of CBM reading probes
The examiner and the student sit across the table from each other. The examiner hands the student the unnumbered copy of the CBM reading passage. The examiner takes the numbered copy of the passage, shielding it from the student's view.

The examiner says to the student: *When I say, 'start,' begin reading aloud at the top of this page. Read across the page* [demonstrate by pointing]. *Try to read each word. If you come to a word you don't know, I'll tell it to you. Be sure to do your best reading. Are there any questions?* [Pause] *Start.*

The examiner begins the stopwatch when the student says the first word. If the student does not say the initial word within 3 seconds, the examiner says the word and starts the stopwatch. As the student reads along in the text, the examiner records any errors by marking a slash (/) through the incorrectly read word. If the student hesitates for 3 seconds on any word, the examiner says the word and marks it as an error. At the end of 1 minute, the examiner says, *Stop* and marks the student's concluding place in the text with a bracket ( ] ).

## Scoring
Reading fluency is calculated by first determining the total words attempted within the timed reading probe and then deducting from that total the number of incorrectly read words.

The following scoring rules will aid the instructor in marking the reading probe:
- Words read correctly are scored as correct:
- Self-corrected words are counted as correct.
- Repetitions are counted as correct.
- Examples of dialectical speech are counted as correct.
- Inserted words are ignored.
- Words read to the student by the examiner after 3 seconds are counted as errors.

- Mispronunciations are counted as errors.
  Example
  Text: The small gray fox ran to the cover of the trees.
  Student: *"The smill gray fox ran to the cover of the trees."*
- Substitutions are counted as errors.
  Example
  Text: When she returned to the **house**, Grandmother called for Franchesca.
  Student: *"When she returned to the **home**, Grandmother called for Franchesca."*
- Omissions are counted as errors.
  Example
  Text: Anna could not compete in the last race.
  Student: *"Anna could not in the last race."*
- Transpositions of word-pairs are counted as a single error.
  Example
  Text: She looked at the bright, shining face of the sun.
  Student: *"She looked at the shining, bright face of the sun."*

## Computing reading-fluency rate in a single passage

The scoring of a reading probe is straightforward. The examiner first determines how many words the reader actually attempted during the 1-minute reading sample. On the completed probe in Figure 3, for instance, the bracket near the end of the text indicates that the student attempted 48 words before his time expired. Next, the examiner counts up the number of errors made by the reader. On this probe, the student committed 4 errors. By deducting the number of errors from the total words attempted, the examiner arrives at the number of correctly read words per minute. This number serves as an estimate of reading fluency, combining as it does the student's speed and accuracy in reading. So by deducting the errors from total words attempted, we find that the child actually read 44 correct words in 1 minute.

---

**Figure3: Example of a scored reading probe**

**Examiner Copy**

| | |
|---|---|
| Summertime! How lovely it was in the country, with | 9 |
| the wheat standing yellow, the oats green, and the hay all | 20 |
| stacked down in the grassy meadows! And there went the stork | 31 |
| on his long red legs, chattering away in Egyptian, for | 41 |
| he had learned that language from his mother. The fields and | 52 |

Total Read Words = 48

Errors = 4

Correctly Read Words = 44

## Accommodating omissions when scoring. . .

When a student skips several connected words or even an entire line during a reading probe, that omission creates a special scoring dilemma. An omission, after all, is considered to be a single error of tracking, no matter how many words were skipped at one time. However, if all words omitted in a line were individually counted as errors, the student's error rate would be greatly inflated. The solution is for the examiner to subtract all but one of the words in each omission before computing the total words attempted.

Let's see how that score adjustment would work. On the completed probe in Figure 4, the student omitted the text of an entire line while reading aloud. The examiner drew a line through all the connected words skipped by the child in that omitted line of text. Because a total of 11 words were omitted, the examiner drops 10 of those words before calculating the total words attempted.

When calculating the number of words the child attempted to read, the examiner notes that the child reached word 48 in the passage. Ten words are then deducted from the omitted lines to avoid inflating the error count. The adjusted figure for total words attempted is found to be 38 words. The child committed 5 errors (4 marked by slashes and 1 omission). These errors are subtracted from the revised figure of 38 total words attempted. Therefore, the number of correctly read words in this example would be 33.

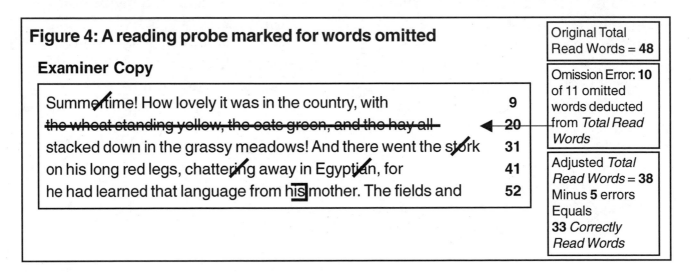

**Figure 4: A reading probe marked for words omitted**

**Examiner Copy**

| | |
|---|---|
| Summertime! How lovely it was in the country, with | 9 |
| ~~the wheat standing yellow, the oats green, and the hay all~~ | 20 |
| stacked down in the grassy meadows! And there went the stork | 31 |
| on his long red legs, chattering away in Egyptian, for | 41 |
| he had learned that language from his mother. The fields and | 52 |

Original Total Read Words = **48**

Omission Error: **10** of 11 omitted words deducted from *Total Read Words*

Adjusted *Total Read Words* = **38** Minus **5** errors Equals **33** *Correctly Read Words*

## Selecting the median reading-fluency rate in a basal

A major difference between basal reading probes and CBM probes in other basic-skill areas is that the examiner is required to give 3 reading probes to arrive at a single estimate of a student's reading fluency in a basal text. In contrast, single administrations of CBM probes in mathematics, spelling, and writing are usually sufficient to yield accurate estimates of student skills. Why does CBM reading alone require 3 probes for each administration? The answer can be found in the nature of basal reading texts.

Although publishers select the contents of a basal reading book to fall within a restricted range of difficulty, instructors know that the material within a basal reader will actually vary somewhat in level of difficulty from story to story. Given the potential variability of text samples taken at random from a basal, there is some danger that reading probes using only a single passage would provide a distorted picture of a child's "true" reading rate. For instance, if the child happened by chance to be given 2 excessively difficult reading probes during successive CBM assessments, the examiner might be misled into believing that the student was making slower reading progress than was actually the case.

To safeguard CBM reading probes against the possibility of faulty estimates of reading ability, the examiner relies on a concept known as central tendency. While this term is adopted from statistics, it means simply that when several samples of a varying behavior are gathered (in this case, samples of reading fluency), there is a much greater chance that one of those samples will be an accurate reflection of a child's "true" ability. But when 3 reading probes are given from a single basal, how does the examiner decide which of the probes represents the "best" estimate of the student's proficiency in reading?

First, the examiner mentally ranks the scores for words read correctly in ascending order (from lowest to highest). Next, the examiner discards the lowest and highest scores, retaining only the middle, or median, score. By dropping low and high scores for each series of 3 reading probes, the examiner is able to greatly enhance the accuracy of the CBM reading probe. The same approach allows the teacher to accurately estimate the number of reading errors that a child makes in each basal.

An example may be helpful here. Let's assume that Jared, a 4th-grade student who has problems with reading fluency, sat down with his teacher one afternoon and was given 3 CBM reading probes taken from the later 2nd-grade reader ('GR 2-Book 2') of the Silver Burdett & Ginn reading series. The instructor then records the results on a recording sheet, as in Figure 5:

---

**Figure 5: Example of a completed score sheet for a CBM oral reading fluency probe**

Date: __Th. 12/5__    Book/Reading Level: ___GR 2-Book 2-P 1-3___

|   | TRW | E | CRW | %CRW |
|---|-----|---|-----|------|
| A. | 93 | 3 | 90 | 97 |
| B. | 72 | 4 | 68 | 94 |
| C. | 83 | 1 | 82 | 98 |

TRW = Total Read Words          E = Errors
CRW = Correctly Read Words      %CRW = Percent Correctly Read Words

---

In order to arrive at the best estimate of the child's actual reading rate, the teacher first decides which of the 3 CRW ('Correctly Read Words Per Minute') reading rates is the middle, or median, score. Since 68 correct words per minute is the lowest score, she discards it. In the same fashion, the instructor eliminates 90 words per minute, the highest score. She is then left with the median, or middle, score of 82 words per minute as the most accurate estimate of Jared's reading fluency in a second grade reading book from the district's basal reading series. Notice that the teacher also uses the concept of the median score to find the best estimate of how many reading errors Jared makes at this reading level. By dropping the low error score of 1 and the high error score of 4, her teacher finds that the most accurate estimate is that Jared makes approximately 3 errors per minute in this 2nd-grade reading book.

In this example, the teacher also computed the student's accuracy of decoding for each reading probe. Strictly speaking, the calculation of a student's accuracy of academic performance is not a part of CBM. However, many instructors find an estimate of student accuracy to be useful diagnostic information. To determine the percent accuracy of a child's reading, the teacher divides the number of words correctly read (CRW) by the total read words (TRW). The resulting figure will be a decimal ranging between 0.0 and 1.0. That decimal figure is then multiplied by 100 to give the instructor the percent accuracy of the child's reading sample.

Referring back to the Figure 4, the instructor administered the first reading probe (line A). In that passage, the student managed to read 90 correct words out of a total of 93 words attempted. Dividing 90 words by 93 words, the teacher came up with a quotient of 097. She then multiplied that decimal figure by 100 (0.97 x 100) to come up with 97 percent as an index of the student's reading accuracy in this individual reading probe. As with number of correctly read words and errors, measures of reading accuracy may be reported as a median figure. However, teachers often choose instead to present reading accuracy as a range of performance. In the above example, the student could be said to read within a range of 94 to 98 percent accuracy in passages take from a second grade reading book from the Silver Burdett & Ginn reading series.

## CBM MATH
### Description
There are 2 types of CBM math probes, single-skill worksheets (those containing like problems) and multiple-skill worksheets (those containing a mix of problems requiring different math operations). Single-skill probes give instructors good information about students' mastery of particular problem-types, while multiple-skill probes allow the teacher to test children's math competencies on a range of computational objectives during a single CBM session.

**Figure 6: A Sampling of Math Computational Goals for Addition, Subtraction, Multiplication, and Division** (from Wright, 2002).

### Addition
Two 1-digit numbers: sums to 10
Two 3-digit numbers: no regrouping
1- to 2-digit number plus 1- to 2-digit number: regrouping

### Subtraction
Two 1-digit numbers: 0 to 9
2-digit number from a 2-digit number: no regrouping
2-digit number from a 2-digit number: regrouping

### Multiplication
Multiplication facts: 0 to 9
2-digit number times 1-digit number: no regrouping
3-digit number times 1-digit number: regrouping

### Division
Division facts: 0 to 9
2-digit number divided by 1-digit number: no remainder
2-digit number divided by 1-digit number: remainder

Wright, J. (2002) *Curriculum-Based Assessment Math Computation Probe Generator: Multiple-Skill Worksheets in Mixed Skills.* Retrieved August 13, 2006, from http:// www.lefthandlogic.com/htmdocs/tools/mathprobe/allmult.shtml

Both types of math probes can be administered either individually or to groups of students. The examiner hands the worksheet(s) out to those students selected for assessment. Next, the examiner reads aloud the directions for the worksheet. Then the signal is given to start, and students proceed to complete as many items as possible within 2 minutes. The examiner collects the worksheets at the end of the assessment for scoring.

## Creating a measurement pool for math computational probes
The first task of the instructor in preparing CBM math probes is to define the computational skills to be assessed. Many districts have adopted their own math curriculum that outlines the various computational skills in the order in which they are to be taught. Teachers may also review scope-and-sequence charts that accompany math textbooks when selecting CBM computational objectives.

The order in which math computational skills are taught, however, probably does not vary a great deal from district to district. Figure 6 contains sample computation goals for addition, subtraction, multiplication, and division.

Instructors typically are interested in employing CBM to monitor students' acquisition of skills in which they are presently being instructed. However, teachers may also want to use CBM as a skills check-up to assess those math objectives that students have been taught in the past or to "preview" a math group's competencies in computational material that will soon be taught.

## Preparing CBM Math Probes

After computational objectives have been selected, the instructor is ready to prepare math probes. The teacher may want to create single-skills probes, multipleskill probes, or both types of CBM math worksheets.

## Creating the Single-skill Math Probe

As the first step in putting together a single-skill math probe, the teacher will select one computational objective as a guide. The measurement pool, then, will consist of problems randomly constructed that conform to the computational objective chosen. For example, the instructor may select the following goal (Figure 7) as the basis for a math probe:

---

**Figure 7: Example of a single-skill math probe:**
**Three to five 3- and 4-digit numbers: no regrouping**

| 105 | 2031 | 111 | 634 |
|-----|------|-----|-----|
| + 600 | + 531 | + 717 | +8240 |
| + 293 | +2322 | + 260 | + 203 |

---

The teacher would then construct a series of problems that match the computational goal, as in Figure 7. In general, single-skill math probes should contain between 80 and 200 problems, and worksheets should have items on both the front and back of the page. Adequate space should also be left for the student's computations, especially with more complex problems such as long division.

To assemble a multiple-skill math probe, the instructor would first select the range of math operations and of problem-types that will make up the probe. The teacher would probably want to consult the district math curriculum, appropriate scope—and sequence charts, or the computational-goal chart included in this manual when selecting the kinds of problems to include in the multiple-skill probe. Once the computational objectives have been chosen, the teacher can make up a worksheet of mixed math facts conforming to those objectives. Using the earlier example, the teacher who wishes to estimate the proficiency of his 4th-grade math group may decide to create a multiple-skills CBM probe. He could choose to sample only those problem-types that his students have either mastered or are presently being instructed in. Those skills are listed in Figure 5.8, with sample problems that might appear on the worksheet of mixed math facts.

---

**Figure 8:  Example of a multiple-skill math probe:**
**Division: 3-digit number divided by 1-digit number: no remainder**
**Subtraction: 2-digit number from a 2-digit number: regrouping**
**Multiplication: 3-digit number times 1-digit number: no regrouping**
**Division: Two 3-digit numbers: no regrouping**

$$9\overline{)431} \qquad\qquad \begin{array}{r} 20 \\ -18 \\ \hline \end{array} \qquad\qquad \begin{array}{r} 113 \\ \times\ 2 \\ \hline \end{array} \qquad\qquad \begin{array}{r} 106 \\ +\ 172 \\ +\ 200 \\ +\ 600 \\ \hline \end{array}$$

---

## Materials needed for giving CBM math probes

Student copy of CBM math probe (either single- or multiple-skill)
Stopwatch
Pencils for students

## Administration of CBM math probes

The examiner distributes copies of one or more math probes to all the students in the group. (Note: These probes may also be administered individually). The examiner says to the students:

*The sheets on your desk are math facts.*

If the students are to complete a single-skill probe, the examiner then says: *All the problems are [addition or subtraction or multiplication or division] facts.*

If the students are to complete a multiple-skill probe, the examiner then says: *There are several types of problems on the sheet. Some are addition, some are subtraction, some are multiplication, and some are division* [as appropriate]. *Look at each problem carefully before you answer it.*

*When I say 'start,' turn the papers over and begin answering the problems. Start on the first problem on the left on the top row* [point]. *Work across and then go to the next row. If you can't answer the problem, make an 'X' on it and go to the next one. If you finish one side, go to the back. Are there any questions?* Say, *Start.*

The examiner starts the stopwatch. While the students are completing worksheets, the examiner and any other adults assisting in the assessment circulate around the room to ensure that students are working on the correct sheet, that they are completing problems in the correct order (rather than picking out only the easy items), and that they have pencils, etc.

After 2 minutes have passed, the examiner says *Stop.* CBM math probes are collected for scoring.

## Scoring

Traditional approaches to computational assessment usually give credit for the total number of correct answers appearing on a worksheet. If the answer to a problem is found to contain one or more incorrect digits, that problem is marked wrong and receives no credit. In contrast to this all-or-nothing marking system, CBM assigns credit to each individual correct digit appearing in the solution to a math fact.

On the face of it, a math scoring system that awards points according to the number of correct digits may appear unusual, but this alternative approach is grounded in good academic-assessment research and practice. By separately scoring each digit in the answer of a computation problem, the instructor is better able to recognize and to give credit for a student's partial math competencies. Scoring computation problems by the digit rather than as a single answer also allows for a more minute analysis of a child's number skills.

Imagine, for instance, that a student was given a CBM math probe consisting of addition problems, sums less than or equal to 19 (incorrect digits appear in boldface and italics):

---

**Figure 9: Example of completed problems from a single-skill math probe**

| 105 | 2031 | 111 | 634 |
| + 600 | + 531 | + 717 | +8240 |
| + 293 | +2322 | + 260 | + 203 |
| 9*8*8 | 4884 | 108*7* | 9*0*77 |

---

If the answers in Figure 9 were scored as either correct or wrong, the child would receive a score of 1 correct answer out of 4 possible answers (25 percent). However, when each individual digit is scored, it becomes clear that the student actually correctly computed 12 of 15 possible digits (80 percent). Thus, the CBM procedure of assigning credit to each correct digit demonstrates itself to be quite sensitive to a student's emerging, partial competencies in math computation.

The following scoring rules will aid the instructor in marking single- and multiple-skill math probes:

- Individual correct digits are counted as correct.
  Reversed or rotated digits are not counted as errors unless their change in position makes them appear to be another digit (e.g., 9 and 6).
- Incorrect digits are counted as errors.
  Digits that appear in the wrong place value, even if otherwise correct, are scored as errors.
  Example

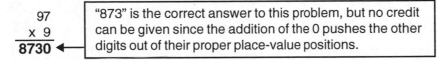

```
   97
 x  9
 8730
```
"873" is the correct answer to this problem, but no credit can be given since the addition of the 0 pushes the other digits out of their proper place-value positions.

- The student is given credit for "place-holder" numerals that are included simply to correctly align the problem. As long as the student includes the correct space, credit is given whether or not a "0" has actually been inserted.
  Example

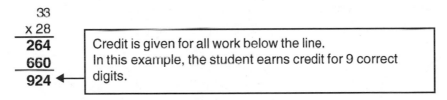

```
    55
  x 82
   110
  4400
  4510
```
Since the student correctly placed 0 in the "place-holder" position, it is given credit as a correct digit. Credit would also have been given if the space were reserved but no 0 had been inserted.

- In more complex problems such as advanced multiplication, the student is given credit for all correct numbers that appear below the line.
  Example

```
    33
  x 28
   264
   660
   924
```
Credit is given for all work below the line.
In this example, the student earns credit for 9 correct digits.

- Credit is not given for any numbers appearing above the line (e.g., numbers marked at the top of number columns to signify regrouping).
  Example

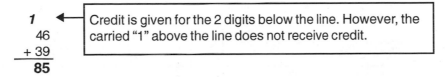

```
    1
   46
 + 39
   85
```
Credit is given for the 2 digits below the line. However, the carried "1" above the line does not receive credit.

# CBM WRITING

## Description

CBM writing probes are simple to administer but offer a variety of scoring options. As with math and spelling, writing probes may be given individually or to groups of students. The examiner prepares a lined composition sheet with a story-starter sentence or partial sentence at the top. The student thinks for 1 minute about a possible story to be written from the story-starter, then spends 3 minutes writing the story. The examiner collects the writing sample for scoring. Depending on the preferences of the teacher, the writing probe can be scored in several ways, as will be explained shortly.

## Creating a measurement pool for writing probes

Since writing probes are essentially writing opportunities for students, they require minimal advance preparation. The measurement pool for writing probes would be a collection of grade-appropriate story-starters, from which the teacher would randomly select a story-starter for each CBM writing assessment. Writing texts are often good sources for lists of story-starters; teachers may also choose to write their own.

## Preparing CBM writing probes

The teacher selects a story-starter from the measurement pool and places it at the top of a lined composition sheet. The story-starter should avoid wording that encourages students to generate lists. It should also be open-ended, requiring the writer to build a narrative rather than simply to write down a "Yes" or "No" response. The CBM writing probe in Figure 10 is a good example of how a such a probe might appear. This particular probe was used in a 5th-grade classroom.

---

**Figure 10: Example of a CBM writing probe**

**CBM Writing Probe**

Name:_____ Grade:_____ Date:_____

One day, I was out sailing. A storm carried me far out to sea and wrecked my boat on a desert island._____

_____

_____

---

## Materials needed for giving CBM writing probes

Student copy of CBM writing probe with story-starter
Stopwatch
Pencils for students

## Administration of CBM writing probes

The examiner distributes copies of CBM writing probes to all the students in the group. (Note: These probes may also be administered individually). The examiner says to the students: *I want you to write a story. I am going to read a sentence to you first, and then I want you to write a short story about what happens. You will have 1 minute to think about the story you will write and then have 3 minutes to write it. Do your best work. If you don't know how to spell a word, you should guess. Are there any questions? For the next minute, think about . . .* [insert story-starter].

The examiner starts the stopwatch. At the end of 1 minute, the examiner says, *Start writing.* While the students are writing, the examiner and any other adults helping in the assessment circulate around the room. If students stop writing before the 3-minute timing period has ended, monitors encourage them to continue writing. After 3 additional minutes, the examiner says, *Stop writing.* CBM writing probes are collected for scoring.

## Scoring

The instructor has several options when scoring CBM writing probes. Student writing samples may be scored according to the

1. number of words written,
2. number of letters written,
3. number of words correctly spelled, or
4. number of writing units placed in correct sequence.

Scoring methods differ both in the amount of time that they require of the instructor and in the quality of information that they provide about a student's writing skills. Advantages and potential limitations of each scoring system are presented below.

*Total words.* The examiner counts up and records the total number of words written during the 3-minute writing probe. Misspelled words are included in the tally, although numbers written in numeral form (e.g., 5, 17) are not counted. Calculating total words is the quickest of scoring methods. A drawback, however, is that it yields only a rough estimate of writing fluency (that is, of how quickly the student can put words on paper) without examining the accuracy of spelling, punctuation, and other writing conventions. A 6th-grade student wrote the CBM writing sample in Figure 11. Using the total-words scoring formula, this sample is found to contain 45 words, including misspellings.

**Figure 11: CBM writing sample scored for Total Words**

| | |
|---|---|
| I woud drink water from the ocean | **7 words** |
| and I woud eat the fruit off of | **8 words** |
| the trees. Then I woud bilit a | **7 words** |
| house out of trees, and I woud | **7 words** |
| gather firewood to stay warm. I | **6 words** |
| woud try and fix my boat in my | **8 words** |
| spare time. | **2 words** |
| | **Total= 45 words** |

*Total letters*. The examiner counts up the total number of letters written during the 3-minute probe. Again, misspelled words are included in the count, but numbers written in numeral form are excluded. Calculating total letters is a reasonably quick operation. When compared to word-total, it also enjoys the advantage of controlling for words of varying length. For example, a student who writes few words but whose written vocabulary tends toward longer words may receive a relatively low score on word total but receive a substantially higher score for letter total. As with word-total, though, the letter-total formula gives only a general idea of writing fluency without examining a student's mastery of writing conventions. When scored according to total letters written, our writing sample in Figure 12 is found to contain 154 letters.

**Figure 12: CBM writing sample scored for Total Letters**

| | |
|---|---|
| I woud drink water from the ocean | **27 letters** |
| and I woud eat the fruit off of | **24 letters** |
| the trees. Then I woud bilit a | **23 letters** |
| house out of trees, and I woud | **23 letters** |
| gather firewood to stay warm. I | **25 letters** |
| woud try and fix my boat in my | **23 letters** |
| spare time. | **09 letters** |
| | **Total=154 letters** |

*Correctly Spelled Words.* The examiner counts up only those words in the writing sample that are spelled correctly. Words are considered separately, not within the context of a sentence. When scoring a good rule of thumb is to determine whether—in isolation—the word represents a correctly spelled term in English. If it does, the word is included in the tally. Assessing the number of correctly spelled words has the advantage of being quick. Also, by examining the accuracy of the student's spelling, this approach monitors to some degree a student's mastery of written language. Our writing sample in Figure 13 is found to contain 39 correctly spelled words.

---

**Figure 13: CBM writing sample scored for Correctly Spelled Words**

| | |
|---|---|
| I woud drink water from the ocean | **6 correctly spelled words** |
| and I woud eat the fruit off of | **7 correctly spelled words** |
| the trees. Then I woud bilit a | **5 correctly spelled words** |
| house out of trees, and I woud | **6 correctly spelled words** |
| gather firewood to stay warm. I | **6 correctly spelled words** |
| woud try and fix my boat in my | **7 correctly spelled words** |
| spare time. | **2 correctly spelled words** |
| | **Total=39 correctly spelled words** |

---

*Correct Writing Sequences.* When scoring correct writing sequences, the examiner goes beyond the confines of the isolated word to consider units of writing and their relation to one another. Using this approach, the examiner starts at the beginning of the writing sample and looks at each successive pair of writing units (writing sequence). Words are considered separate writing units, as are essential marks of punctuation. To receive credit, writing sequences must be correctly spelled and be grammatically correct. The words in each writing sequence must also make sense within the context of the sentence. In effect, the student's writing is judged according to the standards of informal standard American English. A caret (^) is used to mark the presence of a correct writing sequence, as in Figure 14.

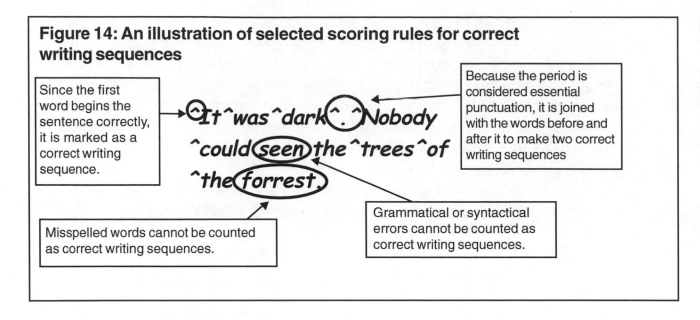

**Figure 14: An illustration of selected scoring rules for correct writing sequences**

Since the first word begins the sentence correctly, it is marked as a correct writing sequence.

Because the period is considered essential punctuation, it is joined with the words before and after it to make two correct writing sequences

^It^was^dark^.^Nobody ^could seen the^trees^of ^the forrest.

Misspelled words cannot be counted as correct writing sequences.

Grammatical or syntactical errors cannot be counted as correct writing sequences.

The following scoring rules will aid the instructor in determining correct writing sequences:

- Correctly spelled words make up a correct writing sequence (reversed letters are acceptable, so long as they do not lead to a misspelling):
  Example

  ^Is^that^a^red^car^?

- Necessary marks of punctuation (excluding commas) are included in correct writing sequences:
  Example

  ^Is^that^a^red^car^?

- Syntactically correct words make up a correct writing sequence:
  Example

  ^Is^that^a red^car ?
  ^Is^that^a^car red?

- Semantically correct words make up a correct writing sequence:
  Example

  ^Is^that^a red^car ?
  ^Is^that^a read car^?

- If correct, the initial word of a writing sample is counted as a correct writing sequence:
  Example

  ^Is that^a^red^car^?

- Titles are included in the correct writing sequence count:
  Example
  > ^The^Terrible^Day

Not surprisingly, evaluating a writing probe according to correct writing sequences is the most time-consuming of the scoring methods presented here. It is also the scoring approach, however, that yields the most comprehensive information about a student's writing competencies. While further research is needed to clarify the point, it also seems plausible that the correct writing sequence method is most sensitive to short-term student improvements in writing. Presumably, advances in writing skills in virtually any area (e.g., spelling, punctuation) could quickly register as higher writing sequence scores. Our writing sample in Figure 15 is found to contain 37 correct writing sequences.

---

**Figure 15: CBM Writing sample scored for correct writing sequence (Each correct writing sequence is marked with a caret(^)).**

| | |
|---|---|
| ^I woud drink^water^from^the^ocean | **5 correct writing sequences** |
| ^and^I woud eat^the^fruit^off^of | **6 correct writing sequences** |
| ^the^trees^.^Then^I woud bilit a | **5 correct writing sequences** |
| ^house^out^of^trees, ^and^I woud | **6 correct writing sequences** |
| gather^firewood^to^stay^warm^.^I | **6 correct writing sequences** |
| woud try^and^fix^my^boat^in^my | **6 correct writing sequences** |
| ^spare^time^. | **3 correct writing sequences** |
| | **Total = 37 correct writing sequences** |

---

**Reference:**

Wright, J. (n.d.). Curriculum-based measurement: A manual for teachers. Retrieved September 23, 2006, from http://www.jimwrightonline.com/pdfdocs/cbaManual.pdf

# Resources: Print and Video Materials
### Available from National Professional Resources, Inc.
### 1-800 453-7461 • www.NPRinc.com

Allington, Richard L. & Patricia M. Cunningham. (1996). *Schools That Work: Where all Children Read and Write.* New York, NY: Harper Collins.

Armstrong, Thomas. *(1996). Beyond the ADD Myth: Classroom Strategies & Techniques* (Video). Port Chester, NY: National Professional Resources, Inc.

Armstrong, Thomas. (1997). *The Myth of the A.D.D. Child.* New York, NY: Penguin Putnam Inc.

ASCD. (2006). *Teaching Students with Learning Disabilities in the Regular Classroom* (Video). Baltimore, MD: ASDC.

Barnett, D.W., Daly, E.J., Jones, K.M., & Lentz, F.E. (2004). *Response to intervention: Empirically based special service decisions from single-case designs of increasing and decreasing intensity. Journal of Special Education,* 38, 66-79.

Basso, Dianne, & Natalie McCoy. (2002). *The Co-Teaching Manual.* Columia, SC: Twin Publications.

Bateman, Barbara D. & Annemieke Golly. (2003). *Why Johnny Doesn't Behave: Twenty Tips for Measurable BIPs.* Verona, WI: Attainment Company, Inc.

Bateman, Barbara D. & Cynthia M. Herr. (2003). *Writing Measurable IEP Goals and Objectives.* Verona, WI: Attainment Company, Inc.

Beecher, Margaret. (1995). *Developing the Gifts & Talents of All Students in the Regular Classroom.* Mansfield Center, CT: Creative Learning Press, Inc.

Bender, William. *Differentiating Instruction for Students with Learning Disabilities.* Thousand Oaks, CA: Corwin Press, 2002.

Bray, Marty & Abbie Brown, et al. (2004). *Technology and the Diverse Learner.* Thousand Oaks, CA: Corwin Press.

Brown-Chidsey, Rachel & Mark W. Steege. (2005). *Response to Intervention.* New York, NY: Guilford Press.

Casbarro, Joseph. (2005). *Test Anxiety & What You Can Do About It: A Practical Guide for Teachers, Parents, & Kids.* Port Chester, NY: Dude Publishing.

Chapman, Carolyn & Rita King. (2003). *Differentiated Instructional Strategies for Reading in the Content Areas.* Thousand Oaks, CA: Corwin Press.

Council for Exceptional Children and Merrill Education. (2005). *Universal Design for Learning.* Atlanta, GA.

Crone, Deanne A. & Robert H. Horner. (2003). *Building Positive Behavior Support Systems in Schools: Functional Behavioral Assessment.* New York, NY: Guilford Press.

Deiner, Penny Low. (2004). *Resources for Educating Children with Diverse Abilities, 4th Edition.* Florence, KY: Thomson Delmar Learning.

Deshler, Donald D. & Jean B. Schumaker. (2005). *Teaching Adolescents With Disabilities: Accessing the General Education Curriculum.* Thousand Oaks, CA: Corwin Press.

Dieker, Lisa. (2006). *7 Effective Strategies for Secondary Inclusion (Video).* Port Chester, NY: National Professional Resources, Inc.

Dieker, Lisa. (2006). *Co-Teaching Lesson Plan Book (Third Edition).* Whitefish Bay, WI: Knowledge By Design.

Dodge, Judith. (2005). *Differentiation in Action.* Jefferson City, MO: Scholastic Inc., 2005.

Elias, Maurice & Linda B. Butler. (2005). *Social Decision Making/ Social Problem Solving A Curriculum for Academic, Social and Emotional Learning.* Champaign, IL: Research Press.

Elias, Maurice, Brian Friedlander & Steven Tobias. (2001). *Engaging the Resistant Child Through Computers: A Manual to Facilitate Social & Emotional Learning.* Port Chester, NY: Dude Publishing.

Elias, Maurice & Harriett Arnold. (2006). *The Educator's Guide to Emotional Intelligence and Academic Achievement.* Thousand Oaks, CA: Corwin Press.

Elliott, Judy L. & Martha L. Thurlow. (2000). *Improving Test Performance of Students with Disabilities. On District and State Assessments.* Thousand Oaks, CA: Corwin Press.

Fad, Kathleen McConnell & James R. Patton. (2000). *Behavioral Intervention Planning.* Austin, TX: Pro-Ed, Inc.

Friedlander, Brian S. (2005). *Assistive Technology: A Way to Differentiate Instruction for Students with Disabilities.* Port Chester, NY: National Professional Resources, Inc.

Friend, Marilyn. (2004). *The Power of Two: Making a Difference Through Co-Teaching, 2nd Edition* (Video). Bloomington, IN: Forum on Education.

Fuchs, D., Mock, D., Morgan, P., & Young, C. (2003). *Responsiveness-to-intervention: Definitions, evidence, and implications for learning disabilities construct. Learning Disabilities: Research and Practice*, 18(3), 157-171.

Fuchs, L. (2003). *Assessing intervention responsiveness: conceptual and technical issues.* Learning Disabilities Research & Practice, 18(3), 172-186.

Fuchs, L.S., & Fuchs, D. (2006). A framework for building capacity for responsiveness to intervention. *School Psychology Review*, 35, 621-626.

Gardner, Howard. (1996). *How Are Kids Smart?* (Video) Port Chester, NY: National Professional Resources, Inc.

Glasser, William. (1998). *Choice Theory: A New Psychology of Personal Freedom.* New York, NY: HarperCollins.

Gold, Mimi. (2003). *Help for the Struggling Student: Ready-to-Use Strategies and Lessons to Build Attention, Memory, and Organizational Skills.* San Francisco, CA: Jossey-Bass.

Goleman, Daniel. (1996). *Emotional Intelligence: A New Vision for Educators* (Video). Port Chester, NY: National Professional Resources, Inc.

Good, R.H. & Kaminski, R.A. (2001). *Dynamic indicators of basic early literacy skills* (6th ed.). Eugene, OR: Institute for the Development of Educational Achievement.

Gorman, Jean Cheng. (2001). *Emotional Disorders and Learning Disabilities in the Classroom: Interactions and Interventions.* Thousand Oaks, CA: Corwin Press.

Gregory, Gale & Carolyn Chapman. (2002). *Differentiated Instructional Strategies: One Size Doesn't Fit All.* Thousand Oaks, CA: Corwin Press.

Gresham, F.M. (2001). *Responsiveness to intervention: An alternative approach to the identification of learning disabilities.* Paper presented at the Learning Disabilities Summit, Washington, DC.

Grimes, J., & Kurns, S. (2003, December). *An intervention-based system for addressing NCLB and IDEA expectations: A multiple tiered model to ensure every child learns.* Paper presented at the National Research Center on Learning Disabilities Responsiveness-to-Intervention Symposium, Kansas City, MO.

Guilford Press (Producer). (1999). *Assessing ADHD in the Schools* (Video). New York, NY.

Guilford Press (Producer). (1999). *Classroom Interventions for ADHD* (Video). New York, NY.

Gusman, Jo. (2004). *Differentiated Instruction & the English Language Learner: Best Practices to Use With Your Students (K-12)* (Video). Port Chester, NY: National Professional Resources, Inc.

Heacox, Diane. (2002). *Differentiated Instruction: How to Reach and Teach All Learners (Grades 3-12).* Minneapolis, MN: Free Spirit Press.

Hehir, Thomas. (2005). *New Directions in Special Education.* Cambridge, MA: Harvard University Press.

Iervolino, Constance & Helene Hanson. (2003). *Differentiated Instructional Practice Video Series: A Focus on Inclusion (Tape 1), A Focus on the Gifted (Tape 2).* Port Chester, NY: National Professional Resources, Inc.

Jensen, Eric. (2000). *Different Brains, Different Learners: How to Reach the Hard to Reach.* San Diego, CA: The Brain Store.

Jensen, Eric. (2000). *The Fragile Brain: What Impairs Learning and What We Can Do About It.* Port Chester, NY: National Professional Resources, Inc.

Jensen, Eric. (2000). *Practical Applications of Brain-Based Learning.* Port Chester, NY: National Professional Resources, Inc.

Kagan, Spencer & Laurie Kagan. (1999). *Reaching Standards Through Cooperative Learning: Providing for ALL Learners in General Education Classrooms* (4-video series). Port Chester, NY: National Professional Resources, Inc.

Kagan, Spencer & Miguel Kagan. (1998). *Multiple Intelligences: The Complete MI Book.* San Clemente, CA: Kagan Cooperative Learning.

Kame'enui, Edward J. & Deborah C. Simmons. (1999). *Adapting Curricular Materials, Volume 1: An Overview of Materials Adaptations—Toward Successful Inclusion of Students with Disabilities: The Architecture of Instruction.* Reston, VA: Council for Exceptional Children.

Katzman, Lauren I. & Allison G. Gandhi (Editors). (2005). *Special Education for a New Century.* Cambridge, MA: Harvard Educational Review.

Kemp, Karen. (2007). *RTI Tackles Reading* (Video). Port Chester, NY: National Professional Resources, Inc.

Kemp, Karen & Mary Ann Eaton. (2007). *RTI: The Classroom Connection.* Port Chester, NY: Dude Publishing.

Kennedy, Eugene. (2003). *Raising Test Scores for All Students: An Administrator's Guide to Improving Standardized Test Performance.* Thousand Oaks, CA: Corwin Press.

Kleinert, Harold L. & Jacqui F. Kearns. (2001). *Alternate assessment: Measuring Outcomes and Supports for Students with Disabilities.* Baltimore, MD: Brookes Publishing Company, Inc.

Lavoie, Richard. (2005). *Beyond F.A.T. City* (Video). Charlotte, NC: PBS Video.

Lavoie, Richard. (1989). *F.A.T. City: How Difficult Can This Be?* (Video). Charlotte, NC: PBS Video.

Lavoie, Richard.(2005). *It's So Much Work to Be Your Friend* (Video). Charlotte, NC: PBS Video.

Levine, Mel. (2002). *A Mind at a Time.* New York, NY: Simon & Schuster.

Lickona, Thomas. (2004). *Character Matters.* New York, NY: Touchstone.

Long, Nicholas, & William Morse. (1996). *Conflict in the Classroom: The Education of At-Risk and Troubled Students, 5th Edition.* Austin, TX: Pro-Ed, Inc.

Maanum, Jody L. (2003). *The General Educator's Guide to Special Education, 2nd Edition.* Minnetonka, MN: Peytral Publications, Inc.

Marston, D., Muyskens, P., Lau, M., & Canter, A. (2003). *Problem-Solving model for decision making with high-incidence: The Minneapolis experience.* Learning Disabilities Research and Practice, 18(3), 187-200.

McCarney, Stephen B. (1993). *The Pre-Referral Intervention Manual.* Columbia, MO: Hawthorne Educational Services.

McDougal, J.L., Clonan, S.M. & Martens, B.K. (2000). Using organizational change procedures to promote the acceptability of prereferral intervention services: The School-based Intervention Team Project. *School Psychology Quarterly*, 15, 149-171.

Minskoff, Esther & David Allsopp. (2002). *Academic Success Strategies for Adolescents with Learning Disabilities & ADHD.* Baltimore, MD: Paul H. Brookes Publishing.

Moll, Anne M. (2003). *Differentiated Instruction Guide for Inclusive Teaching.* Port Chester, NY: Dude Publishing.

Munk, Dennis D. (2003). *Solving the Grading Puzzle for Students with Disabilities.* Whitefish Bay, WI: Knowledge by Design, Inc.

National Association of State Directors of Special Education (NASDSE). (2005). *Response to Intervention: Policy, Considerations, and Implementation.* Alexandria, VA: NASDSE.

Nelsen, Jane, Lynn Lott & H. Stephen Glenn. (2000). *Positive Discipline In The Classroom: Developing Mutual Respect, Cooperation, and Responsibility in Your Classroom.* Three Rivers, MI: Three Rivers Press.

Nolet, Victor & Margaret McLaughlin. (2000). *Accessing the General Curriculum: Including Students with Disabilities in Standards-Based Reform.* Thousand Oaks, CA: Corwin Press.

Norlander, Karen. (2006). *RTI Tackles the LD Explosion: A Good IDEA Becomes Law (Video).* Port Chester, NY: National Professional Resources, Inc.

Purcell, Sherry & Debbie Grant. (2004). *Using Assistive Technology toMeet Literacy Standards.* Verona, WI: IEP Resources.

Reider, Barbara. (2005). *Teach More and Discipline Less.* Thousand Oaks, CA: Corwin Press.

Renzulli, Joseph S. (1999). *Developing the Gifts and Talents of ALL Students: The Schoolwide Enrichment Model* (Video). Port Chester, NY: National Professional Resources, Inc.

Rief, Sandra F. (1998). *The ADD/ADHD Checklist.* Paramus, NJ: Prentice Hall.

Rief, Sandra F. (2004). *ADHD & LD: Powerful Teaching Strategies & Accommodations* (Video). Port Chester, NY: National Professional Resources, Inc.

Rief, Sandra F. (1997). *How to Help Your Child Succeed in School: Strategies and Guidance for Parents of Children with ADHD and/or Learning Disabilities* (Video). Port Chester, NY: National Professional Resources, Inc.

Rief, Sandra F. & Julie A. Heimburge. (1996). *How to Reach & Teach All Students in the Inclusive Classroom: Ready-To-Use Strategies, Lessons, and Activities for Teaching Students with Learning Needs.* West Nyack, NY: Center for Applied Research in Education.

Robinson, Viviane & Mei K. Lai. (2006). *Practitioner Research for Educators.* Thousand Oaks, CA: Corwin Press.

Rose, D. & A. Meyer (Editors). (2002). *Teaching Every Student in the Digital Age.* Alexandria, VA: ASCD.

Rose, D. & A. Meyer (Editors). (2005). *The Universally Designed Classroom: Accessible Curriculum and Digital Technologies.* Cambridge, MA: Harvard University Press.

Rutherford, Paula. (2002). *Instruction for All Students.* Alexandria, VA: Just Ask Publications.

Sailor, Wayne. (2004). *Creating A Unified System: Integrating General and Special Education for the Benefit of All Students* (Video). Bloomington, IN: Forum on Education.

Sailor, Wayne. (2002). *Whole-School Success and Inclusive Education: Building Partnerships for Learning, Achievement, and Accountability.* New York, NY: Teachers College Press.

Salovey, Peter. (1998). *Optimizing Intelligences: Thinking, Emotion, and Creativity* (Video). Port Chester, NY: National Professional Resources, Inc.

Shaywitz, Sally. (2003). *Overcoming Dyslexia: A New and Complete Science-Based Program for Reading Problems at Any Level.* New York, NY: Knopf Publishing.

Shinn, M. (1989). *Curriculum-based measurement: Assessing special children.* New York: Guilford Press.

Shumm, Jeanne Shay. (1999). *Adapting Curricular Materials, Volume 2: Kindergarten Through Grade Five—Adapting Reading & Math Materials for the Inclusive Classroom.* Reston, VA: Council for Exceptional Children.

Smith, Sally. (2001). *Teach Me Different!* (Video). Charlotte, NC: PBS Video.

Snell, Martha E. & Rachel Janney. (2000). *Collaborative Teaming.* Baltimore, MD: Paul H. Brookes Publishing Co., Inc.

Snell, Martha E. & Rachel Janney. (2000). *Social Relationships & Peer Support.* Baltimore, MD: Paul H. Brookes Publishing Co., Inc.

Sousa, David A. (2001). *How the Special Needs Brain Learns.* Thousand Oaks, CA: Corwin Press.

Sprick, R.S., Borgmeier, C., & Nolet, V. (2002). *Prevention and management of behavior problems in secondary schools.* In M.A. Shinn, H.M. Walker & G. Stoner (Eds.), *Interventions for academic and behavior problems II: Preventative and remedial approaches* (pp. 373-401). Bethesda, MD: National Association for School Psychologists.

Strichart, Stephen S., Charles T. Mangrum II & Patricia Iannuzzi. (1998). *Teaching Study Skills* and Strategies to Students with Learning Disabilities, Attention Deficit Disorders, *or Special Needs, 2nd Edition.* Boston, MA: Allyn & Bacon, 1998.

Thompson, Sandra, Rachel Quenemeen, Martha Thurlow, & James Ysseldyke. (2001). *Alternate Assessments for Students with Disabilities.* Thousand Oaks, CA: Corwin Press.

Thurlow, Martha L., Judy L. Elliott & James E. Ysseldyke. (1998). *Testing Students with Disabilities: Practical Strategies for Complying With District and State Requirements.* Thousand Oaks, CA: Corwin Press.

Tilton, Linda. (2003). *Teacher's Toolbox for Differentiating Instruction: 700 Strategies, Tips, Tools, & Techniques.* Shorewood, MN: Covington Cove Publications.

Tomlinson, Carol Ann. (2001). *How to Differentiate Instruction in Mixed-Ability Classrooms, 2nd Edition.* Alexandria, VA: ASCD.

Villa, Richard A. & Jacqueline S. Thousand. (2004). *A Guide to Co-Teaching.* Thousand Oaks, CA: Corwin Press.

Watson, T. Steuart & Mark W. Steege. (2003). *Conducting School-Based Functional Behavioral Assessments: A Practitioner's Guide.* New York, NY: Guilford Press.

Witt, J., & Beck, R. (1999). *One minute academic functional assessment and interventions: "Can't do it… or "won't" do it?* Longmont, CO: Sopris West.

Wood, M. Mary & Nicholas Long. (1991). *Life Space Intervention: Talking with Children and Youth in Crisis.* Austin, TX: Pro-Ed, Inc.

Wormel, Rick. *(2006). Fair Isn't Always Equal. Portland*, ME: Stenhouse Publishers.

Wunderlich, Kathy C. (1988). *The Teacher's Guide to Behavioral Interventions.* Columbia, MO: Hawthorne Educational Services, Inc.